# Words on Paper

# Words on Paper

A Manual of Prose Style
for Professional Writers, Reporters, Authors,
Editors, Publishers, and Teachers

BY

ROY H. COPPERUD

*With an Introduction by*

ERWIN D. CANHAM

Editor of *The Christian Science Monitor*

HAWTHORN BOOKS, INC.

*Publishers*

NEW YORK

FIRST EDITION August, 1960

*For my wife, Mary*

# Introduction

WORDS, words, words.

We live in an age of words, of talk, of constant oral expression. Language is getting progressively looser. Oral expression is sometimes graphic, but it is often flabby. It is almost always repetitive. Nobody can speak quite as well as he can write, certainly as well as he ought to be able to write if he doesn't tie himself into knots of affectation.

If we are to save our precious language from being bloated into oral inanity, we must work harder at the sharpening and simplifying of prose. Roy H. Copperud makes herewith a mighty contribution to better writing. Primarily he is working on journalistic writing, but what he says applies to most other forms of writing. And, believe me, the language of many learned professions needs reform and simplification even more than newspapers do.

In a time when our knowledge is increasing with breathless speed, particularly in specialized areas, it is important that we understand one another. Altogether too many in the learned disciplines write and speak only in their own language, their own jargon. Nobody is more incomprehensible than the sociologists, unless it is the philosophers. The natural scientists, when they try, are often able to express themselves with remarkable clarity.

So all of us in the world need to learn to write more comprehensibly. This book tells how to do it. In large part, it makes its point through horrible examples of what not to do. This method is very effective. We remember the lessons. It concludes with a lengthy lexicon of wayward words, a handy list of things to do and not to do. The list, like Mr.

Copperud's total approach, is right down to earth. It will offend some purists. But it is itself purism of the highest order, for it aims above all at rugged, simple clarity.

Since newspaper writing is one of the prime targets and examples of the book, it is worth recalling how badly reform is needed. The printed word these days is under attack. People are being washed over with the spoken word, and the spoken word possesses power the printed word does not have. The spoken word, especially face-to-face or on television, is used through the living medium of human personality. Words which would bore us in print have new impact as they are impelled into our consciousness by a vivid personality. People are very indiscriminating in the face of the spoken word. Often, too, the spoken word—with all its repetitions and flabbiness—comes at a pace timed to human comprehension. Most people's minds work slowly, and the spoken word is about all many of them can absorb.

I can illustrate the point. With editors of three other newspapers, I have engaged for over 10 years in a weekly half-hour television discussion. It is a cracker-barrel kind of discussion. It is unrehearsed, unwritten, almost unprepared. We utter some 3,000 to 4,000 words during the half hour. Most of it is ungrammatical, repetitious, excitable—oral language at its most typical. And yet we have a high penetration into the thinking of viewers. We have a large audience. People who would never read 3,000 words any one of us has written will listen with avid interest.

All of which proves that if we are to preserve the purity and power of the written word, we must work at it, and write in style that will have the maximum chance of entering the human mind. The purpose of writing is communication. It is of no importance until somebody reads it. Therefore it must be simple and readable. It must command attention.

Nothing needs saving more urgently than the purity of language. The power-seeking despots of this world, the propagandists, have long known the power of words. They have been trying to steal the finest and dearest words that free society has inherited, in order to subvert them to the purposes of tyranny. The word "peace" is the best example.

"Democracy" is used lavishly by those who would destroy it. "The people" are enshrined in the formal titles of nations which deny the rights of people. So it goes.

Mr. Copperud's practical, precise, experienced discussion of the use of words may do more than help newspapers to survive and flourish. By imbuing us with new awareness of the importance of words, it may even help us—indirectly and in the long run—to preserve all our freedoms. For freedom, as many have said, is indivisible, and purity is a seamless robe.

ERWIN D. CANHAM
Editor of *The Christian Science Monitor*

# Preface

*Words on Paper* is intended to assist and encourage clear, direct expression. The book is based on errors, gaucheries, and misconceptions that have appeared in print. Examples have not been invented to point a moral, as the brothers Fowler put it. Nor has any attempt been made to include obvious fundamentals that any reasonably literate person knows already, as, for example, that sentences start with capital letters and end with periods. This kind of comprehensiveness is the province of the grammar. Because this is no more a dictionary than it is a grammar, it also stands clear of the dictionary's primary field, which is definition, except for meanings that are often misapprehended.

The plan of the book, utilizing chapters for material that lends itself to some cohesive grouping, and a glossary for material that does not, was adopted after careful consideration of other possibilities, with the aim of making the book as easy as possible to use. The glossary, which deals mainly with usage, also constitutes a detailed index to the chapters.

No attention is given to matters of pronunciation or to expressions peculiar to speech, because people will hardly endure having their writing corrected, much less their conversation. Conversation is conducted on many more levels of usage than writing, and thus pretty much eludes criticism.

Theoretically, there are at least two levels of written usage, the formal and the informal, but no well-defined line separates them. The word *formal* is distasteful because it suggests the tone considered suitable for the fustier academic journals. It is also, in general, associated with the pompous, the stiff, and what is written with a self-conscious effort to convey an impression of intellectuality. This subject is explored further in Chapter IV.

Regardless of what *formal* means as applied to writing, it is evident that magazines, well-edited newspapers, and nonacademic books today use a direct, conversational, workmanlike prose that, whatever it may be, is decidedly not formal. This book aims at the standard exemplified by the best such prose. It is the style referred to by Dr. Johnson as "familiar but not coarse, and elegant but not ostentatious."

Since, in the end, usage is a matter of opinion, the reader is sure to disagree with some of the views set forth here. The writer of such a book can only hope that the reader will concur in most of his ideas. The avoidance of specific errors is unimportant. What is important is the cultivation of a critical habit of mind toward writing, to ensure that it is as explicit, concise, and readable as possible. No one can be taught how to write, but everyone can be taught how not to write.

The books I have consulted are mentioned in the text and bibliography. The dictionary used as the standard in this book is *Webster's New International Dictionary,* second edition, and its abridgment, *Webster's New Collegiate Dictionary*. References to *Webster* mean these dictionaries. Comparisons have been made, however, with the *American College Dictionary,* the *Oxford English Dictionary,* and, to a lesser extent, other works in this field. For permission to quote from H. W. Fowler's *Dictionary of Modern English Usage,* I am indebted to the Oxford University Press.

*Words on Paper* had its genesis in a column, "Editorial Workshop," that has appeared since 1954 in *Editor & Publisher,* the journal of the newspaper field. Much of the material in this book was used in the columns in somewhat different form. Considerable material has been added. I warmly appreciate the response of readers and the encouragement, of both the column and the book, that has come from Jerome H. Walker, executive editor, and Robert U. Brown, publisher and editor, of *Editor & Publisher*. Material that appeared in the columns is reprinted by permission of *Editor & Publisher*.

One more thing remains to be said. How does one come

by the audacity to offer a book on such a multifarious and difficult subject as usage? The answer is contained, I believe, in a passage from an excellent little volume, *Grammar Without Tears,* by Hugh Sykes Davies, used here by permission of The John Day Company, Inc.:

"A century ago, an industrious American called Goold Brown wrote a book of rather more than a thousand pages on *The Grammar of English Grammars.* Several hundred pages are filled with exercises consisting of errors for correction, and they are drawn from the writings of his fellow grammarians."

Mr. Davies added in a footnote:

"This does not reflect any great discredit on grammarians, still less does it disqualify them from their office. On the contrary, the principle of 'set a thief to catch a thief' holds good in the business of giving advice on the use of language. The man best qualified to give it is not he who writes with ease and almost unfailing correctness, but he who has a constant struggle to say anything at all without making howling mistakes. The style and grammar of this book will, I hope, be judged on this principle."

ROY H. COPPERUD

# Contents

PART THREE
WAYWARD WORDS

# PART ONE

# GRAMMAR AND STYLE

# CHAPTER I

# Modifiers Gone Mad

Piled-up Adjectives; Limiting Adjectives; Dangling Participles; Participles and Time Sequence; Misrelated Appositives; Tricky *ics*; False Possessives; Nouns as Adjectives; Lost Articles (*a, an, the*); *A* vs. *an* Before *h*).

## Piled-up Adjectives

THE URGE to condense, while generally commendable, is to blame for some odd effects that place an unnecessary burden on the already weary reader. Behold, then, the puny noun, staggering under a load of adjectives so heavy they all but crush it:

"He was arrested on *conspiracy and concealing stolen property* charges." (The modifiers are italicized.)

"Next on the docket were *two disturbing the peace* suspects."

"*Former San Anselmo County Sheriff's Deputy* Wolfgang Schmalz is in trouble again."

"*A 15 cent per $100 assessed valuation road tax* increase was proposed."

What price terseness? Howard B. Taylor, managing editor of the *San Diego Union,* hit it off neatly in a memo to his staff:

"Mouth-filling strings of compound adjectives force the reader to go back and retrace the meaning of a sentence: 'The strikers presented *a 20-cent-an-hour wage-increase* demand.' The compound adjective is too big to swallow. Let's make it 'The strikers asked an increase of 20 cents an hour.' A wire story recently read, 'The strikers are seeking a *25-cent-an-hour* wage hike, contending that *a 10-cent-an-hour* jump, which gave them *a $2.10 hourly pay* scale, is insufficient.' That's really making life tough on the reader.

"A string of titles preceding a name likewise is difficult to digest: 'Signers included *former Salt Lake City mayor* Albert Sprague.' Let's make it 'Signers included Albert Sprague, former mayor of Salt Lake City.' "

Another variation of this quirk gives us "a 9 a. m. February 26 meeting" instead of "a meeting at 9 a. m., February 26," and "the 1939 erection of the Oakdale School" instead of "the erection of the Oakdale School in 1939."

*The AP Log* told how a bureau chief who had been taken to task for "*Glass jar manufacturing heir John A. Kerr's divorce* decree" came back with:

"All I can say is it's a good thing for Associated Press members that Kerr's old man didn't invent the International Harvester Company's two-row cotton-picking machine."

## Limiting Adjectives

Limiting adjectives are often used in a way that has an ambiguous effect, especially in writing where concision is desired at the apparent expense of exactness.

"His labor turnover is nominal, and he is proud of the loyalty of his nonunion workers." This sounds as if the man might have had two kinds of employees, union and nonunion, and as if only the nonunion ones were loyal. In this instance, however, all the employees were nonunion, so the writer should have said, "He is proud of the loyalty of his workers, who are nonunion."

"The reception was held in Mrs. Nelson's San Francisco home." Does Mrs. Nelson have homes elsewhere, as this seems to suggest? If not, it would better be "in Mrs. Nelson's home, in San Francisco" ("in Mrs. Nelson's home in San Francisco"—omitting the comma—would be open to the same objection as the example).

It is undesirable, for the same reason, to write "Burglars invaded the 424 W. Oak home of Al Fresco last night." Since this was Fresco's only home, it would have been better to say "the home of Al Fresco, at 424 W. Oak, last night."

Unnatural placement of modifiers also appears in other contexts: "Receipts were 25 per cent ahead of the same 1959 month." This is disagreeably unidiomatic; better, "the same month in 1959."

"The speaker cited Professor A. M. Low, Britain's inventive version of Thomas A. Edison." Here the adjective *inventive* has been dragged in to tip off the reader about the basis for the comparison, but the effect is to say that Edison was not inventive. A piece about the use of television to train teachers spoke of the program's *electronic objective*. Here the use of the adjective *electronic* is not misleading, but merely obtrusive and silly, which may also be said of *inventive* in the foregoing example.

## Dangling Participles

"Dear Sir:

We enclose herewith a statement of your account. Desiring to clear our books, will you kindly send us a check in settlement?"

The reply ran:

"Sirs:

You have been misinformed. I have no wish to clear your books."

This little exchange, adapted from an example in Fowler, neatly illustrates the question, when is a dangling participle? Or, more properly, when is a participle dangling?

To start at the very beginning, let us first settle the question, what is a participle? Elementary, my dear Watson. A participle is a verb form usually ending in *ing* or *ed*, like *desiring* or *settled*, and used, as far as this discussion is concerned, as a modifier. The past participle, of which *settled* is an example, is sometimes formed irregularly, as in *born, seen,* and the like. Participles may also take auxiliaries: *having settled, being seen, having been born*. This does not exhaust the technical distinctions, by any means, but should be enough to give the idea.

Writers are often tripped up by phrases containing participles and occurring at the beginnings of sentences. Such phrases usually modify the subject of the clause that follows. The trick in handling them correctly is to be sure that this subject *is* the element intended to be modified.

The fellow being dunned in Fowler's example, who was probably only a grammatical dead beat, took his creditors literally, and applied the force of *Desiring to clear our books* to *you*. Now, you may say, the scoundrel really knew better than that.

So he undoubtedly did. Dangling participles rarely confuse meaning. At the least, they cause the reader a moment of hesitation while he pairs up the modifier with the modified. At the worst, they create an absurd effect, making the writer sound like an ass and perhaps creating an opportunity like the one our dead beat seized.

"In applying the brakes, the car skidded off the road." Power brakes are with us, indeed, but even cars equipped with them do not apply their own.

"Born of a poor but proud Catholic family, few would have predicted greatness for young Konrad." But it was Konrad who was born, not *few*, as this sentence reads.

What is the cure for dangling? There is none, perhaps, except close attentiveness to what one is writing, which of course is more of a panacea than a specific. Like Indian Snake Oil, it will cure whatever ails you, including hyphenitis, comma coma, and disorders of the colon, as well as the dangles.

Bob Considine once quoted D. C. Claypoole, the newspaperman to whom George Washington confided his plans not to run again, as having written:

"He received me kindly and after paying my respects to him desired me to take a seat near him."

Did George pay Claypoole's respects to himself, and if so, how was it managed? Well, that's what the man said, if not what he meant, showing that the crazy, mixed-up participial phrase is not new to American prose.

## Participles and Time Sequence

Modifying phrases containing present participles often become structural atrocities in the hands of inexpert writers. There can be no gap between the time of such a phrase and that of the main part of the sentence. The timing must be either that of a connected sequence, or simultaneous:

"Going to the door, he turned the key." (*connected sequence*)

"Laughing gaily, she turned to go." (*simultaneous occurrence*)

If there is an interval between what happens in the participial phrase and what happens in the main part of the sentence, a past participle should be used, or some other change should be made.

"Joseph Doakes is a graduate of Columbia, *receiving* his degree in 1960." This is painfully awkward for *"having received* his degree in 1960." The linkage here is not close enough for the present participle to fit happily. Recasting to *"who received* his degree in 1960" is, of course, another solution.

"The mother said her daughter fell out of the car, apparently *opening* the door when no one was looking." Here, similarly, *having opened* is required to indicate the sequence and perhaps even the agent.

"Eriksson has been a resident of the city for fifteen years, *coming* here during the war as a naval architect." *having come*.

"He has been in the service since 1927, *starting* as a clerk." *having started*.

Often a participial phrase inadvisedly subordinates an idea that is of equal rank with the main part of the sentence.

"The Van Gilders were married on Christmas Day, 1907, in Anabel, Mo., *moving* to the West Coast shortly afterwards." This would be improved by substituting *"and moved* to the West Coast . . ." A phrase containing a present participle cannot be used to convey a time *after* that of the main clause.

"By 1918 he was president, *moving* up to the chairmanship in 1940." Same trouble: *and he moved* up to.

"Miss Jones began her studies at the college in September, 1956, *receiving* her degree last June." *and received* her degree.

"This is one of the most sensational of the many revelations *coming* from behind the Iron Curtain in several years." *that have come*.

## Misrelated Appositives

Grammarians have been so preoccupied with the dangling participle they have taken little notice of another kind of misplaced modifier. This error grows out of a common appositive construction, but I have failed to find it identified in any of the grammars I keep at hand. If it needs a name, perhaps *misrelated* or *dangling appositive* would be appropriate.

"Until recently a resident of San Carlos, *Peaches' real name* is Mrs. Ralph Willson." It was Peaches herself, and not her real name, that was a resident of San Carlos. The basic fault here may be the attempt to jam unrelated material together into one sentence. Still, all this can be done grammatically: "Until recently a resident of San Carlos, Peaches is known formally as Mrs. Ralph Willson."

"A devout, old-fashioned Moslem, *his concubines* are numbered by the hundreds." The fault is evident; a possible cure is "A devout, old-fashioned Moslem, he numbers his concubines by the hundreds."

"A widow of seventy, *her health* is poor." The woman herself, not her health, is the widow of seventy. "A widow of seventy, she is in poor health."

Dangling adjectival phrases are somewhat similar. "Tiny and slender, *Yuomi's straight hair* is clipped close in the trademark of a nurse." Tiny, slender hair? "Tiny and slender, Yuomi wears her hair straight and clipped close . . ."

"Now forty-four years old, *his assignments* have taken him around the world." Forty-four-year-old assignments will not gladden the heart of the editor. "Now forty-four years old, he has had assignments that have . . ."

"At thirty-five, *the people of France* made Poujade the undisputed master of the fourth largest party in their National Assembly." It was Poujade, and not the people of France, who was thirty-five. "The people of France made Poujade, at thirty-five, the undisputed master . . ."

While we're at it, let's consider one that looks right, at first glance, but isn't:

"Now sixty-eight, *he and his second wife* live in a Colonial-style house." The writer here was led astray by a compound subject—not *he* alone, but *he and his second wife*. Husband and wife could have been the same age, but were not, and the descriptive adjective was intended to apply only to the husband. The correction that suggests itself is recasting in some such form as "Murgatroyd, now sixty-eight, and his second wife live . . ."

"Now a widow, *she and her husband* moved to New York in 1956." The way this sentence stands, both the woman and her husband are characterized as *a widow*.

"An inveterate traveler, *Mr. Parkinson and his wife* have visited all the national parks." Diagnose this one for yourself—you're on your own.

## Tricky *ics*

Is there a difference between *a dramatic* instructor and a *dramatics* instructor? It seems apparent that any instructor who used stage techniques in putting his lessons across would be *a dramatic instructor,* but that a *dramatics* instructor could only be one who taught dramatics.

The distinction between *athletic* and *athletics,* used as adjectives, is technically the same, but is less observed. On the sports pages, most athletics directors have long since become athletic directors, disregarding the fact that they may be paunchy and inert. The difference between an *athletic* director and an *athletics* director is, grammatically, the same as that between a *musical* critic and a *music* critic.

We often read of *electronic* engineers, who (or which?), strictly speaking, would be robots, but this is not the meaning intended—nor even the one the reader assumes, if we are going to be honest about it. The writer has in mind *electronics* engineers; that is, engineers who are trained in electronics.

*Politics,* although capable of being pressed into service as an adjective, fortunately has a distinct and well-accepted adjective form, *political. Politic,* of course, is something else again.

*Narcotics, cosmetics,* and *economics* can and sometimes do give the same kind of trouble as *athletics* and *dramatics.* Narcotics agents, who deal with drug-law violations, often see themselves referred to as *narcotic agents.* This designation, which describes them as "tending to stupefy," would better fit after-dinner speakers.

The point in all this is the difference between a true adjective (*athletic*) and a noun (*athletics*) that is being made to do service as an adjective. There is nothing wrong, incidentally, with putting words to other than their primary uses.

I hesitate to press this matter of *ic* vs. *ics* any further, because it has become all but puristic to insist on a distinction between, for example, *athletic* director and *athletics* director. The likelihood of misunderstanding is negligible, if it exists at all. There is about as much chance of impressing the difference on the sporting fraternity as there is of getting *athletics* pronounced in three syllables instead of four.

## False Possessives

Now let us take up a dido that might be called a false possessive. Many modifiers of the general kind we have been considering end in *s* and, especially when they are proper names, some writers feel compelled to regard them as possessives and clap apostrophes on them. Note these examples:

"He accepted a *General Motors'* scholarship."

"The applicant was a *United States'* citizen."

"The scene did not pass muster with the *Hays' Office.*"

There is really no idea of possession here, and so the apostrophes are uncalled for. *General Motors, United States,* and *Hays* are being used simply as adjectives, like *roads* in *roads appropriations* and *athletics* in *athletics director*.

This brings us to a shadowy realm inhabited by names once regarded as possessive forms, but now often written without the apostrophe: *Odd Fellows*['] *Lodge, Lions*['] *Club, Taxpayers*['] *Association, master*[']*s degree, in ten years*['] *time,* and even *Hell*[']*s Canyon,* from which the federal government removed the apostrophe by ukase. It looks as if such words are coming to be felt primarily as describing, and not as indicating, possession.

## Nouns as Adjectives

Any flat ban on pressing nouns into service as adjectives is foolish. One part of speech easily assumes the role of another; this is one of the most distinctive and useful characteristics of English. Sometimes, however, a bad taste is left with the fastidious when nouns are forced into the role of adjectives. Most of us, I think, will concede that these are undesirable examples of this practice:

"The officer expressed reluctance to discuss the case for *security* reasons."

"The general was retired for *health* reasons."

"The architect warned that the situation soon may reach *disaster* proportions."

"The service will be discontinued for *economy* reasons."

It is noticeable that three of these four examples have *reasons* as the objectionably modified noun. Locutions of this kind are recognizable as journalese. The difficulty cannot be with the words used as modifiers, for *health, security, disaster,* and *economy* all sound acceptable as adjectives in other combinations: *health* insurance, *security* measures, *disaster* preparations, *economy* drive.

What's the difference? It looks as if (1) all these combinations have evolved from prepositional modifiers (reasons *of* health, measures *for* security) and (2) those in which the preposition is *of* cannot tractably be forced into the adjective-noun relationship.

In the first example, *reasons* of *security, reasons* of *health, proportions* of *disaster,* and *reasons* of *economy* sound undeniably better than *security reasons, health reasons, disaster proportions,* and *economy reasons*.

It should be possible to play by ear in these situations. Furthermore, *security reasons, health reasons,* and the rest can also be recast as *for the sake of security, for* (or *because of*) *his health, may amount to disaster,* and *for economy*. This often means more words, you say? Certainly. Nothing is more noxious than the idea that there is some all-redeeming virtue in condensation. This delusion is responsible for the telescoped expressions readers continually stumble over.

## Lost Articles

Articles are a species of modifier. In the last twenty years, the notion has got around that opening sentences, particularly in newspaper stories, would be the better if they did not start with *the, a,* or *an.* The idea, as once explained to me, is that the articles convey little or nothing, and only stand in the way of the reader, who is panting to get at the meatier words.

Fortunately, this dictum appears to be falling from favor. But like the lie that runs twice around the earth while the truth is lacing up its shoes, it persists, and prejudice against—or neglect of—articles is still to be found in odd corners.

The unhappily missing article is nearly always *the,* perhaps because far fewer sentences start with *a* or *an.* It seems, too, that leaving off *a* or *an* has an even more indigestible effect than leaving off *the.* Some writers, conscious of the prejudice against starting with articles, and at the same time unwilling to commit abortion, cunningly rearrange their sentences so that some other element comes first. But in this labor there is no profit, and there may even be a loss, if the rearranged version is less readable or direct.

It is not true, of course, that articles convey nothing. If this were so, they would be dropped from conversational speech, especially at the least literate level, which hews to essentials. *The* particularizes what it precedes; *a* and *an* designate one of a class. Meaning of a sort *can* be put across without these subtleties. But not the sort of meaning that is the most readable and lucid.

Does it really speed the reader on his way to leave an article off the beginning of a sentence? Surely not if he pauses, as he will, to wonder what happened to it, and finds himself obliged to choose between possible shades of meaning. The writer's job has thus been foisted on the reader, and he has every right to feel irked.

One day I stumbled through this sentence: "Crux of the situation is belief expressed by board members that legislation should govern the use of the reservoir by the public." If the aim is to be telegraphic, why not go whole hog: "Crux of situation is belief expressed by board members that legislation should govern use of reservoir by public"?

As a sidelight, we may note that *the* has been dropped in popular use of the name *Congress.* Who can say why? Certainly it never occurs to anyone to drop the article from *the Supreme Court, the Cabinet,* or *the Senate.* It is noticeable that recent Presidents have meticulously referred to "*the* Congress."[1]

[1] Alexander Sloan of the *Newark News* kindly called my attention to an interesting commentary, which appears in the introduction to *The President, Office and*

As another sidelight, let us consider the expressions *in future* and *in interim* as against "in *the* future" and "in *the* interim." The omission of the articles makes the terms Anglicisms, which in itself is nothing against them, but until they are naturalized they will sound affected in this country.

It is a tortuous business to generalize about the places where *the* is or is not normally required. The matter is governed by idiom, which does not yield to rules, anyway. Let's admit this: We all know very well when we are leaving out a desirable *the*; it is never done by accident.[2]

Careless use of *the* may confer a distinction that is either inaccurate, unintended, or both. Referring to John Jones as "*the* vice-president of the Smith Corporation" implies that the corporation has only one vice-president. "Laurence Olivier, *the* actor" is acceptable on the assumption that he is well enough known so that his name will be recognized. On the other hand, referring to a movie starlet, Hazel Gooch, lately of Broken Bottle, Iowa, as "*the* (rather than *an*) actress" leaves the reader with an inferior feeling that he has not recognized a name he should know, although in fact his ignorance of Miss Gooch is nothing to be ashamed of.

## A vs. an Before h

The use of *an* before words beginning with *h* (*an hotel, an historic event*) is now an undoubted affectation—in the United States, at least. It was formerly the practice to use *an* before unaccented *h*'s, but apparently no one could decide which ones were unaccented. In 1909, crotchety Ambrose Bierce wrote, "The contrary usage in this country comes of too strongly stressing our aspirates." Too bad, old boy, it's all over now; our aspirates have aspired and are beyond aspersion.

Some exceptions remain: *hour, honor,* and *heir,* where the *h* sound is

---

*Powers,* fourth edition, by Edward S. Corwin, New York: New York University, 1957.

Corwin noted that the Constitution says *the Congress* twenty-six times and *Congress* only five times. Although the Congress established by the Constitution was the last of a succession of congresses, "no sooner did the Constitution go into effect than the term *the Congress* was scrapped by all and sundry." Washington, Jefferson, and Chief Justice Marshall, among others, all said *Congress.*

Professor Corwin attributed the recent reversion to the archaic expression, "to which Presidents Truman and Eisenhower and Chief Justice Warren have all succumbed," to Franklin D. Roosevelt, "who was never disinclined to resort to the bizarre when it was calculated to focus attention on himself; besides, FDR may have reckoned that his pious revival of the original expression ought to stop the mouths of the critics of his Court-Packing Plan."

[2] "Remember what the Bible says: 'If I forget *the,* O Jerusalem, let my right hand forget her cunning.' "—Bernstein, Theodore M., *Watch Your Language.* Great Neck, New York: Channel Press, 1958.

not merely unstressed, but nonexistent. There will always be some Uriah Heeps around saying "an 'umble," however.

Expressions like *an habitual* tend to indicate to the American reader that the *h* is not to be sounded. Instead of achieving the elegance aimed at, such affectations impart a kind of Cockney flavor. One halmost hexpects to find the missing *h*'s prefixed to the words that start with vowels.

*An Historian's Approach to Religion* by Arnold Toynbee, incidentally, was a worthy sequel to his *A Study of 'istory.*

The use of *an* before words beginning with *u* or *eu,* for example *an utopia,* or *an eulogy,* is a related peculiarity. These words in fact begin with a consonant sound, *y,* and call for *a* as their article. It is hard to pronounce *an eulogy* and, by the same token, faintly irksome to read it (at least to us lip-readers).

Webster speaks of expressions like *an union* as often employed by British writers. As far back as 1926, however, that British oracle on usage, Fowler, advised against the locution and at the same time called *an humble* "meaningless & undesirable."

*A* is mistakenly used instead of *an* before figures, initials, and even words that begin with vowel sounds. Instances: *a $800 salary, a RCA contract, a Amazonian feat.* This quirk can be regarded only as a manifestation of illiteracy, or perhaps deafness. English-speaking people learn to put *a* before consonant sounds and *an* before vowel sounds when they learn to talk, and most people are grown before they become aware what the basis of the distinction is. Few lack the right instinct in this matter, although some of them are apparently breaking into print.

# CHAPTER II

# Verbs and Their Vagaries

Sequence of Tenses; Split Infinitives; Infinitives of Purpose; Misleading Infinitives; Division of Compound Verbs; *Shall* and *Will*, *Should* and *Would*; Passive Voice; *Was Given*.

## Sequence of Tenses

MANY an absurdity is committed in the name of a widely misapplied rule of grammar, the one governing sequence of tenses. The general idea is that the tense of the verb in the main clause of a sentence governs the tense in a subordinate clause. Sometimes this state of affairs is called attracted sequence; that is, the tense of the verb in the clause that follows is attracted to the tense of the verb in the main clause.

So far, so good. Let's look at an example to make clear what we are talking about: "He *said* he *was* tired of everything." The verb in the main clause, *said*, is in the past tense, so the verb in the dependent clause, *was*, naturally falls into the past tense. Most of the time, this is not the kind of rule it is necessary to stop and think about. Here are some other examples of normal sequence of tenses:

"The man *wore* a pained expression as the officer *forced* his car to the curb."

"The motorist *explained* that he *tried* to buy a replacement for his defective headlamp."

"She *promised* that she *would be* there."

Some writers seize upon the basic rule of sequence and follow it out the window—or, what is just as bad, into the next sentence. The basic rule has an important exception, which can be relied upon to forestall a good deal of nonsense, to wit: The *present* tense, rather than the past, is used in the subordinate clause to express a continuing or timeless state of affairs. Consider: "He *said* the world *is* round." Applying the basic rule of sequence, *is* here would be *was* because the main verb, *said*, is in the past tense. But that would make it sound as if the world no longer were round.[1]

---

[1] A sentence concerning the roundness of the earth is invariably cited in discussions of sequence of tenses, and for all I know it may be illegal not to do so.

In the name of common sense, exceptions to the basic rule of sequence are properly made to describe any condition that continues in effect at the time of writing. Here are some examples:

"The surveyor *reported* that the terrain *is* [not *was*] rugged."

"Hoover *pointed out* that there *are* [not *were*] seventy-five to eighty independent government agencies, each of which *consumes* [not *consumed*] the President's time."

Although the basic rule of sequence applies properly to one sentence at a time, some writers allow succeeding sentences to be attracted into the past tense, sometimes with preposterous results. Here is an example:

"The chances of Richard Roe, candidate for Congress, *were considered* good. Roe *was* a Catholic from a predominantly Catholic district."

Since Roe's candidacy continued at the time of writing, this gave the unintended impression that he might have changed his religion. Lapses like this, which can be prevented by understanding the rule of sequence and knowing when to make an exception to it, have drawn indignant protests to editors, to say nothing of having confused readers.

For all this, sequence of tenses is still good for a battle royal. One such battle raged for weeks in the bulletin circulated by a press association among its customers. It concerned this sentence:

"Nehru *said* he *would go* before the U. N. tomorrow to seek a vote on Hungarian intervention." Obviously, the squabbling revolved around whether it should have been "Nehru said he *will go*." Although the disputants freely made use of pious appeals to "good grammar," only one of them seemed to have a clear idea of what the grammar of this situation really is.

Who won? Well, nobody did. Considerable spleen, righteous indignation, sarcasm, and the like were vented, but when the smoke had cleared the situation was left, if anything, more confused than before. Now, which is correct—"Nehru said he *would go*" or "Nehru said he *will go*"? Both versions are. But the use of *will* is a modern trend.

The basic rule of sequence, as we have noted, requires the tense in a subordinate clause to correspond with the tense in the main clause. Consequently, the past-tense *said* requires a past-tense *would go*. But several participants in the discussion held that "Nehru said he *will go*" is more direct and thus preferable.

These fellows could find some support in a pronouncement by George O. Curme, a grammarian's grammarian. In his *Syntax,* regarded by scholars as a classic, he took note of "a tendency in indirect discourse to break through the old sequence when a more accurate expression suggests itself."

One of the more interesting aspects of the debate was the confusion over the function of *would* in *Nehru said he would*. Several of the disputants mistook it for a subjunctive form indicating uncertainty. They seized on this as affording a wonderful excuse in the event Nehru did not carry out his intention.

A certain type of editor, I have noticed, loves to hedge. The reasoning seemed to run like this: Suppose Nehru failed to appear and some reader came roaring into the newspaper office with a complaint that he had been misled. The editor who had used *would* supposedly could point it out, saying, "See? We said Nehru *would* appear—not *will*—*would*, that is, unless something prevented him. We're in the clear."

*Would* in this instance, however, is not a subjunctive form, but simply the past tense of *will*. Of the half-dozen-odd participants in the debate, only one appeared to recognize this. "I *would* if I could" illustrates the subjunctive, indicating a conditional state, but "I said I *would*" illustrates the past indicative, indicating simple intention.

Those timid editors who fear that readers may hold them accountable for the promises of news-makers will have to look for another way out. Maybe they could find it in appending an editor's note, along these lines:

"While the *Bladder* has no reason to believe Mr. Nehru does not fully intend to appear before the U. N., in accordance with his statement, there's many a slip, etc., and any number of mischances, including a change of mind on his part, may prevent it. This newspaper wants it fully understood by its readers that it cannot undertake to guarantee the fulfillment of intentions expressed by others as reported in its columns."

## Split Infinitives

One might think the revered Henry Watson Fowler had the last word on the split infinitive more than thirty years ago when he divided the English-speaking world into five classes, namely:

"(1) Those who neither know nor care what a split infinitive is; (2) those who do not know, but care very much; (3) those who know & condemn; (4) those who know & approve; & (5) those who know & distinguish."

But no; here we are, still in doubt about the split infinitive, although his conclusion remains the consensus of grammarians today. In a nutshell: a split infinitive is not an error of itself, horrifying as this may sound to the dogma-damned fuddyduddies who compile style manuals. The acceptability of a split infinitive depends only on whether it damages the rhythm or meaning of the sentence.

Let's start from scratch. An infinitive is a verb form containing *to*: *to go, to run, to eat, to walk*. It is split when something separates *to* from its partner:

*to* quickly *go, to* clumsily *run.* Splitting an infinitive objectionably is only one of the many ways a sentence can be spoiled by poor arrangement of its parts. Yet a big red flag has been hung on verb forms containing *to,* and unnumbered browbeaten writers believe they will not enter heaven if they split the infinitive. They go to any lengths to avoid it, on all occasions, even though half the time the cure is worse than the disease.

Those who are impatient with grammatical definitions and distinctions, a category that seems to include most of us, may rely on the ear as a pretty good guide. If a sentence doesn't sound right, it isn't any good, whether the infinitive is split, rewoven, braided, or sawed in half.

These split infinitives are objectionable because they sound awkward: "I want to *consistently* enforce discipline"; "His purpose was to *effortlessly* be promoted"; "Jones was ordered to *immediately* embark." Such sentences call for recasting even if you don't know a split infinitive from an ablative absolute. The adverb (italicized) fits easily at the end in each instance.

But listen to this: "Production of food fats is expected to *moderately* exceed domestic use and commercial exports." The nonsplit fanatic is likely to do one of two things with this. He may make the sentence read "is expected *moderately* to exceed," which is no good because it raises a doubt as to whether the expecting or the exceeding will be moderate; or he may move *moderately* to the end of the sentence, but that's too far away from *exceed,* which it modifies.

This sentence was criticized as containing an undesirable split: "This will permit the nation to *quietly* drop her violent opposition to the treaty." Because there was no other comfortable place for the adverb, rewording was prescribed. Why? This kind of thing only illustrates Fowler's comment to the effect that reasons are not the strong point of the critics of split infinitives.

Life might be pleasanter if the existence of the infinitive were forgotten and if the mischief sometimes caused by splitting it were cured in each instance for its own sake. If splitting the infinitive merely hurts the poor little thing, let it suffer. That goes double for sympathetic pedants.

## Infinitives of Purpose

Ever trip over a sentence like this: "He made the trek in four days to arrive here exhausted"? You might easily get the impression that the poor guy had traveled with the intention of wearing himself out. That seems absurd, so you decide that what the writer really meant was "He made the trek in four days, arriving here exhausted."

Evidently it is possible to guess what is meant, in spite of what is written. Indeed, the reader must become adept at a kind of steeplechase, because ambiguous constructions like this are freely employed. They make some reading a sporting proposition, and may even transform a dull account into a moderately interesting game of chance.

Constructions like *to get* in "He went to the store *to get* some ice cream" are sometimes called infinitives of purpose. It is not necessary to know what they are called to sense that they convey an intention. They ought to be saved for that purpose; if they are used when no intention exists, a double meaning results.

"Increased sales are announced by many companies, to confound the pessimists." One would think those diabolical companies announced increased sales just to confound the pesky pessimists. This is an interesting idea, but hardly a likely one. What seems more probable is that the confounding of the pessimists was an unpremeditated sequel to the announcements, such as would be expressed by "Increased sales are announced by many companies, confounding the pessimists."

Here's a three-way weirdie:

"George Fox, the itinerant preacher-mystic, defied Oliver Cromwell to found the Society of Friends in the seventeenth century." At first blush it seems as if Fox might have said something like, "Look here, Cromwell, you go founding any Society of Friends and I'll fix *your* clock." Fox, however, was himself the founder of the society, so the foregoing can't be right. Could it be that Fox defied Cromwell *for the purpose* of founding the society? Not much logic here, either. What the writer had in mind, of course, was "George Fox . . . defied Oliver Cromwell *by founding* the Society of Friends."

Moral: When you use an infinitive (*to arrive, to confound, to found*) see that you are not unconsciously indicating an intention.

## Misleading Infinitives

Infinitives find their way into places where they are obtrusive, ambiguous, or both: "It was the largest maneuver ever *to be* held in the South." This may easily be read as meaning "the largest maneuver that *will ever be* held," but the intention was "that *has ever been* held." The writer could have achieved his purpose explicitly by leaving out *to be*: "It was the largest maneuver ever held in the South."

Sometimes an infinitive displaces a relative clause: "This is one of nineteen communities *to have* such a program." Here, too, there is a suggestion of the future. The intended meaning, however, was *that have,* and these words might better have been used than *to have.*

"One of the most determined suicide attempts *to be* recorded locally was a failure yesterday." Again, the infinitive does nothing but give a misleading suggestion of the future; it should have been omitted. *Ever* would contribute any desirable emphasis.

"He was one of three speakers to address the meeting." Misinterpretation is unlikely here, although this might be understood as "who were scheduled to address." The writer meant "one of three speakers *who addressed,*" and might as well have said so.

These objectionable and unnecessary uses of the infinitive seem related to, or descended from, its occasional use to indicate the future: "He is to leave in the morning." Curme points out that this construction has some modal force, conveying the idea of necessity or compulsion. Very often, however, writers who use the infinitive in this way intend a simple future. They say "I am to meet the 5:15" when they mean simply "I will meet the 5:15." In no sense do they mean "I am required to meet the 5:15."

The use of *am to, is to,* and *are to* for *shall* or *will* should be discouraged. This usage is probably fostered by newspaper headlines, in which the convention is to indicate the future with the infinitive: "Statesmen To Meet in London." Headlinese, whose characteristics grow out of space limitations, often finds its way into text, where the limitations do not exist. It is easy to see how one might expand that headline into "Statesmen *Are To* Meet in London." But the preferable form would be "Statesmen *Will* Meet in London."

## Division of Compound Verbs

The idea that newspapermen, for all their supposed cynicism, are romantics at heart finds some support in their tender attitude toward compound verbs such as *has been, must approve,* and *will block.* They seem to see a connubial relationship between the halves of the verb forms, and are determined that nothing shall injure it. Thus we have a large breed who spend part of their time plucking adverbs out of such elements. This energy might better be expended in other directions.

All the commentators on this foible, starting with Fowler, seem agreed that it is the illegitimate offspring of a disreputable parent, namely, the split-infinitive phobia. As we have seen, Fowler, the spokesman of a more conservative age, held that there really is nothing wrong with the split infinitive as such.

Numerous authorities since then have called the fear of the split infinitive a superstition. The *coup de grâce* has recently been administered by an English scholar, Robert Davies, in *Grammar Without Tears.* Davies shows how the entire mix-up grew out of one of numerous misapplications of the rules of Latin grammar to English.

But back to our subject, the divisibility of compound verbs. Look at:
"The budget was *tentatively* approved."
"The matter was *automatically* delayed."
"Experts are *now* pinning their hopes on the House."
The words in italics separate the parts of compound verbs, and many objectors would wish them elsewhere. Don't ask them why. They have no reason, except perhaps that someone once told them "That's the way it oughtta be." Indeed, the very notion that reasons should support rules of usage and grammar will strike them as a rude surprise in itself.

Consider these points:

1.   In many sentences, an adverb falls naturally among the parts of a compound verb and not nearly so naturally anywhere else. Juggle the quoted sentences around and see for yourself.

2.   The splitting of compound verbs is essentially a question of word order. Considerations of emphasis, euphony, and meaning—rather than some irrational phobia—should govern here.

3.   It is impossible to be consistent about keeping compound verbs together, even for those willing to ignore nuances of emphasis and the like. Sentences containing negatives illustrate this: "I will *not* concede the election" and "The decision will *not necessarily* block action." Note also questions like "How has *your health* been?" (Again, the divisive elements are italicized.)

Fowler was inclusive, specific, and emphatic in refuting the superstition that division of compound verbs is undesirable, and went so far as to say that putting the adverb anywhere except within the parts of the verb requires special justification.

Those who go through copy carefully remarrying split-verb constructions belong to the same lodge as the *which*-hunters, who are bound and determined that *which* is always preferable to *that*. Let us try to be as enlightened in our attitude toward words as toward people and not compel them to stay together when they would be happier apart.

## Shall and Will, Should and Would

If you paid attention in school, you learned a little formula for the use of the verbs *shall* and *will* and *should* and *would*. It went like this: to express the simple future, or let us say to indicate a simple intention, use *shall* with the first person and *will* with the second and third persons.

This gives us "I shall grow old one day" and "You (he, she, it) *will* grow old one day." Plurals follow the same pattern: "We *shall* . . ." but "You (they) *will* . . ."

Then, to express determination, or insistence, the pattern is reversed: "I *will* demand my share, no matter what they say" and "You *shall* obey the law like everyone else."

The mass mind that decides on questions of usage appears to have rejected this method of making the distinction between simple future and determination, however. Even the textbooks, although they carefully recite the formula so as to stay within the law, are conceding that usage now largely ignores it.

For better or worse, *shall* and *should* have taken on a distinctly flossy overtone, at least in the United States, and few can use them without a twinge of self-consciousness, except in certain circumstances. We mentally note down the person who says, "I shall take the 5:15 home as usual" as putting on the dog, linguistically speaking. Those who insist that they use *shall* not as an affectation but as the unconscious result of careful training can only be insensitive or uncommonly resistant to what they hear all around them.

*Shall* reportedly is losing face even in England, although it continues to be much more frequently used there than in America, especially on the literary level. The purists among the English lump Scots, Irishmen, and Americans together when they fix the blame for the downfall of *shall*.

"The story is a very old one," writes Sir Ernest Gowers, "of the drowning Scot who was misunderstood by English onlookers and left to his fate because he cried, 'I will drown and nobody shall save me!' " Fowler mentioned the same story, calling it much too good to be true. The time may now have arrived when it is necessary to explain that the Englishmen, construing their grammar strictly, understood the Scot as insisting that he was determined to drown and would allow no one to save him.

*Shall,* then, seems well on the way to extinction, much like the hapless Scot, except in certain constructions where it is used idiomatically without hesitation; e.g., questions, like "Shall I answer the telephone?" and "Shall we dance?" *Shall* also remains firmly entrenched as a means of expressing compulsion or obligation, especially in legal contexts: "The sum shall be repaid in monthly installments."

To the ignorant, *shall* has a tonier sound than *will,* and this causes them to put it in impossible contexts: "I look forward to the time when delegates like yourselves shall meet in every country of the world."

*Should* has fallen under much the same shadow as *shall*. "I should like to attend the premiere" and "If the price fell, I should buy the property" grate on the ears of most Americans as intolerably precious, if not effete, hightoned, or all three. *Should* is generally used now only in the sense of *ought to*: "We should put the car in the garage before it rains."

The nice distinctions of determination vs. simple future that once hung on the choice between *shall* and *will* are now made in speaking by the tone of voice and in writing by a choice of words that cannot be misunderstood ("you *must*" rather than "you *shall*"). An extreme example of this might be, instead of saying "You shall apologize," to growl "You will damn well apologize."

## Passive Voice

The use of the passive voice ("The door *was opened*" rather than "Someone *opened* the door") is a favorite object of excoriation in style manuals, usually without further qualification or explanation. Sweeping indictments of this kind are meaningless, but they are nevertheless characteristic of the vaporings of self-appointed stylemasters, especially on newspapers.

Critics say the passive is undesirable in description or narration. The real issue is whether the subject brought into prominence by use of the passive voice is of any consequence. "The door was closed quietly" and "The issue was discussed for an hour" are hardly objectionable if the closer of the door and the discussers of the issue are of no moment.

As a device for varying sentence structure, however, the passive is not only objectionable but conspicuous. In the course of a biographical sketch "Further education *was received* at Brown University" is absurd because it places an unexplainable emphasis on *further education*. "France and Germany *were visited* next" illustrates the same fault.

For other considerations involving the passive, see in Part Three *drowned, was drowned; married, was married; graduated, was graduated.*

## Was Given

The *was given* phobia, a classic symptom of style craziness, appears to have had its origin in one of the strictures of Ambrose Bierce. The supposition is that such a sentence as "The soldier was given a rifle" is inadmissible because, Bierce wrote, "What was given is the rifle, not the soldier. . . . Nothing can be 'given' anything." How easy it is to go astray handing down rules *ex cathedra* is demonstrated by the fact that Bierce broke his own rule by using *was given* in the very lines he composed to forbid its use.

"The soldier was given a rifle" is a variant arrangement of "A rifle was given to the soldier." Curme writes that sentences in which the accusative becomes nominative "are often preferred in choice expression," and cites as an example, "They were given ample warning."

Simeon Potter, in *Our Language,* says: ". . . in spite of loud protests from proscriptive grammarians, 'Me was given the book' has become 'I was given the book' by the most natural process in the world."

The *Oxford English Dictionary* quotes as an example of the uses of *give* "He was given the contract." When we read sentences like this, do we get the impression, even for a moment, that it was the *soldier, they, I,* or *he* that was given? The idea is obviously nonsense.

Ambrose also forbade us to say "The house was given a coat of paint." But then he didn't like *coat of paint,* either; he insisted it should be *coating*.

# CHAPTER III

# *As* You *Like* It

## Conjunctions

D*on't use* like *as a conjunction.*

How many ages hence this conjunctional injunction will go ringing down the windy corridors of grammatical right and wrong would be hard to say. The odd thing is that, while the rule itself is still marching down the main street as proudly as a drum major, actual practice is increasingly drifting off into side alleys.

To apply this rule, it is necessary to know what a conjunction is. This is the parting of the ways for many would-be purists. Observation shows that the sternest followers of the rules don't quite know what many of them mean, when you get right down to it.

Of this much they are sure: *like* has a curse on it, and is to be avoided whenever possible. This approach produces some strange contortions, of which more anon. What disturbs the purists is the use of *like* in sentences like these:

"He said the movies are not going to stand still, *like* they have for twenty-five years."

"She walked to the altar *like* she said she would."

Note in the above that the groups of words introduced by *like* have subjects and verbs; that is, they are clauses. *Like,* under strict application of the rule, is correctly used only to introduce words or phrases: "He ate *like* a beast" and "She trembled *like* a leaf." The same principle applies to *like* for *as if*: "The Kremlin has been making noises *like* [strictly, *as if*] it wants such a meeting."

*Like* is poaching more and more on the preserves of *as,* and few warrants are being sworn out. What often makes the distinction seem artificial is that the examples quoted last may be thought of as possessing implied verbs. If these verbs are expressed, the phrases become clauses, and *like* is required under the rule to introduce them: "He ate *as* a beast eats" and "She trembled *as* a leaf does."

If you tremble like a leaf yourself at the danger of straying from the path of righteousness in this respect, a useful rule of thumb propounded by Frank O. Colby will keep you on it:

"If *as, as if, as though* make sense in a sentence, *like* is incorrect. If they do not make sense, *like* is the right word."

This rule is easy to use, as will be found by making some trial substitutions, and will keep you infallibly in the good graces of the purists without your even knowing what a conjunction or a subordinate clause is. Mr. Colby, no purist himself, said he had given up as a lost cause the fight against *like* as a conjunction. So have other authorities.

Now, will you join me in a brief excursion out the window with those who are so terrified by *like* that they won't use it even when it's right? First, we have the *as with* aficionados, who write: "The helicopter, *as with* the horseless carriage of an earlier day, is here to stay." There may be a place for *as with,* but the one belonging to *like* is not it.

Then there are those who would walk a mile, not just for a Camel, but to evade *like*:

"The unique plane stands on the ground *in a manner similar to* a camera tripod."

One of the biggest fusses in the history of usage was stirred up by a slogan of the R. J. Reynolds Tobacco Company, "Winstons taste good—like a cigarette should." Reynolds no doubt rubbed its hands gleefully over the extra attention its colloquial use of *like* attracted. Yet, as we have noted, the fact is that the rule against *like* as a conjunction has seen its best days, and so Reynolds really did nothing very heinous.

Grammarians would agree that Reynolds was well within the pale of informal usage. Shakespeare, John Dos Passos, the *New York Times,* and H. L. Mencken are among those cited by Rudolf Flesch in *The Art of Readable Writing* as *like*-likers. *Like* for *as* still will not pass muster in *formal* writing, whatever that is. But it is astonishing that such an uproar should have been created by its use in ads aimed at the lowest common denominator.

My favorite grammarian, Porter G. Perrin, the author of *Writer's Guide and Index to English,* pretty well sums up the views of the grammarians when he says *like* as a conjunction "is obviously on its way to becoming generally accepted and is a good instance of a change in usage, one that we can observe as it takes place."

I wonder how the ultrafastidious felt when they read Liggett & Myers' "Live modern—smoke an L&M." If they had to be critical, *modern* as an adverb is worse than *like* as a conjunction. Here, again, the choice of words no doubt was made with great care, to strike a homey, down-to-earth note among the great unwashed.

Criticizing the admen for things like these is like criticizing Joel Chandler Harris for not having had Uncle Remus talk the King's English, or Finley Peter Dunne for having allowed Mr. Dooley an uncommon liberty with syntax.

Yet the admen are sometimes sensitive, and go on the defensive. For several months I was enchanted by a radio jingle advertising Franco-American spaghetti as the "Best spaghet you ever et." It was not explained whether the reason was a flood of letters from spaghetti-loving purists, or spontaneous remorse, but suddenly that line was changed to "Tastiest spaghetti yet"—carefully preserving, you will notice, the meter and the rhyme, while tidying up the usage.

## As vs. Since

*As* in the sense of *since* or *because* is avoided in careful writing; partly, perhaps, because sometimes it may be confused with *as* in the sense of *during the time that,* but mostly because it grates on the well-tuned ear, a not unimportant organ when it comes to words.

"As the door was locked, he turned and walked away" is ambiguous, for *as* here may be understood as meaning either *during the time that* or *because*. Even when there is no real ambiguity, *as* for *because* is objectionable because it creates a momentary uncertainty for the reader.

"Porter's design is called the Revised Springfield, as he made it while living in Springfield, Mass.," is improved by exchanging *as* for *because*—and perhaps even more by removing the comma.

## While

*While* is best reserved to mean *at the same time as* and is less happily used in the senses of *and, but,* or *although.* "One brother was born June 9, 1893, at Oakland, while the other was born July 19, 1898, at San Jose" unnecessarily makes the reader hesitate, and may make him smile—not with, but at, the writer.

"The cannon will be based on Okinawa while the rockets are being sent to Japan" is ambiguous, because what the writer intended was "*but* the rockets are being sent to Japan." "While architecture flourished in Rome, sculpture was less cultivated" would have been understandable at once as it was meant if it had been written, "*Although* architecture flourished . . ."

### As...as; Not so...as

The pairs _as . . . as_ and _not so . . . as_ sometimes give difficulty. "He likes to be known as a philosopher as much as a theologian" lacks an essential _as_. With the construction filled out, it would be "He likes to be known _as_ a philosopher _as_ much _as as_ a theologian." The third _as_ is required to complete the comparison, and the fourth one is a preposition that is needed with _theologian_ just as much as the first one is needed with _philosopher_. As revised, of course, this sentence is impossible; it might be called half-_as_'d in spite of its abundance of _as_'s. The only cure here is recasting: "He likes to be known equally as a philosopher and as a theologian."

"The critic said the play was as good or better than last season's hits." Another omitted _as_, but this one can be slipped in without difficulty: "as good _as_ or better than."

The idea that _so_ is required with _not_, rather than _as_ ("The moon is not _so_ large as it was last night") has no grammatical basis. The sentence as quoted is correct, but so is "not _as_ large as"; indeed, this is the more natural way to say it. Supposed distinctions like this, which have no merit but give play to intellectual snobbery, are what keep the purists happy.

### That

Although almost any style manual you pick up will contain the admonition to leave out _that_ as a conjunction ("He said _that_ he was starving") when possible, it's actually good advice, in contrast to many stylebook dicta, which are likely to be (a) Victorian purism, (b) superstition, (c) prescriptions for decapitation as a cure for dandruff, or (d) nonsense.

Often, however, we encounter instances when essential _thats_ have been omitted; they have been left out not only when possible, but also when impossible. That's the big trouble with rules, even good ones. Writers tend to clutch them like a life preserver, and jump overboard.

I hesitate to go into the question of where _that_ is called for and where it is not, because it is one that yields only to the capricious law of idiom. Idiom is something that must be felt. _That_ should be retained, in any event, to mark the beginning of a subordinate clause when a part of the clause otherwise may be wrongly associated with some part of the main clause. Often a time element will cause confusion if _that_ is left out.

"Metzman said on Jan. 1 the fleet stood at 1,776,000 cars." The speaker was citing the size of the fleet on Jan. 1, but it is an open question, without a _that_ after _said_, whether Jan. 1 was not the date on which he made the statement.

"The speaker said last November the outlook improved." This is another example of the same problem. *That* is needed after either *said* or *November,* depending on what the time element is intended to modify. It may be argued that the context is likely to supply the answer to this question, but the reader deserves to be spared even momentary doubt.

Sometimes the omission of *that* sends the reader off on the wrong scent as to the force of the verb: "He added the proposed freeway could follow the existing route." "He added *that . . .*" would read unequivocally, but the first version may appear, for the moment, to make *freeway* alone the object of *added,* as in "He added the proposed freeway to the list of essential projects."

At least one *that,* and preferably a pair of them, should be used with co-ordinate clauses: "The deputy foreign minister said last night that Panama does not receive its fair share of Panama Canal revenues, and sentiment for a 50 per cent increase is likely to grow." Now, who is to say, offhand, whether the words about growing sentiment for a 50 per cent increase were a part of the deputy foreign minister's statement, or an observation by the writer? The sentence should have read ". . . and *that* sentiment . . ."

The first *that* of a pair like this is sometimes dropped, perhaps out of the general eagerness to dispense with the word: "The board was told the point is really one of economics, and that if the ordinance were repealed, meat markets would be driven out of business." On the whole, however, the two clauses are more clearly balanced if both are set off by *that* (". . . was told *that* the point . . .").

Before a complete direct quotation, as distinguished from a fragment, *that* is clearly excess baggage: "The Point Four director in Iran reported *that* 'More than half the population of the village have been killed under the falling walls of their homes.' " *That* in this position—or inside the quotation marks, for that matter—smacks of an earlier age.

*But that* sometimes sticks in the craw of the critical, in such sentences as "I do not doubt *but that* society feels threatened by homosexuality." Technically, *but* here is excessive. Yet usage by good writers as well as those not so good has gained it a respectable place.

## Preposition at End

A couple of English professors (professors, that is, of English) were mountain-climbing on vacation, when all at once they saw an avalanche bearing down on them.

"Heaven help us," cried one. "We're done for."

"For God's sake, Henry," returned the other, "don't end your last sentence with a preposition."

This may be funny enough on the surface, but it is a joke that could not have been made up by a grammarian. (If, in fact, any joke could.) The *for* in *done for* is not really a preposition but an adverb that has merged with the verbal modifier *done* to form a new expression, whose meaning depends on both words taken together. Anyway, who could imagine an English professor, even on vacation, using a colloquialism like *done for*?

The notion that it is wrong, or undesirable, to end a sentence with a preposition has been flayed by Fowler and many another authority on language. The most recent blow was struck by Sir Winston Churchill, who, when accused of ending a sentence with a preposition, is said to have replied: "This is the type of arrant pedantry up with which I shall not put."

You can show that sentences with the preposition at the end are more forceful than those that have been recast to avoid it; you can cite masters of English prose from Chaucer to Churchill who employ end prepositions freely and consciously; and you can prove that such usage is established literary English, but superstition-ridden writers will still wince at it.

In writing, as distinguished from rule-reciting, the avoidance of the end preposition is most evident, perhaps, in structural detours that start with a preposition followed by *which*. Few care about making the world a better place *to live in,* but nearly everyone wants to make it a better place *in which to live.* "The car she was riding in," after editing with zeal and ignorance, becomes "The car in which she was riding."

The use of circumlocution to find another place than the end for the preposition not only weakens the sentence but gives it a stilted sound. "What are we coming to?"; "There was nothing to talk about"; "It was something he had always dreamed of"; and "The situation was too much to contend with" are perfectly good English in any context. Shame on him who wads these sentences up into "To what are we coming?"; "There was nothing about which to talk"; "It was something of which he had always dreamed"; and "The situation was too much with which to contend."

The origin of the superstition forbidding the preposition at the end of a sentence is sometimes considered a mystery, but actually it came, again, from applying Latin rules of grammar to English. In Latin, it is said to be all but impossible to detach a preposition from its object. Linguists now, however, have decided that the rules of one language make a Procrustean bed for another.

## Choice of Prepositions

Idiom is often flouted, these careless days, in the choice of prepositions. Let us start with *between* and *among*. No one would use *among* with only two objects ("Among you and me"), but there is a misguided though prevalent idea that *between* cannot be correctly used with more than two objects: "Agreements were reached *between* six nations." The proper use of *between* does not depend on the number of objects, but on whether they are being considered in pairs. Even this is open to question as a limiting rule.

Pointless efforts are sometimes made to prescribe *in* or *at,* depending on the prescriber's prejudice, as the correct preposition to use with a place, such as a city, building, or street. Either *in* or *at San Francisco,* or *the Municipal Auditorium,* is correct. Some insist that a house is *in* a street and, as a corollary, that people live *in* a street. Whatever justification may be advanced for this peculiar usage, popular acceptance is not it. In unaffected parlance, people live *on* a street, not *in* it, and that is where a house stands, too.

"He turned himself into the Fourth Precinct Police Station" sounds like a feat of magic that would have shamed Houdini. We have here a phrasal verb, *turn in,* and the *in* has unfortunately been fused with the preposition *to.* It should have been "turned himself in to." *Turn into,* however, is possible, as in "We turned into a side street." If *this* be magic, make the most of it.

People used to die *of* things, rather than *from* them, and in spite of the widespread use of *from* in this connection, it is still not regarded as acceptable. Nor should *of* be used with *off*: "He jumped off of the bridge."

People are increasingly being accused *with* crimes, rather than *of* them, as they should be. Sometimes they *confess to* the misdeeds, rather than simply confessing them. The use of *confess to* produces some striking gaucheries: "Joan Crawford and Phil Terry also confessed failure to their marriage." From some backwoods weekly, you say? Not at all; this appeared in one of the country's leading news magazines.

*Confess to* appears to have encouraged, by analogy, *admit to,* for which sanction can be found nowhere: "Greene frankly admits to a youthful membership in the party"; "She admits to having been a brat as a child"; "He admits to a gourmet's interest in food." Fowler said *confess to* is idiomatic and *admit to* is not. Nevertheless, it is observable that *to* is unnecessary with either *confess* or *admit* and, further, that these constructions are usually found in diseased contexts.

When the defendant is in luck, it is often written that "the charge was dismissed against Jones." This is a sad arrangement of words, since it tends to link *dismissed* with *against,* and thus to suggest nonsense. Surely it would be preferable to say "The charge against Jones was dismissed." Sometimes we have suspects being exonerated *from* a charge, but here the right preposition is *of*. Likewise, they plead (guilty, not guilty) *to,* not *of,* charges.

Some of us harbor the delusion that it is wrong to say a man was hit *over* the head, unless the blows missed him. This is a standard sense of the word ("down upon from above"), however, and instantly clear except to those who willfully misunderstand. Those perverse ones would probably insist that a person could not wander over the face of the earth except in an airplane.

*Over*, however, sometimes *is* called into play illogically, as in "Considerable reductions over single-performance prices are again being offered." These reductions, it seems plain, are *from*, not *over*, which suggests an increase.

Grammatical folklore has it that *to compare with* is to liken and *to compare to* is to contrast. But it's not that simple, by puristic standards. Why don't we admit the truth—that the finely drawn distinction between these expressions is neither observed in writing nor perceived in reading, and that the attempt to preserve it may as well be abandoned as useless? For a fuller discussion of this point see *compare to, with,* and *contrast,* in Part Three.

*As* as a preposition is unnecessary after such words as *named, appointed, elected*: "He was appointed as vicar" might as well be "He was appointed vicar."

## On

Standardization, by making mechanical parts interchangeable, gave the industrial age a big push, if I was not misinformed in my early brushes with the science of economics. This process is also at work in language, and has been for centuries. The specialists in that field call it not standardization but leveling. That is to say, diverse forms which do the same or similar jobs tend to merge, or to kill one another off. One evidence of this is the disappearance of *thee, thou, ye,* and the like from all but archaic or specialized usage. *You* has put them all out of business.

The losing fight being made by *whom* against *who* is an example of leveling that is under way in our own time. It seems predictable that *whom* will go the way of all flesh, in spite of the fact that people who are trying too hard to be correct sometimes make it displace *who*. *The New Yorker* calls attention to this from time to time under the heading, "The Omnipotent Whom."

The prize contender for omnipotence, in my opinion, is neither *who* nor *whom*, but rather the preposition *on*. Like a bandwagon-climber who has scented a promising dark horse, I began some time ago to note down evidence of *on*'s increasing popularity, especially in the press. I have found it nosing out *about, at, for, from, in, into, of, to,* and *toward*. Drunk with success, it may easily press forward and knock all other prepositions out of the language.

Would this be a good thing? Some linguists regard as the most advanced those languages in which leveling has gone the farthest. Certainly it makes communicating simpler. In this instance, the effort now spent on choosing among prepositions would be saved. But *on,* despite its popularity in the press, is not being accepted as a proxy elsewhere.

Let us see how *on* has gone beserk:

"His worried fans can be reassured *on* one thing, however." My candidate here would be *about,* or perhaps *of.*

"The officer questioned the woman *on* her wounds." Sounds deucedly uncomfortable for the woman, and downright inconsiderate of the officer, who might have settled himself elsewhere. *about* or *concerning.*

"The mayor was dismayed *on* the permit denial." *at* or *by.*

"Don't wait *on* me." This remark was addressed, not to a waitress, but to a friend by a man who did not want to be waited *for.* This is a Far-Western barbarism, common in conversation. From there it oozes into the newspapers: "The trustees must wait *on* approval by the State Allocations Board." *await* or *wait for.*

"Complaints *on* dogs running loose are increasing"; "I'll call him *on* that." *about.*

"The man has an elephantlike memory *on* abuse he has taken"; "Support will be sought *on* the proposal." *of* and *for.*

"The wraps may be lifted soon *on* dramatic defense developments." *from.*

"Developments *on* Middle East problems dominated the session." *in.*

"The defendant was convicted *on* a charge of theft"; "A study *on* psittacosis has been undertaken"; "Complaints *on* violations of waterway rules have been received." *of.*

"Science is finding clues *on* possible causes." *to.*

"Little progress has been made *on* racial integration." *toward* or *in.*

And, finally: "The aim is to educate the populace *on* the proper use of English." Let's start now, if it's not too late.

## With

"Only citizens of the United States will be eligible for permits with all of them to be issued on a competitive basis."

"Smith was struck in the chest and right hip with the third shot going wild."

"The United States ranks ninth in infant mortality with Sweden having the best record."

Sentences of this ilk are as thick as thistles, and about as easy to penetrate. They can be figured out, all right, but not without a pause after *with* to decide which way the wind is blowing. If you want the grammar of it, let's call in a grammarian, Easley S. Jones, the author of *Practical English Composition,* who describes such *with* constructions as nonrestrictive adverbial prepositional phrases.

The main points are that *with* phrases can be legitimate, and that they must be set off by commas. Here is an example of an unobjectionable *with* phrase, which unmistakably modifies the main part of the sentence, as it should: "The bandit raced through the corridor, with the police gaining slowly."

But many *with* phrases are clumsy substitutes for clearer construction. On close inspection, *with* is seen to be introducing elements that ought to be clauses. *With* phrases are used sparingly by good writers, because they seldom fit happily. Let us see whether a little carpentry will not improve the sentences quoted at the beginning:

"Only citizens of the United States will be eligible for permits, all of which will be issued on a competitive basis."

"Smith was struck in the chest and right hip, but the third shot went wild."

"The United States ranks ninth in infant mortality. Sweden has the best record."

The moral: If you must use *with* phrases, put commas in front of them. But remember that a sentence containing this construction is often a poor job in the first place.

## Piled-up Prepositions

It must be an uncontrollable passion for exactness that causes us to pile up prepositions, or in some instances to use them when they could be better omitted altogether. Doubled prepositions often occur when a range is specified: "Its control spreads *into between* 25 and 30 per cent of the economy." Such constructions are clumsy because the reader must figure out that the object of *into* is the whole six-word phrase beginning with *between*. "Into 25 or 30 per cent" reads more easily.

"The airlift is expected to speed the delivery of mail *by from* twenty-four to forty-eight hours" would be smoother going with *from* left out.

"Investments *of from* two to four million dollars were reported." Here too, *from* is superfluous.

"The weatherman predicted a low temperature *of between* 75 and 80 degrees." In this instance *of* seems expendable. Newspaper weather stories seem especially hospitable to intrusive prepositions. The italicized words would never be missed in "A low temperature *of* near 45 degrees is expected" and "The Sierra received *from* 2 to 4 inches of slushy snow." *At about* may be trimmed to *about*: "About nine o'clock last night."

Some extra prepositions do not fall into any readily apparent category, but are none the less objectionable: "The Justice Department is expected to keep hands off *in* the dispute." This looks like a variant of *off of,* scorned of old and no more reputable now than ever.

# CHAPTER IV

# Diction, Dictionaries, and Word Order

Colloquialisms; Contractions; Technical Terms; Redundancy; Repetition of Defining Modifiers; Ellipsis; Variation; False Comparison; Parallelism; Euphemisms; Dictionaries; Word Order (Inversion); Misplaced Prepositional Modifiers; Gerund Construction.

## Colloquialisms

I F THE admonitions we often hear were scrupulously and literally followed, much of what we read would sound like a cross between a mayor's proclamation and a frosty exchange of courtesies between ambassadors. What I am getting at is the distinct, and deplorable, tendency favoring stuffy writing. The encouragers wouldn't want to hear it put that way, of course. They would be likely to say that they prefer a formal tone of expression, or that they want dignity.

This attitude is nothing more or less than a facet of the pomposity that has afflicted writing since the Year One. The professorial, textbook style is repellent wherever it is encountered. Reviewers apologize for books that are pedantically written but otherwise have merit.

Stuffiness is especially repellent in news reportage. The news is all narrative, and narrative that isn't breezy is hard going. News situations, in general, are repetitious enough in their outlines. The reader should not be bored even more by starchy prose.

Now, this subject has endless ramifications, and I want to narrow this disquisition down to one aspect, namely, the old-maidish alarm caused by words the dictionary identifies as colloquialisms. To judge by the fright they create, colloquialisms may well be less acceptable to some people than slang, vulgarisms, or obscenity. There is good reason to believe that most of these fussers simply do not know what *colloquial* means. Let us penetrate the fine print in the front end of Webster's *New International Dictionary* to see what is said there on this subject:

"It is unfortunate that with some the term *colloquial* has somewhat fallen into disrepute, the impression having gained ground that a word marked *colloquial* in a dictionary or similar work is thereby condemned as not in the best use. See the definition of *colloquial* in the vocabulary."

Here it is:

"Colloquial, adj. Pertaining to, or used in conversation, esp. familiar conversation; hence, informal."

The opposite of *informal* is *formal,* and in further discussion Webster says that colloquialisms are appropriate in informal writing, among other places, *but not in formal written discourse.*

Well, what is formal written discourse, anyway? Proclamations and diplomatic communications, turgid and often laughable in their choice of language, surely come under this heading. So do legal documents, about whose pomposity even lawyers are growing uneasy, to judge from indictments of legal lingo in bar-association journals. But come now, do we want communicative writing of any kind to be bracketed with dull stuff like this? Formal prose of every description is reached by the same road, one marked NO COLLO-QUIALISMS.

We have no business shunning the conversational or the informal, unless we also want to drive off the reader. Even the academician turns with a sigh of relief from the mealy prose out of which he grinds his daily bread to something written with the comfort of the reader in mind.

## Contractions

The avoidance of contractions is another aspect of the fear of informal writing. The attitude toward them usually ranges from outright prohibition to discouragement "except when appropriate." Qualified discouragement of this kind would be all right except that experience shows it is usually interpreted as a general ban. Many of us seemingly often lack confidence in our ability to decide when contractions *are* appropriate.

My own observation is that the objectionable use of contractions is all but nil. Thus the bad breath blown upon them might as well be saved, or aimed instead at one of the numerous real vices that are prevalent but seldom singled out for criticism.

Rudolf Flesch, in *The Art of Readable Writing,* came to this conclusion: "If you want to write informal English, the use of contractions is certainly essential."

I remember a story about a little girl who had to walk through a graveyard on her way home. She was asked, "Aren't you afraid?" After this question had gone through the hands of an editor whose mother had been frightened by a stylebook, however, it came out "Are you not afraid?"

Then there was the headline on a feature story that read: "It Is Official! June Was Hot!" Well, "It Is Official" is simply not idiomatic; many a reader will boggle at it, wondering what reason could be given for sidestepping "It's Official."

It is easy to imagine the editor responsible for "Are you not afraid?" and "It is official" staidly announcing to his friends, upon being presented with an heir, "It is a boy!" On second thought, such a lackluster remark would hardly take an exclamation point. It might, however, prompt "Here is to you" as a toast in reply. But here is, or here's, hoping that all such follies will be forestalled by judicious acceptance of contractions.

## Technical Terms

In everyday communication, should we use technical terms that are not common currency in preference to readily understandable substitutes? Experts on readability would probably say no. Nevertheless, the use of technical language, or of the cant belonging to a specialized field, is a temptation to the writer who thinks it will make his stuff sound learned and impressive.

The use of technical terms is hard to avoid in writing that deals with advances in physics, medicine, and the other sciences, and often no satisfactory synonyms are available in plain language. The writer who keeps his audience in mind, however, will be careful to follow the unfamiliar technical terms he must use with definitions rendered in language as simple as possible.

Science writing, a special case, is usually handled by writers who make it a specialty and who have no need to be warned of such pitfalls. But what about writing that deals with such everyday subjects as automobile accidents? These accounts often abound with *contusions, abrasions, lacerations, fractures,* and other terms redolent of the hospital. Everybody knows, of course, that a fracture is a break, although that's not what everybody ordinarily says. Lacerations are cuts, for practical purposes, although the doctor may mean something more complex by this expression. It is doubtful that *contusions* presents any clear picture to the layman. What's wrong with *bruises* instead of *contusions, cuts* instead of *lacerations,* and *sewing* instead of *suturing?* This much is certain: although many readers may know what some medical terms mean, there are many more who do not.

*Hemorrhage* is certainly inexcusable for *bleed* in anything but a medical journal. *Coronary occlusion, carcinoma, thrombosis,* and *first-, second-,* and *third-degree burns* all require translation for the ordinary reader.

Some writers, having learned the meaning of some technical terms, are so proud of themselves they cannot resist showing off. Others never bother to find anything out, and lazily relay what has been given them by medical men.

It is a good principle not to send the reader to the dictionary, but to send the writer there instead. Let the reader relax.

In one city, an outbreak of sleeping sickness (encephalitis) was attributed to the *culex tarsalis* mosquito. Newspaper stories on the subject, which caused considerable public alarm, ran for weeks before anyone thought of describing *culex tarsalis* and its habits, giving some idea how common this variety was among the dozen or so in the area.

In another instance, the term *low low water line* was used again and again in connection with an important water-front project. Yet no one but seafarers knew what that line was, and the newspapers failed to give any help to the others.

## Redundancy

The sportsman does not use a shotgun when a rifle will do. When it comes to writing, the rifle can't be beat. The writer who closes his eyes, pulls the trigger, and lets fly with a barrage of words ought to be told that somehow they lose their force in bunches. A single, well-chosen shot will bring the quarry down every time. In general, the fewer the words the better the writing.

The soporific habit of using several words where one will serve may be illustrated by *a sufficient number of* vs. *enough, at the present time* vs. *now,* and *in the immediate vicinity of* vs. *near.* These woolly expressions, which occur so often they pop readily into the mind, are readily used by the uncritical writer. Hunting them down and nailing them to the wall is a salutary exercise.

A repulsive pair of expressions has grown onto the word *future*: *in the near future* and *in the not-too-distant future.* Translated, *in the near future* means *soon,* and *in the not-too-distant future* can mean *before long, eventually, finally, next year, sometime,* or *sooner or later.* The reader, poor fellow, must decide.

The word *case* is the progenitor of a hardy breed of villains that seem impervious to attack: *in case* (if), *in most cases* (usually), *if that were the case* (if so), *not the case* (not so), *in the case of* (which often may be omitted entirely, and if not, replaced by *concerning*), and *as in the case of* (like).

Here is a little beauty: "It is possible that this material may become mixed with clouds in some cases and induce rain sooner than otherwise would have been the case." Stripping this down to what counts, we get: "This material may become mixed with clouds and induce [cause?] rain sooner."

Some redundancies have become classical targets of critics: *"at the intersection of* Market and Main" (at); *"consensus of opinion"* (consensus); *"entirely* destroyed" (destroyed). Also undeservedly popular are *despite the fact that* (although), *due to the fact that* (because or since), *during the period from* (from), and *for the purpose of* (for).

Redundancy is a vast and overfertilized field. Among its varieties, as classified by scholars, are pleonasm (using more words than necessary), tautology (repeating an idea in different words), and circumlocution or periphrasis (talking around the subject). The point of this preachment is not so much to urge the outlawing of the particular expressions cited as to encourage the critical sense. Nevertheless, the examples have been chosen for their prevalence, and any writer who does forego them will certainly not harm his work.

Ignorance of what common words mean, or unwillingness to trust them to do their job unaided, is responsible for some specimens of redundancy. *Experience, records, custom,* and *history* come only from the *past*; thus there is no occasion for *past experience, past records, past custom,* and *past history*. *Gifts* and *passes* are by definition *free,* even if the advertising gentry cannot be made to see it. An *innovation* is by its nature *new,* as are a *beginner* and a *tyro,* and an *incumbent* is inescapably of the *present. Plans* are willy-nilly of the *future,* as must be *prospects* and *developments. Planning* can be nothing but *advance.*

What is *friendship* if it is not *personal*? And what is *business* if not *official,* oh bumbling bureaucrats? *Both agreed* offends the thin skinned, for *both* is two taken together and *agreement* is a coming together. *Equally as* is a horse of the same color. *On account of* is distasteful for *because of,* and *in excess of* is even worse for *more than,* because it is not only redundant but pompous.

"*In order to* balance the budget," or what have you, might better be simply *to balance. In back of* is a gaucherie for *behind,* though *in front of* (a building, for example) serves a purpose that *before* does not. *Advance reservations* seem to be getting ahead of themselves. *In which* is often superfluous, as in "Each candidate will be given fifteen minutes *in which* to express his views." An accident victim is taken to a hospital *for treatment,* inevitably; why labor it?

*New construction* is Navyese for a ship abuilding; why apply it to buildings, when nothing is more self-evident than the newness of what is under construction? These random examples show, if nothing else, that the pen is mightier than the pitchfork.

## Repetition of Defining Modifiers

Redundancy is evident also in the useless repetition of defining modifiers. Once a man has been identified as a hotel porter he should be referred to as *the porter* rather than *the hotel porter*. (This is not to be interpreted as discouraging the use of *he* or *him* when possible.) The examples that follow illustrate other instances of excessive identification. The descriptives that should be omitted are in italics:

"George Jones was found guilty of second-degree murder today. A jury composed of seven men and five women returned the *second-degree* verdict after five hours. The *second-degree-murder* conviction carries a penalty of five years to life."

"A dinner will be held Sunday at 7 P.M. Reservations *for the dinner* may be made by telephone."

It is a mark of an undeveloped style to review, or sum up, or restate purposelessly what has just been said. Summaries should be made deliberately, with a view to assisting the reader, and should not betray fuzzy-mindedness in the writer, as in these instances:

"He became pastor of the church when it was completed two years ago. Prior to accepting the pastorate, he was a student." Better: "Before that, he was a student."

"They tried to break a safe out of a 500-pound block of concrete. Failing to free the safe from the concrete, they fled." Better: "Failing, they fled."

"Sixteen people were killed in a tragic crush on New Year's Day. Those victims were killed when a tremendous crowd surged across a narrow bridge." Better: "Sixteen people were killed in a tragic crush on New Year's Day when a tremendous crowd surged across a narrow bridge."

## Ellipsis

Ellipsis is the grammarian's word for omission of what is readily understood. It is a useful device that should be encouraged, short of ambiguity or conveying a misleading idea. Let us consider instances in which ellipsis is and is not desirable.

An element may usually be profitably omitted from the second of parallel constructions in which it would be repeated in the same position. Often such constructions involve numerical comparisons. In the examples cited, the words in italics would be better left out:

"McDonald said 189,344 members are on leave and 257,026 *members are* on part-time schedules."

"In 1958 there were twenty-one days of 100-plus readings and in 1953 there were twenty *days of 100-degree or higher weather*." Here, afraid to repeat *100-plus readings,* the writer strained to invent a variation; he might better have saved his effort and ended on *twenty.* More of the same:

"The plant is capable of handling 650 tons per hour, but is handling only 500 *tons per sixty minutes*." The substitution of *sixty minutes* as a variant for *hour* may strike some readers as ingenious, but it will strike many others, alas, as stupid.

"Jones was cited for driving without due caution, and Smith *was cited* for driving without a license."

"Turnover totaled 420,000 shares, well below Monday's 570,000-*share figure.*"

"The college has enrolled 10 per cent more full-time students this year than *were registered for classes* at the end of the first week of school last year."

The words that may be omitted may involve a comparison, rather than a repetition:

"Mohammed Reza is now more firmly on his throne than *he ever had been* since he became Shah."

Sometimes, however, it will not do to fail to repeat verb forms:

"On his arrival, he was told the job was filled and *offered* $100 as expense money." This should read *was offered* to complete the parallel construction with *was filled*. As it stands, *offered* may be taken as active instead of passive.

"The spokesman said another firm *has* or is about to file for a franchise." This should be *has filed*, for the missing word is not smoothly supplied by the reader. Careless ellipsis may be confusing in other constructions: "The men forced the singer to take sleeping pills after they stripped and photographed her in the nude." Who, then, was nude?

Another form of ellipsis is recommended in relative clauses, usually those starting with *which, who,* or *that.* The idea has sometimes been stated in this way: Cancel the pronoun (*which, who, that*) plus companion forms of *to be* (*is, are, was, were*). This is how it works:

"There is a difference between what they announce as crop yields and the amount [that is] available to the people."

"Work is under way on an ice rink [that is] scheduled to open next month."

"The bridge would give access to the island, [which is] now served by a ferry."

"Members of the Pioneer Methodist Church, [which was] built in 1858, will celebrate next week."

"Elman, [who was] an amateur musician before he escaped, now performs professionally."

*That* or *which* may also be omitted when they are the subjects of other verbs: "Sibelius was stricken with a brain hemorrhage at the villa [which] he built near Helsinki fifty-three years before."

"Local issues were responsible for the clobbering [which] the Republicans took in the Maine election." Technically, those two *whiches* should have been *thats,* anyway. For this aspect of the problem, see *that* vs. *which,* Chapter VII.

Ellipsis of a different kind is employed to shorten quotations for the writer's purpose, and in these instances the reader must be placed on notice that he is getting a curtailed version: "The speaker said the book was 'ill-conceived, hastily written . . . and obviously the work of an ignoramus.' " The use of three spaced periods for this purpose has become such a standardized and well-accepted convention there is no excuse for using *x*'s or asterisks.

## Variation

Variation merely to avoid repetition of a term is not only worse than repetition, as Fowler said, but may suggest a distinction that does not exist.

The problem is often neatly solved by ellipsis:

"He *played with* Charlie Barnet's Orchestra and *worked with* Red Norvo's Sextet." Play and work are two different things, but the writer here was merely straining to avoid repeating the same words to express the same idea. Yet he might have said "played with Charlie Barnet's Orchestra and with Red Norvo's Sextet."

"Russia's army newspaper *Red Star* claims there are now 33 million Communist Party members in seventy-five nations. The breakdown gave Indonesia one million. France was said to have 5 million Red voters; Italy, 1.8 million card-carriers." Are Communist Party members, Red voters, and card-carriers all the same? The writer assumed this to be true, but of course it is not. The changes are rung unnecessarily. Once it has been established that *Communist Party members* is the idea under discussion, the writer might have trusted the reader's memory beyond Indonesia to: "France was said to have 5 million; Italy, 1.8 million."

In other common instances, such variation is merely silly:

"About 76 per cent of Russia's doctors are *women,* while in the United States only 6 per cent are *female*." *Women* would have sounded better repeated; or "but the proportion in the United States is only 6 per cent."

"Cigarette smokers *puffed* a record 205 billion cigarettes in the first six months of this year, 4.4 per cent more than they *lit up* in the same time in 1956." Lighting up and puffing are different things, and the variation has an absurd sound: "4.4 per cent more than in the same time in 1956."

"In cases where both parents are *obese,* 72 per cent of the offspring also are *fat.* When one parent is *fat,* 41 per cent of the children are *overweight.* When neither parent is *obese,* only 4 per cent of the offspring are *fat*." This writer danced an ungainly dance between *obese, fat,* and *overweight* on one hand, and between *children* and *offspring* on the other. What about "When both parents are fat, 72 per cent of the children are. When one parent is fat, 41 per cent of the children are. When neither parent is fat, only 4 per cent of the children are"?

One aspect of what Fowler called elegant variation might be described as the geographical fetish, since it requires that the second reference to a place be in the form of a geographical description. In California, under these ground rules, it is permissible to name San Francisco once, but the second time it is mentioned it must become *the northern city*. Other samples of this aberration:

"The caravan plans a dinner in Podunk and an overnight stop in the Razorback County city" and "A three-day international convention opened today in Nagasaki on the anniversary of the atom bombing of the southern Japanese city."

There is something to be said for this practice. It conveys information to the reader about the location of the place named, in the event he happens not to know where it is. But there is also something to be said against the practice—it's an asinine way to write. Desirable information about locale or anything else should be offered for its own sake and not made a device to avoid naming the place again.

From map-making, the fashioners of this kind of prose often graduate into zoological classification:

"Children who want to enter a frog in the event may pick up an amphibian at the Chamber of Commerce office." Here pearls of another branch of knowledge are being cast before readers, but they probably will not appreciate it, the swine. As a swine-lover, I will defend them if they prefer *an overnight stop there* to *an overnight stop in the Razorback County city,* or *may pick one up* to *may pick up an amphibian.*

"A search for a mountain lion was abandoned when no sign of *such a carnivore* was found." *Such a carnivore* is a pompously stupid substitute for *such an animal* or even *one.* Here are some common latter-day examples of elegant variation: *simian* for *monkey, jurist* for *judge, bovine* for *cow, feline* for *cat, quadruped* for any four-legged animal, *equine* for *horse, optic* for *eye, tome* for *book, white stuff* for *snow.*

The printed word is a powerful educative force, but it is questionable whether calling an oyster *a bivalve,* an elephant *a pachyderm,* a dog *a canine,* gold *the yellow metal,* legislators *solons,* or professors *savants* has contributed anything to public uplift.

## False Comparison

Careless writers, apparently by carrying ellipsis too far, often stumble into false comparison. They write "Older houses are still selling here, unlike many cities" or "Like many patient folk, Russian violence can be brutal." If these writers stayed awake, they would see the need for "unlike *those in* many cities" and "like *that of* many patient folk." The difficulty in such instances is that a relative pronoun (usually *that*) and a preposition have been inadvisedly squeezed out. In the examples, as a result, *older houses* are compared with *many cities,* and *patient folk* with *Russian violence.*

Here are other examples, in which the originally omitted, but necessary, words have been italicized:

"Addiction in California appears to differ from *that in* other states."

"Robert Sarnoff, president, admitted that NBC's situation was in some ways tougher than *that of* the other networks."

"Five bids were lower than *that of* the American Seating Company."

Sometimes the error is caused by omitting the preposition alone, as in "Receipts from livestock sales were 7 per cent less than the corresponding period last year." The receipts were not less than the corresponding period, as reported, but less than *in* the corresponding period.

"An illusion of reality can be more completely brought to an audience on the screen than *by* any other medium."

## Parallelism

Parallelism is the name given to following the same pattern with constructions that naturally fall into it. It makes for ease in reading and, therefore, is to be encouraged. Most offenses against parallelism consist in switching verb forms: "It is a matter *of letting* tavern owners know their rights and *to avoid* confusion." *Of letting* should be matched by *of avoiding.*

"Benson said the only real answer to the dairy-surplus problem seems to be *to push* consumption of butter through regular marketing channels and *encouraging* farmers to get rid of inefficient cows." *to push* :: *to encourage.*

"The unit will contain air-to-ground voice equipment *for transmitting* traffic-control instructions and *to obtain* position reports from aircraft." *for transmitting* : : *for obtaining.*

"Vladimir Petrov was reported as *having asked for* and *was granted* asylum in Australia." This construction not only flouts parallelism but also shifts awkwardly from the active to the passive voice: *having asked for* and *having obtained.*

"Stringfellow *had returned* to Ogden, Utah, *became* a radio announcer, *gone* into politics, and *been elected* to Congress." Either *had returned, had become, had gone,* and *had been*; or *returned, became, went,* and *was elected.*

"A welcome will be extended by Joe Blow, and Wolfgang Ethier will speak on 'My Reform School Career.' " An awkward shift from the passive to the active: "Joe Blow *will extend* a welcome, and Wolfgang Ethier *will speak* on . . ."

"The state *suspended* sixteen driver permits, and one was revoked for vehicle violations." *suspended* sixteen . . . and *revoked* one.

Parallelism is desirable in other instances than those involving verb forms: "Mr. Ziegfeld selected girls for their good looks, personality, and good figures." *personalities*.

"The fight ends when the losing cricket breaks away from *his* conqueror and is promptly removed from the cage by *its* owner." Either *his* or *its* should be used consistently.

"One of the officers was suspended *for ten days,* and the other for *a five-day period.*" *for ten days,* and . . . *for five days.*

"The production models will have *a speed* of 85 miles an hour, *a range* of 150 miles, and *carry* 800 pounds." And *a capacity* of 800 pounds.

## Euphemisms

Life is a hard business, as someone has said, and we often seek to soften its blows by giving them agreeable names. This device—for example, saying *passed away* instead of *died*—is known technically as euphemism, or pleasing talk. Euphemism is not something that can or should be done away with. In many instances, the bluntest names for things are intolerable in polite society and censorable in print. The so-called four-letter words fall in this category. On the rare occasions when they appear in print—in novels, for example— the effect on the reader may be one of shock, refreshment, amusement, or a mixture of all three.

Writers should at least be aware when they are using terms that are at one or more removes from the most explicit versions. Euphemisms are distasteful when they indicate unnecessary squeamishness. The trend of our ordinary expression for many years has been away from the complex, the pretentious, and the flowery, and toward the simple, the unassuming, and the unadorned.

It is not so long ago that *social disease* was as close as anyone but a doctor would come to saying *syphilis* or *gonorrhea*—and even the euphemism was used with reluctance. In fact, the medical campaign to curb syphilis was seriously impeded by the refusal, at first, of mass publications even to name the disease. Few now boggle at it.

Prudery is far from dead, however. I am reminded of the commanding officer of a naval station with a complement of several thousand civilians. He objected in horror when the editor of the base paper publicized the presence of an infectious disease in the community that affected the sexual organs of little girls. The same week, as the speaker at a mixed dinner of the Petty Officers Club, he told a joke involving toilet paper that gave offense to many persons present.

Let's skip around among some typical euphemisms. A cut or increase in wages or prices is often glossed over, when it seems desirable, as *a downward revision* or *an upward revision* (or *adjustment*). In the jargon of business, especially, prices are never raised, but delicately *revised upward*. This may be all right for the public relations man, whose vocation is to gloss, but certainly such genteelisms should not be adopted by others with the idea that they possess some desirable elegance.

*Heart condition* used to be more popular than it is now for *heart ailment*. *Heart condition,* more than one critic has said, is meaningless, since every heart has a condition, better or worse. *Heart attack,* while we are on this subject, is a useful workaday term that has been unaccountably denounced as denoting an attack by the heart. The publicity recently attending heart ailments in high places has led to widespread lay use of *coronary* as an illegitimate noun (for what was once *heart attack*). *Cardiac,* too, has been enthusiastically taken up by the laity.

*Realistic* is a key euphemism in collective and other kinds of bargaining. *Realistic,* in this connection, is what its user's proposals are, in contrast to those of the other side, which are invariably *unrealistic*.

During the war we became familiar with *planned withdrawal,* the military's euphemism for *a retreat*. General Jonathan Wainwright was so outraged by this kind of mush that he described one reverse in these unequivocal terms: "We took a hell of a beating."

The name *Woman's Christian Temperance Union,* as nearly everyone must be aware, is a misnomer, for its members advocate abstinence, not temperance. *Abstinence* has an unyielding sound, however, and it may be that the temperance ladies can stand the shock of solid words no more than they can stand the fumes of hard drink. *Belly,* to follow the liquor down, is all but indecent; genteel people speak only of the *abdomen*. I wonder when the Nice Nellies will succeed in cleaning up the Bible to "Thy abdomen is like an heap of wheat set about with lilies."

## Dictionaries

The differences between reputable dictionaries on points of usage are negligible. It must be conceded, however, that such differences may be fairly conspicuous, for obvious reasons, between the *Oxford English Dictionary* (by and for Englishmen) and *Webster's New International* (by and for Americans).

A lack of esteem for dictionaries prevails in some quarters on the ground that they are not infallible. This, of course, is so, as it is of all human endeavors. Disesteem for dictionaries was encouraged by testy Ambrose Bierce, who acidly wrote them off as bloated, absurd, and misleading. In their place, presumably, or perhaps to counteract their evil influence, he offered his own revelation, *Write It Right* (1909). This little book, now pretty much a curiosity, contains considerable patches that don't make much sense any more.

If you turn from the dictionary in haughty superiority, what are you going to turn *to*? Your own notions of usage, meanings, and mechanical practices? They are likely to be only prejudices, not very well founded. Reputable dictionaries, with all their faults, are the work of boards of lexicographers who assiduously study words, consult experts in special fields, and analyze writing and speech at all levels to determine what accepted practice really is.

About the worst thing that can be said about dictionaries, and substantiated, is that they are likely to be behind the times. This is hardly avoidable, because a major revision takes years. Sometimes a new word may be born, live gloriously, and die in the interim between editions. Scientific terms, especially in these times, are invented and come into fairly wide use between editions, too.

Instances of rapid changes like those above are comparatively rare. The great body of the language shifts and takes new directions, but hardly faster than a glacier. Divergence from the fiats of the dictionary might most constructively take the form of a more liberal attitude toward slang and toward old words that are swimming into new orbits.

Many are misled by the order in which dictionaries list the various senses of a word. The Merriam-Webster dictionaries, for example, explain in a preface that as far as possible the order of definitions is that of the historical order of development of the meanings. But many lookers-up assume that the first definition is the most widely accepted one, or at least the one that is unexceptionable in modern usage. Listing meanings in the order of development is a scholar's device that places noncurrent, archaic, and even obsolete significations ahead of modern ones. The practice of numbering meanings is open to quibble on the ground that it seems to denote rank, although of course this is not the intention.

When I write my dictionary, the healthiest, most current definitions will come first; the ailing and dead later. And definitions will be separated by some non-rank-happy typographical mark.

The *American College Dictionary* follows such a plan, in that central or common meanings are put first, and the obsolete, archaic, and rare at the end. The Merriam-Webster editors say, in defense of their plan, "The historical arrangement is of especial value to those interested in the development of meanings." Whistling in the dark, they continue that it "offers no difficulty to the user who is merely looking for a particular meaning." Oh, no? And assuming they are right about this, it is the rare user indeed who is interested in the development of meanings.

The *Oxford Universal Dictionary*, the most recent abridgment of the great *Oxford English Dictionary*, uses the same plan as Webster, but redeems it with a system for indicating the current status of the word, although this system is not apparent to the casual user.

## Word Order

Atmospheric inversion has been blamed for smog. The inversion of sentences creates a kind of linguistic smog that puts the reader to work sorting out the disarranged words, causes his eyes to smart, and perhaps makes him wish he were reading something else. A desperate straining for variety in sentence structure seems to be at the heart of it all. Tired of starting with the subject and adding the predicate, some writers make a mighty effort and jump right out of the frying pan into the smog.

Commonly they grab a hapless auxiliary verb by the ears, yank it out of the protective shadow of its principal, and plop it down at the beginning of the sentence. Like this: "Encouraging the United States were Britain and France." The normal, painless way to say this is "Britain and France were encouraging the United States"; or, passively, "The United States was being encouraged by Britain and France."

The usual word order has been varied by moving *encouraging* up front, but the variety may have been gained at too high a price. Americans, unlike Germans and ancient Romans, are not used to holding some element of a sentence in suspension until the other pieces of the jigsaw puzzle come along, and there is no reason why they should get used to it. Inversion, of course, is not wrong; it is just pathetically overdone, particularly in newswriting.

Versifiers have an excuse for this kind of thing, when they find it necessary to place the word with the desired rhyme at the end of the line, regardless of how the chips fall. But these fellows at least can plead poetic license.

When a fellow who wrote "Hiring the men will be ranchers in the vicinity" was asked whether he had a license to mangle prose, he only reddened and fell silent. It was noticed, however, that he amended the sentence to "The men will be hired by ranchers in the vicinity."

Stuff like "Damaged were the cars of two motorists" and "Suffering minor injuries in the crash was his wife, Viola" and "Caught in the school during the explosion were twenty girls" is gawky and inexcusable. These examples call to mind the line from Wolcott Gibbs' classic satire on *Time*: "Backward ran sentences until reeled the mind." No word-mincer, Gibbs.

Sometimes writers start sentences with auxiliary verbs only because they think there is no other way out when introducing a series of names: "Passing their intermediate tests were George Simms, Ernest Worth, Alben Smith, Nelson Raddle, and Alex Jones." But there *is* another way out: "Those who passed their intermediate tests were . . ." ("Intermediate tests were passed by . . ." is possible, but would be a clumsy use of the passive.)

It should be kept in mind that emphasis is acquired by a word that is taken out of its normal position in a sentence. When a sentence is disarranged for

no other reason than to gain variety in its structure, the effect may be awkward. The reader gets an impression of emphasis where emphasis makes no
sense. Better methods are available for structural variety, such as beginning
with subordinate elements.

The uprooted word is not always an auxiliary verb; it may be an adjective,
as in "Responsible for all cultural questions is a key member of the city
administration." There is still no good reason for standing a sentence like this
on its head.

## Misplaced Prepositional Modifiers

FOR SALE: *Piano, by a lady going to Europe with carved legs.* The authors
of books on grammar are so fond of quoting examples like this that we might
expect such errors to be extinct by now. There is a cure for this kind of
thing, but it is so magical I hesitate to divulge it. Oh well, here it is: *stay
awake.* And beyond this, reread critically what you have written.

"Details are slipping out of plans for the first Soviet-bloc beauty contest."
"Details of plans for the first Soviet-bloc beauty contest are slipping out."

"Hospital attendants said the baby had a history since birth of heart disease." ". . . a history of heart disease since birth."

"They held at gunpoint the woman in her home for four hours." "They
held the woman at gunpoint . . ."

"The group opposed a proposal calling for a written definition of the positions on disarmament of the great powers." ". . . of the positions of the great
powers on disarmament."

"The Israelis were accused of firing on the Egyptian post of Deir el Balat
for ten minutes without causing casualties." This sounds like a reproach for
poor marksmanship.

Here are two more examples that fit in with the others, although the misplaced elements are not prepositional:

"He said every chance would be given to complete satisfactorily the negotiations." This is too Teutonic for the American ear. Make it "to complete
the negotiations satisfactorily."

"An applicant for a federal job should have a chance to explain informally
derogatory information." ". . . to explain derogatory information informally."

## Gerund Construction

An unnecessarily maladroit construction comes of putting a gerund between *the* and *of*, on the model of *The Taming of the Shrew* and *The Shooting
of Dan McGrew.* In these instances, of course, it accomplishes what is desired; namely, setting the gerunds (*taming* and *shooting*) in the forefront.

"Stevens repeated that the responsibility for *the filing of* the charges was his." In this and other examples that will be held up for criticism, it is recommended that *the* and *of* be left out, making the succeeding element the object of the gerund: "the responsibility for filing the charges." As Perrin notes in *Writer's Guide and Index to English,* "This emphasizes the verbal phase of the word and makes for economy and force."

"Officials plan to save considerable time in *the* conducting *of* the charity drive." *in conducting.*

"The contract calls for *the* spending *of* $100,000." *for spending.*

"He proposed psychological tests for *the* screening *of* candidates for the priesthood." Some examples of this practice are more objectionable than others, and this is one of the worst. Even after making it *for screening,* we would have two *for* phrases in succession. *Tests to screen candidates* is smoother.

"Improvement in *the* gathering *of* and reporting on such data is needed." *improvement in gathering.*

"The proposal calls for *the* setting up *of* a joint staff." *Up* and *of* are hideous side by side; *setting up.*

The worst has been saved for the last: "The kids made their own caps out of box-tops, and cheesecloth served for *the* holding on *of* the hats." *and cheesecloth held them on*; or *and used cheesecloth to hold them on.*

# CHAPTER V

# Possessives and Plurals

Possessive Forms; *Persons* vs. *People; None;* Collectives; Plural
Oddities; Editorial (and Royal) We.

## Possessive Forms

HAVE you, too, sometimes puzzled over forming possessives, especially of words that already end in *s?* It's all very simple. To decide whether you want just the apostrophe, or apostrophe plus *s,* you need note only:

1. The number of syllables in the word.
2. Whether the accent (primary or secondary) falls on the last syllable, the penult, the antepenult, or elsewhere.
3. Whether the last syllable begins, or ends, or both begins and ends with an *s* sound.
4. Whether the word falls into certain categories of ancient classical, Biblical, or foreign proper names.

Then all you have to do is apply the right one of the half-dozen or so rules prescribed for various combinations of these conditions.

Haw. Is there a revolver in the house?

As usual when rules run rampant, confusion is the only thing that clearly emerges. Words like *antepenult* are an affront to those of us too lazy to look them up, and may even be obscene. But pronunciation can be relied on for a rule of thumb in forming the possessives of both singular and plural forms. If you add an *s* sound in speaking the word in its possessive form, add apostrophe *s;* if the pronunciation is unchanged, add just the apostrophe.

This gives us, by way of examples, *the boy, the boy's bike; the boys, the boys' bikes; Louis, Louis's pencil; Dulles, Dulles's memorandum; Moses, Moses' tablets* (you would not say *Moseses,* which is how *Moses's* would sound); *the boss, the boss's order; the bosses, the bosses' orders.*

The rule of letting the pronunciation govern is not only easy to follow most of the time, but also conforms to the predominant trend of usage. There may be legitimate differences about pronunciation, in any event. Some argue that they would not add another syllable in speaking the possessives of names like *Dulles* and *Dickens,* writing the possessive forms as *Dulles'* and *Dickens'.* These forms are acceptable, and furthermore the possessive of *any* name that ends in *s* may be formed by adding only the apostrophe: Louis', Doris', Thomas'.

It is also considered correct to form the possessive by adding only the apostrophe to words that end in *s* sounds, though not in the letter *s* itself: *Dr. Schultz' office, Mr. Chance' car, Cortez' discovery, innocence' evidence.* These forms, however, have a strange look, and carefully edited writing seems to be consistent in using apostrophe *s* rather than the apostrophe alone in such instances.

Funny examples will turn up. Few writers would make it *Illinois's,* because the basic word properly pronounced does not end with an *s* sound. The *s* sound is added, of course, in speaking the possessive, which leads to the fleeting notion it should be written *Illinoi's.* But that way madness lies.

A prevalent solecism in Suburbia is displayed on countless fancy mailboxes and front-yard lamp posts in the form of the householder's name bedecked with a misplaced apostrophe. *The Smith's* is what the scrollwork usually announces; the proud owner is apparently unaware that this does not quite make sense. It might better be *The Smiths* or *The Smiths'.* This little bobble is even more prevalent, come to think of it, on millions of imprinted Christmas cards (*The Glotz',* for example, rather than *The Glotzes*).

It is generally considered objectionable to make possessives of the names of inanimate things, as in *the water's temperature* and *the sky's color. The temperature of the water* and *the color of the sky* are smoother and more idiomatic.

## Persons vs. People

The superstition is still pretty vigorous that *people* cannot be used freely as the plural of *person* and that *people* correctly denotes only a nation or a large and indefinite group, as in *the British people* or *We, the people.* According to this law, which usage has in fact repealed, one may not speak of *sixteen people,* or any other definite number, but must say instead *sixteen persons.* The *Dictionary of Contemporary American Usage,* however, says the use of *people* in this way "is now fairly standard English, and is generally preferred to the word *persons.* We may now say *three people were present* or *three persons were present,* as we please. Most people now prefer the first form, and *persons* now sounds pedantic or bookish."

Or, they might have added, newspaperish. The basis for these conclusions is perfectly evident, apparently, except to newspaper editors, whose feeling for usage often seems about two generations in arrears. Foolish rules have a way of running amuck, leading to such absurdities as, "The job of the comedian is to make persons laugh." Those who will not accept the opinion cited are referred to *Webster's New International,* which gives as examples "many or a few *people*; thousands of *people*; a cockpit built for two *people.*"

In a strange coincidence, three press associations made *persons* vs. *people* the subject of comment in their bulletins within the space of a month. The first comment, in *Copy Talk,* put out by the Canadian Press, could have pointed the way for the other two, because it reasonably followed the example of usage and criticized a couple of curious examples that came of going hog wild with the case-hardened rule: *elderly persons of Ivor* and *an elderly persons' party.*

"*Persons* is perhaps defensible," *Copy Talk* noted, "but people just don't think or talk that way. *People* and *people's* would have been better and more natural."

Not long afterwards another press-association bulletin dogmatically recited the old rule at the behest of a subscribing editor, adding its own blessing. That was too much for two other subscribing editors, who offered indignant rebuttals in the next issue. One of them correctly identified the problem as one of changing usage, rather than misuse, and the other used words like "snobbism" and "stultifying" to describe the attitude of the diehard who had started it all.

A few days later this ukase appeared in a bulletin issued by a third press association: "Ten persons may be killed in a fire, but not ten people." And that was all. Ah, the splendid isolation of it—isolation from usage, from books on language, from common sense, from observation, from everything but hand-me-down, newsroom "grammar." Yet this bulletin quickly recanted in the face of concerted objections, many of them from members of the press association's own staff.

Now, anyone is entitled to be mistaken, and I would be first to assert this right for myself. But the writers of wire-service bulletins, who are more or less laying down the law for thousands of their own staffers and are also offering guidance that credulous editors are likely to take as gospel, too often go off the deep end in these matters. More doubt and less dogma would serve the great cause better.

## None

About the first thing any cub reporter learns, after being told the location of the men's room, is that the word *none* is singular and consequently always takes a singular verb. He must never write *none are, none were,* but always *none is, none was.* This is an article of faith, a first principle as firmly established as the conviction that it's a sin to split an infinitive. If the cub should question the invariable singularity of *none,* some kindly but condescending veteran will explain: "It's a basic rule of grammar, my boy. *None* comes from *not one,* and what else can *not one* be but singular?"

It's a persuasive theory, and the chances are that the cub will take the old hand's word for it and not look it up. This may be just as well, because if he did look it up he would get a surprise that might cause him to inquire into a number of other supposedly immutable principles and thereby discover that some of them are about as soundly based as old wives' tales.

Let us assume that some less credulous cub does undertake to look up *none.* We might peek over his shoulder as he turns the pages:

"As subject, *none* with a plural verb is the commoner construction."—*Webster's New International Dictionary,* 1953.

"*None* may be considered singular or plural according to the implied meaning, but is generally used with the plural form of the verb."—Clark, Davis, Shelley, *Handbook of English.*

"*None* may be either singular or plural."—Woolley, Scott, Bracher, *College Handbook of Composition.*

"*None, most, some, such* may be singular or plural."—Easley S. Jones, *Practical English Composition.*

"With the indefinite pronouns *all, any, none,* and *such,* use a singular verb if the group is considered as a unit and a plural verb if the members of the group are considered individually."—Sanders, Jordan, Magoon, *Unified English Composition.*

Fowler also concurred in this, or perhaps set the stage for it, since his comment was the earliest. But even before him, as he points out, the *Oxford English Dictionary* had described the plural construction as commoner.

Had enough? All right, but it is evident that somewhere, somehow, *none* apparently was anointed as singular, although the records of the proceedings seem to have been lost. Harry Shaw, Jr., author of *Writing and Rewriting,* speaks of a "standard rule" that *none* requires a singular verb. But first he says that it may be used with either singular or plural and that studies of its use by good writers have shown that it is as often plural as singular. Even sour Ambrose Bierce in *Write It Right* hedged in deference to usage.

Is one small word worth all these others? For its own sake, no. But as a sample of the indefensibility of many so-called rules, perhaps yes.

## Collectives

It is written, in the apocrypha of journalism, that a certain editor deemed the word *news* to be plural. This was a curse and an abomination to his staff, but being wage-earners and dependent on him, they held their peace. And it came to pass that one day he sent forth a scribe to a far city, where great tidings were awaited.

But many hours passed and there was no word, and this same editor chafed in his impatience. At length he dispatched a message saying, "Are there any news?"

And lo, the scribe was strained beyond endurance, and gnashing his teeth, he answered straightway: "Not a single new."

That editor is probably dead, if he ever lived, but his intransigent and not altogether reasonable spirit lives on in many today who insist that words like *couple, group,* and *team* are invariably singular. This leads to such sentences as "The *couple is* considered the best *performers* of Shakespeare on the New York stage"; "The *group has been* discussing the problem among *themselves*"; and "The *team* that *wins* the game will have *their names* engraved on the cup."

The way out of this trap is embarrassingly easy. The general principle is one that will show the way out of other quandaries. Don't adopt any rule on hearsay; make sure it has some basis in usage, grammar, and common sense. Whatever rules you do adopt, don't follow them out the window. Words like *couple, group, team,* and other collectives, including *crowd, committee, class, jury, herd,* and *number,* are either singular or plural according to the way they are used. *Number,* perhaps the most frequently used, has its own rule of thumb: preceded by *a,* it is plural; preceded by *the,* it is singular.

Thus it ought to be "The handful of faithful *were* well rewarded" (*was* would make that devoted handful seem squeezed into a fistful); "A score *were* injured in the wreck" (the singular is patently absurd here); "The crowd *was* dispersed"; "The crowd *were* waving their programs"; "The number of rooms *was* too small"; "A number of us *are* going on a picnic."

Common sense, that uncommon attribute, will show the way. Don't strain to put in print something you would not naturally speak. This principle ought to take you blindfolded through a sentence like "An ever-increasing number of students spend their first two years in junior college," which sounds fine and is correct as it stands, but may lead you astray if you pick it apart.

It is well to be consistent. If you say "the team *is*," don't use *their* as a reference, at least in writing; say *its. Their* in this construction is condoned in talking, however.

The words *couple* and *pair,* without which the society pages would have to go out of business, deserve additional mention. In reference to a man and a woman, *couple* should always take a plural verb. Not even marriage should extinguish individuality to the extent of justifying reference to two people as one. Sentences like "The couple will spend *its* honeymoon in the Bahamas" are preposterous.

## Plural Oddities

Idiom, that perverse old dictator, requires that the singular—rather than the plural, which would be logical—be used in expressions like *a ten-year-old boy, a six-mile race, a three-month investigation* (not *ten-years-old, six-miles, three-months*). The possessive is acceptable (*a three months' investigation*) but this construction seems to be fading away.

Likewise, it was a *10-foot* pole Ed Wynn used for not touching things.

Idiom calls for the plural, however, when the modifying phrase follows, rather than precedes, the noun. None but the rustic speak, or write, of *a man 6 foot tall,* or *a ditch 9 foot wide.*

Some compounds develop mix-ups in their plurals. *Court-martial* (actually, a martial, or military, court) becomes *courts-martial,* not *court-martials.* The tendency to make it one word, *courtmartial,* does not help matters. Likewise, *right-of-way* becomes *rights-of-way, passer-by* becomes *passers-by,* and *son-in-law* becomes *sons-in-law.* Such is the inconsistency of English, however, that the possessives of such expressions are formed on the last element: *court-martial's finding, mother-in-law's temper.*

Names of people that end with *s* (Jones, Dithers, Adams) call for the addition of *es* to form their plurals. Thus the Jones family are the *Joneses*; not, as we too often see, the *Jones,* the *Jones',* or even the *Jone's.* In "Blondie" one day Chic Young had Dagwood saying, "The Ditherses have invited us over to play bridge." This forthright use of the correct form may have been a milestone in comic-strip diction.

Conservative usage still calls for the apostrophe in plurals of letters, figures, signs (the *B's,* the *1940's*) and the like, although there is a strong trend away from it. There is nothing wrong with *1940s* or *GIs.* An inflexible rule calling for omission of the apostrophe will lead to trouble now and then, however, as in *As,* which comes out more intelligibly *A's.* This is an argument not against the apostropheless forms, but against inflexible rules, which are likely to lead to trouble anyway. Even when the apostrophe is dropped in plurals like *GIs,* it is needed to indicate possession (*the GI's uniform*) and seems desirable in verb forms like *O.K.'s* and *O.K.'d.*

Another curiosity has to do with using plurals when there seems no reason to, and when, in fact, the singular would be more exact. Consider, for example: "Church *services* were held at 11"; "*Charges* of vagrancy were lodged against the transient"; and "The dedication *ceremonies* were canceled." In the foregoing, the reference is to a single service, a single charge, and a single ceremony. The plural usage seems fairly prevalent and probably does no harm for the most part, except perhaps when the mistaken impression may be given that more than one charge is lodged. How, we may wonder, did this quirk get started? The tendency to inflate things larger than life size may be the answer.

## Editorial (and Royal) We

The editorial *we* seems to be falling rapidly into disrepute as intolerably stuffy. It is probably justifiable in newspaper editorials, at least when the ideas being presented are actually those of more than one person. But under a by-line, the use of *we* can only suggest a split personality in the writer. Few things sound more absurd than *we ourself.*

The use of *I* has been denounced, of course, as immodest. Some writers, then, when they have occasion to bring themselves into the act, coyly masquerade as *this writer, the present writer, the present reporter,* etc. *The present writer* may indeed be present, but one may be left with the suspicion he's not all there. The fact is that *this writer, the present writer,* and the like are more obtrusive than *I* and thus really less modest. Rudolf Flesch, among others, has shown how the creation of a personal link between the writer and his audience promotes readability. So when the writer under a by-line speaks for himself, let him have the honesty to come out with *I* and not don a false face, or pretend he's two other people.

The fear of frankly speaking out for oneself looks like an aspect of the fetish for objectivity that nearly drained all the blood out of journalistic writing before the wind shifted to another quarter. Basil Walters of the Knight Newspapers, in a tribute to newspaperwomen, gave them credit for setting a good example by letting a little fresh air into the stuffy pigeonholes of journalism. The trend toward movable prose may yet come to be recognized as the greatest boon to newspaper readers since the invention of movable type.

Gerald Ashford, amusements editor of the *San Antonio Express,* invited readers to offer their opinions on *I* vs. the editorial *we*; he put up prizes for the three best letters. Now, this is a novel and enlightened approach to problems of expression. Many of us, when our linguistic preferences are challenged, tend to fly into a dudgeon and asperse the intelligence of the challenger. When it turned out that an overwhelming proportion of his readers preferred *I*, Mr. Ashford changed his own usage to conform, after a brief transition period during which he mixed in a few *we*'s, just to get the feel of the thing gradually.

Although no contest, poll, or opinion, however authoritative, will ever settle any language problem, Mr. Ashford's approach recognized a great and constructive principle: the preference of the literate majority governs these matters in the end. The winner of his contest, Roberta Young of Victoria, Texas, wrote, among other things:

"There are fashions in writing just as there are in clothes. The editorial *we*, I (not *we*) think, is today a journalistic hoop skirt, or at least a bustle. What's wrong with saying *I*, anyhow? Everybody knows that's what you mean, so why beat around the bush with a bogus *we* that fools nobody? Writers, of all people, should not pretend to be lacking in ego . . . in my opinion, an ounce of forthrightness offsets several pounds of ego. The editorial *we* is not only awkward, stuffy, and pompous, but downright ridiculous. I recommend that it should henceforth be reserved exclusively for the use of expectant mothers and schizophrenics."

The consensus of the many criticisms of the editorial *we* in other letters was similarly to the effect that its use is old hat as well as objectionably impersonal. Some of the critics expressed the opinion that the modesty it is supposed to indicate rings false. Many of them cited the use of *I* by such essayists as G. K. Chesterton, Charles Lamb, Robert Louis Stevenson, William Lyon Phelps, Joseph Addison, and Thomas Huxley. One reader commented that even in editorials, naming the newspaper (e. g., "The *Bladder* believes . . .") is more explicit and thus preferable to the editorial *we*.

The editorial *we* is likely to be associated by many with the royal *we*, the style affected by royalty and the princes of various churches in official pronouncements. Readers are thus likely to associate *we* less with modesty than with hauteur, and with presumptions to power and status. Queen Victoria, you will remember, sniffed, "We are not amused." A possible reply to that might have been, "You and who else, your double-talking royal highness?"

Investigation shows that the editorial *we* is old stuff, for it had a counterpart in classical Latin. The royal *we* goes back to the time in Roman history when it was used in joint decrees of two or three men. Thus it may be said to have had an honest origin, unlike the editorial *we*, which often creates a misleading impression of multiple authorship.

# CHAPTER VI

# Beset by Demons

Hyphens in Compound Modifiers; with Numbers; with Phrasal Verbs; in Word Division; with Prefixes and Suffixes; *Non, Co; Ex;* Abbreviations (*Kas., Kan., Kans.*); State Names; Alphabetical Designations; Spelling (British Preferences, Spelling as Humor).

## Hyphens in Compound Modifiers

To BEGIN with, let us bow our heads and meditate on the text for the day. It comes from the gospel according to John Benbow, in *Manuscript and Proof,* the stylebook of the Oxford University Press, and runs: "If you take hyphens seriously you will surely go mad."

Yet some big, strong journals that do not hesitate to beard a vested interest in its den every week are so terrified of this all but imperceptible mark that they have banished it from their pages. Somehow, it makes one think of the elephant and the mouse—or perhaps the elephant and the flea.

On the other hand, there are publications that cannot abase themselves enough before what they conceive to be a minuscule deity, and in their style manuals devote page after page of homage to it in the form of ritualistic dogma setting forth in minute detail when it shall be invoked and when not. How the hyphen got such a reputation for merciless power is a mystery, for actually he is a self-effacing little fellow, always ready to perform a needed task but just as ready to stay on the shelf when people feel they can get along without him, as they often can.

The first thing to remember about the hyphen is that it is a joiner—not like George Babbitt, the super-Rotarian, but like a Gretna Green parson. Let us pass over both the more obvious and the rarer kinds of jobs done by the hyphen to consider the two uses that seem to give the most trouble. One of the hyphen's jobs is linking compound modifiers before a noun. In this instance, the hyphen weds two ordinarily separate words used in such a way that they form a single idea. There is some leeway here, for many such combinations are perfectly understandable in the intended sense without the hyphen, though the purist would insist on it. In spite of the purist, however, the tendency is to drop the hyphen.

Strictly, the correct forms would be *snow-covered hills, an odd-looking man, dark-brown cloth,* and *a power-driven saw*; but who would be likely to misconstrue *snow covered hills, an odd looking man,* or *a power driven saw*? You will often see such expressions written without the hyphen, and it seems stupid to quibble when the sense is clear.

But *strong navy agitation,* which conveys "strong agitation by (or concerning) the navy" is a horse of another color from *strong-navy agitation,* or "agitation for a strong navy." Contrast also *an old time clock* (an old-time clock or an old time-clock?); *a single tax organization* (a single organization concerned with taxes or one concerned with the single tax?); *a small animal hospital* (a small hospital for animals or a hospital for small animals?).

## Hyphens with Numbers

The hyphen is often carelessly omitted part way through compound modifiers, especially those containing numbers: *a 25-mile an hour speed* is properly *a 25-mile-an-hour speed*. Likewise, *a 500-foot long relief map* should be *500-foot-long,* and *a 12-foot thick concrete wall* should be *12-foot-thick*. On the other hand, numbers preceding nouns as simple modifiers are sometimes mistakenly followed by hyphens: "sentenced to *180-days* in jail" should be *180 days*. Similarly, "*400 million dollars'* worth of business" should not be *400-million-dollars' worth*.

Writers should remember that compound modifiers other than those containing numbers may have more than two parts, all of which should be linked. "Contributors of the *most sought-after* items" was intended to be "contributors of the *most-sought-after* items." The versions have differing senses.

## Hyphens with Phrasal Verbs

Hyphens often insinuate themselves into those combinations of verb and adverb that really are new verbs, like *cash in, hole up, pay off*. Confusion arises because some such expressions can be used as modifiers, and then the hyphen is required. Thus,

"The Communists *stepped up* infiltration" (a verb in two parts, no hyphen); and "A *stepped-up* campaign is planned for spring" (compound adjective modifying *campaign,* hyphen required).

The hyphen is out of place, too, after adverbs ending in *ly*: *a widely advertised event*. Other adverbs forming parts of compound modifiers take it, however: *the well-known human race*.

When it is used to join two figures, the hyphen means *through* and serves as a handy, word-saving device. "The convention will be held February 16-20" means the convention will start on the 16th and continue through the 20th.

To prevent misinterpretation, use of the hyphen must be based on good judgment. The distinctions necessary in the examples cannot be made in publications that ban the hyphen, without recasting the sentence. What is likely to happen is that the required hyphen will be struck out in conformity with the ban, thereby confusing the sense. The no-hyphens rule is, of course, worse than the evil (too many hyphens) it would suppress, because it is likelier to alter the meaning. That is something the disease we might call hyphenitis seldom does, however much it may annoy the discriminating.

## Hyphens in Word Division

It seems hardly necessary to note that the commonest use of the hyphen is to divide words that are broken at the ends of lines. This is primarily a problem for the printer, except when he falters and changes must be made on proofs. The basic rule is that words are properly divided only on syllables. The way to resolve questions about this, and they are many, is to consult a dictionary.

Words are often divided in typescript, but this is generally discouraged, especially in material intended to be set in type. Hyphens at the ends of lines in manuscript can raise unnecessary questions for the printer. The lines as he sets them will not correspond to the way they break in the manuscript, and thus he cannot always be sure whether the hyphen in a compound modifier, for example, that happens to fall at the end of the line is intended if the break occurs elsewhere.

Single-syllable words, no matter how long, cannot be divided: *through, though, would, smooth*. Divisions on one letter, as *a-round*, are improper. *English for Printers*, the instruction manual of the International Typographical Union, says: "Singular nouns of one syllable, pronounced as if they were words of two syllables when pluralized, cannot be divided: as, 'horse,' *horses*; 'inch,' *inches*; 'fox,' *foxes*; 'dish,' *dishes*."

Divisions of figures and of names of people are to be discouraged, but are unavoidable in printing set in narrow measure—newspaper text, for example.

## Hyphens with Prefixes and Suffixes

Hyphens, as we have noted, have a strong tendency to fade away. In certain common uses, they are called on for a time to link ordinarily separate elements. After a while people seem to get used to seeing those elements together, and the engagement, so to speak, is followed by a wedding; the elements are joined and the hyphen is forgotten. This is particularly true of the hyphen's use with prefixes and suffixes (like *pre-, bi-, anti-, co-, -down, -goer*). Thus *mid-summer* becomes *midsummer,* and *pre-war* becomes *prewar.* Yet many writers not only hang onto the hyphen like grim death in instances like these, but also wedge it into words like *react, intercede, excommunicate, retroactive,* and others where it has not belonged in the memory of living man, if ever.

The dictionary-makers are often thought of as stick-in-the-muds who don't catch up with accepted usage until thirty years too late. But they are way ahead of many of us when it comes to dropping hyphens that have served their purpose. It seems like a good idea to get rid of hyphens when usage has sanctioned it to the extent that the dictionaries agree. There is an easier solution to the hyphen problem than creating a morass of rules for individual combinations. Just shift the whole thing onto Webster's shoulders. The result will be a heap of discarded hyphens, which may be thrown away, combined to make dashes, or chopped up into periods.

For ready reference, here is a list of prefixes usually set solid: *a, ante, anti, bi, by, co, counter, down, electro, extra, hydro, hyper, in, infra, mal, mid, multi, non, out, over, pan, post, pre, re, semi, sesqui, sub, super, supra, trans, tri, ultra, under, up.*

Prefixes usually hyphenated: *all-, ex-, extra-, no-, off-, self-, vice-, wide-* (*wide-angle,* but *widespread*).

Suffixes usually set solid: *down, fold, goer, less, like, over, wise.*

Suffixes usually hyphenated: *-designate, -elect, -odd, -off, -on, -to, -up, -wide. Headon, leanto, closeup, nationwide* are not merely on the way but already here, although Webster has not yet approved.

## Non, Co

As a general rule, *non* as a prefix is set solid; another rule is that the hyphen is used to keep prefixes from doubling vowels. This combination gives rise to *nonco-operation,* an odd-looking beast. Webster's version is *non-co-operation,* which seems unnecessarily clumsy, especially since the *New Collegiate* concedes in a discussion of hyphenation that *cooperate* and *coordinate* are often written thus because of their great frequency and familiarity. What's wrong, then, with *noncooperation*? That's what the *American College Dictionary* offers, although it does put a dieresis over the third *o.* Doubled vowels or no, *reelect* and *reenter* are also solidly entrenched in many reputable quarters.

*Co* in the sense of *associate* is sometimes distinguished from its other senses by being saddled with the hyphen. This leads to *coextensive, coexist,* but *co-producer, co-signer.* The distinction seems worthless, however, as long as *coproducer* and *cosigner* are understandable at sight. Some deem the hyphen necessary to distinguish *correspondent* from *corespondent,* but Webster does not.

## Ex-

May *ex-* properly be attached only to its noun, and not to the noun's modifier? This niggling question was manfully tackled, and resolved, by the *New York Times* critique, "Winners & Sinners." For example, should it be *Waldorf ex-headwaiter* rather than *ex-Waldorf headwaiter*? The answer is that *ex-Waldorf headwaiter* is beyond criticism. The fellow was, of course, a former headwaiter at the Waldorf, and the only way to express this smoothly is to put the *ex-* in front of *Waldorf*.

It is not possible, anyway, to keep *ex-* attached only to nouns and not to their modifiers; witness *bathing ex-beauty*. "Winners & Sinners" said anything like that would be the work of a copy ex-editor. It may be (and has been) argued that ambiguity may arise from the likes of *ex-Democratic attorney general* (that is, *ex-Democrat, ex-attorney general,* or both?), but only the determinedly wrongheaded will see a problem here, for *ex-* obviously modifies all three words as a unit. At any rate, the problem of the placement of *ex-* is pretty much limited to headlines, because otherwise it can be side-stepped by using *former*.

Before exiting on *ex-*, let's have a look at *ex-felon,* a puzzling creation that pops up now and then. It evolved, probably, on the model of *ex-convict,* and in a strict sense both expressions may be open to the same objection. *Convict,* however, has come to mean almost exclusively "one serving a sentence," and thus *ex-convict* fills a distinct need. But *felon* is not associated with imprisonment; it means simply "one who has committed a felony." *Ex-felon,* then, may well be meaningless, and he who commits a grievous offense against the law may proudly take his stand with the Englishman and declare, "Once a felon, always a felon." Still, maybe we could save *ex-felon* for the felon who has reformed, to some extent, and limits his lawlessness to misdemeanors.

\* \* \*

The whole question of the hyphen is fraught, as they say, with peril, and the only point concerning it on which grammarians agree is that confusion reigns supreme. Many an open-minded writer will go along with Webster on setting prefixes solid until he reaches something like *antilabor,* which may stick in his craw even after he figures it out as the consistent treatment of *anti-labor.*

John Dos Passos, with combinations like *welldressed, sportsclothes,* and *panamahats,* may be so far ahead of the parade that it will never catch up. On the other hand, many British publications use *to-day. To-day* is an odd fish in America, but it may be of interest that even back in his time, Fowler commented on the lingering of the hyphen in this word as singular conservatism. Its persistence may reflect a last-ditch effort by the British to preserve the fiction of linguistic individuality.

Is there hope for those who write *radio-active* for *radioactive, over-turn* for *overturn, thorough-going* for *thoroughgoing, re-admit* for *readmit, one-time* (single occasion) for *onetime* (*sometime* or *quondam*)? I say there isn't, unless they can be persuaded to stop, look, and look up before striking the hyphen key.

Let us close with a wistful comment from the Fowlers in *The King's English*: "Hyphens are regrettable necessities, to be done without whenever they reasonably may."

## Abbreviations

Some little improprieties occur in the use of abbreviations. It is considered not quite kosher, for example, to abbreviate the month without the date (*He left last Dec.,* as against *He left last December,* or *last Dec. 21*); nor is it proper to abbreviate the state without the city (*The factory is in Ala.,* as against *The factory is in Alabama,* or *in Mobile, Ala.*).

Nor should proper names be abbreviated by anyone except their owners: *Wm.* for *William, Robt.* for *Robert,* and the like. When a clipped form of a proper name is used, however, it is not regarded as an abbreviation, and does not take a period: *Ed.* is properly *Ed* for *Edward, Edmund, Edwin,* etc.

The urge to dispense with what might well be omitted does not seem to have touched the use of periods after *Mr., Mrs.,* and *Dr.* in most editing. Yet there is a trend in this direction, especially in books, and more especially in British usage. Here's how it looks: "Dr Livingston, I presume?" Not so bad, really.

When it became known, early in his emergence as a figure of international importance, that the *S* in *Harry S. Truman* stands for nothing, but was merely adopted by Mr. Truman with the idea of rounding out his name, there was a great flurry among lint-pickers to make sure that it was given *Harry S* (look, Ma, no period) *Truman.* But to what grammatical Utopia will such fussiness lead us?

## Kas., Kan., Kans.

Kansas, to the casual eye, is a peaceful enough place, but appearances are deceptive. For beneath the surface civil rebellion seethes. The bone of contention is how to abbreviate *Kansas.* Some prefer *Kan.,* which may be regarded as more or less the orthodox version; others favor *Kas.* The disagreement is not without a tinge of bitterness.

It was, I believe, with a piece entitled "What's the Matter With Kansas?" that William Allen White first attracted national attention. His successors in Kansas journalism today are demanding, "What's the Matter With *Kan.* (or *Kas.*)?" depending on their preference. As a journalistic controversy, this difference appears to date back at least to a 1952 meeting of Kansas members of the Associated Press. It was debated at the 1954 and 1955 meetings, too. The trouble is that the Associated Press uses *Kan.* in the other forty-nine states, and Kansas members who see nothing wrong with it are irked by the confusion resulting from the intrastate use of *Kas.,* which, of course, is not uniform even in Kansas.

The chief proponent of *Kas.* is F. W. Brinkerhoff, editor and manager of the Pittsburg, Kansas (taking no chances), Publishing Co. Mr. Brinkerhoff concedes that the choice between *Kan.* and *Kas.* is a matter of taste, but adds, "Kansans themselves should say what the abbreviation should be. Kansas is independent and would not appreciate having the other states choose its abbreviation."

It is good to be able to report that democracy rules in this crisis, because the current use of *Kas.* by the Associated Press (in Kansas, that is) is the result of a vote by AP members.

Illustrious example figures on both sides of this affair. The *Topeka Capital* and the *Topeka State Journal,* it is said, have always used *Kan.* But the mighty *Kansas City* (Missouri, that is) *Star* uses *Kas.* If the *Kan.* and *Kas.* camps are not utterly unreconcilable, they may yet find common ground in the *U. S. Postal Guide.* Its version is *Kans.*

## State Names

Most publications use the *Postal Guide* as their authority for abbreviations of state names, although sometimes they may only think they are doing so. The *Postal Guide* specifies *N. Dak.* and *S. Dak.,* not *N. D.* and *S. D.;* *N. Mex.,* not *N. M.; Nebr.,* rather than *Neb.;* and *Oreg.,* rather than *Ore.* (but who ever uses *Oreg.?*); *Calif.* and *Colo.,* not *Cal.* and *Col.* (for evident reasons); *Pa.,* not *Penna.* The often seen *Wisc.* has no sanction; it's *Wis.* Nor is *Wn.* acceptable; it's *Wash. The Postal Guide* recognizes no abbreviations for *Alaska, Idaho, Maine, Ohio,* or *Utah.*

## Alphabetical Designations

If there is a prize for the most irritating form of cryptography, I nominate the little trick of reducing the name of an unfamiliar organization or agency to initials after its first appearance. The press associations consider this great stuff, but to many critics it is confusing, exasperating, and unnecessary. I have my own theory about how it got started. After the upsurge of alphabetical agencies in Roosevelt days, some of them (AAA, NRA, FHA, CCC) became so familiar that writers took to using the abbreviations without spelling out the names even once. Some thoughtful editor, to jog the memories of readers, directed that the names of such agencies be given the first time in each story and followed by the abbreviation: *Federal Housing Administration* (*FHA*).

Use of the abbreviation alone thereafter is fine, for agencies as well known as the FHA. But the thing has gone full speed into reverse. Instead of helping the reader to learn the full names of organizations whose abbreviations are relatively familiar, the press-association reporters (and their sedulous apes on newspapers) use the device to manufacture new and baffling abbreviations for organizations that are all but unknown. Now hear this:

"A security board has found doubt of the loyalty of an official of the International Monetary Fund (IMF). The finding was made after a hearing by the International Organizations Employes Loyalty Board (IOELB). Because the IMF is an international body, the IOELB worked in cooperation with foreign agencies."

It's bad enough when only one such abbreviation figures in a story, but when there are more, we have confusion compounded. Readers no brighter than myself have to fumble back to the beginning for the key every now and then, meanwhile cursing the diabolical cleverness of the abecedarian who encoded the names. But you don't want to repeat unwieldy titles, you say? You don't have to. Just use a key descriptive that the reader will recognize instantly. This is less complicated, and may be less fun. But the reader will like it.

In the example cited, the International Monetary Fund might have been referred to, after having been named once, as—steady, now—*the fund*. The International Organizations Employes Loyalty Board could have become *the loyalty board,* or even just *the board.*

The practitioners of alphabetism know no shame. They will start out with the translated version of a foreign name, for example *General Confederation of Labor,* and in going on with the story will use an abbreviation based on the original (*CGT* for *Confédération Générale du Travail*). This is a game for polyglots, devised by stupes.

There is a place, of course, for FHA, ICC, and other abbreviations that are widely known. Every town has its own handful that everyone recognizes, and they come in very handy, especially for headlines. But the writer who converts Associated Society of Locomotive Engineers and Firemen into *ASLEF* belongs in the acrostics department.

## Spelling

Remember the spelling demons back in grammar school? Those were the words some statistical pedagogue had ascertained to be the most troublesome from one grade to the next, and how we were drilled on them! Anyone who has served much time editing knows that writers are beset by their own legion of demons. The most indestructible of them all is *accommodate*. Two *m*'s after two *c*'s seem to be just too much to expect.

But before trotting out the horrible examples, let us muse on some peculiarities. Newspapers dearly love to insist on their own spelling preferences, many of which are Webster's second choices. The press is nearly unanimous in favor of *cigaret* over *cigarette* and *employe* over *employee*. These forms probably are specified because they are the naturalized versions of what were originally foreign words and because they are shorter. Yet the joker is that, although newspapers unquestionably command a wider readership than any other printed medium, they have failed to unhorse *cigarette* and *employee* from favored usage.

That absolute tyrant of the language, the public, seems remarkably conservative in its resistance to variant spellings. Brevity and convenience seem to count for nothing; witness the hard sledding of such simplified forms as *tho* and *thru*. Americans, though they are likely to look up to the English as mentors when it comes to language, reject their handily telescoped forms like *spoilt* and *connexion*.

It is apparent that any attempt to influence spelling appreciably in the direction of simplicity is doomed. Periodicals that attempt this are likely to accomplish nothing more than to inconvenience their staffs and make their readers smile. The fact that not one of the *Chicago Tribune*'s millions of readers commented on its virtual abandonment of fonetic (oops) phonetic spelling in 1955, after years of persistence in such oddities as *frate* for *freight* and *sofomore* for *sophomore,* seems to indicate the public thought they were seeing typographical errors all those years.

But large-scale, consistent efforts to simplify spelling are more logical, at any rate, than the random, freakish deviations found in some style manuals. An example of this is the insistence by one periodical for many years until recently on *hight* for *height*. *Hight* is in the dictionary as a dialectal variant, but its presence there at all stunned every new staff member. Copyreaders delighted in working *hight* into big headlines, where readers took it for a glaring typographical error.

Here is a list of words that seem to give the most trouble:

*Accommodate* (not *accomodate*), *accordion* (not *accordian*), *anoint* (not *annoint*), *exorbitant* (not *exhorbitant*), *existence* (not *existance*), *fictitious* (not *ficticious*), *fluorescent* (not *flourescent*; the word comes from *fluorine,* not *flour*); *incidentally* (not *incidently*—but when you come down to it, why not?), *inoculate* (not *innoculate*), *liquefy* (not *liquify*), *marshal* (not *marshall;* there is no such word), *nickel* (not *nickle*), *objet d'art* (not *object d'art,* if you must show off your French), *Philippines* (not *Phillipines*), *rarefy* (not *rarify*), *resistance* (not *resistence*), *restaurateur* (not *restauranteur*), *skulduggery* (not *skullduggery;* the word is an American version of the English *sculduddery* and apparently is not related to *skull,* for its origin is said to be obscure), *violoncello* (not *violincello,* though the long form is disappearing in favor of *'cello* or *cello*).

## British Preferences

British preferences in spelling, while hardly incorrect, are conspicuous when used in America, and the writer who favors them may be suspected of affectation. British preference is for *ou* in certain words where American usage calls for *o*: *behaviour, labour,* for *behavior, labor.* Other such words: *ardour, clamour -ous, colour -ed, dolour -ous, favour -ite, honour -able, mould, moult, odour -ous, smoulder, splendour -ous, valour -ous, vapour -ous, vigour -ous.* Note, however, that *glamour* is preferred to *glamor* in both Britain and America.

*ce* is used where Americans use *se*: *defence, offence, pretence.*

*ss* is used where Americans use *s*: *biassed.*

A terminal *e* is used where Americans drop it: *axe.*

*que* is used where Americans prefer *ck*: *cheque.*

*xion* is used where Americans prefer *ction*: *connexion, inflexion, reflexion.*

*oe* is used where Americans prefer *e*: *homoeopathy, oecumenical, oesophagus.*

*ough* is used where Americans prefer *ow*: *plough.*

*s* is used where Americans prefer *c*: *practise.*

*e* is used where Americans prefer *a*: *grey.*

*y* is used where Americans prefer *a*: *pyjamas.*

*ise* is used where Americans prefer *ize*: *apologise, capitalise, focalise, visualise.*

*dge* is used where Americans prefer *dg*: *abridgement, acknowledgement, fledgeling, judgement.*

*re* is used where Americans prefer *er*: *accoutrements, centre, fibre, lustre, metre, sabre, sceptre, spectre, theatre.*

*ae* is used where Americans prefer *e*: *aeon, aesthetic, aestivate, anaemia, encyclopaedia.*

*ll* is used where Americans prefer *l*: *apparelled, councillor, counsellor, empanelled, jeweller, quarrelled.*

*l* is used where Americans prefer *ll*: *dulness, enrol, fulfil, instal, skilful, wilful.*

## Spelling as Humor

In his preface to *A Subtreasury of American Humor,* E. B. White transfixed a foible that he noted particularly, he said, in the humorous writing of fifty to one hundred years ago. It is still to be seen in print today, however, particularly in comic strips and syndicated stuff of the folksy or old-hometown persuasion.

Mr. White wrote,

"It occurred to me that a certain basic confusion often exists in the use of tricky or quaint or illiterate spelling to achieve a humorous effect. For instance, here are some spellings from the works of Petroleum V. Nasby: he spells 'would' *wood,* 'of' *uv,* 'you' *yoo,* 'hence' *hentz,* 'office' *offis.* Now, it happens that I pronounce 'office' *offis.* And I pronounce 'hence' *hentz,* and I even pronounce 'of' *uv* . . . the queer spelling is unnecessary, since the pronunciation is impossible to distinguish from the natural or ordinary pronunciation . . ."[1]

He has something there. Not only is such spelling pointless as humor when spoken words, rather than written misspellings (e. g., *Dere Mable*) are being represented, but it may strike many readers as simple-minded.

If any dissenters are lissening, I want to express my appreesheayshun for yore attenshun, and natcherally hope it did not make you impayshunt to here about this.

[1] By permission; copyright 1941, E. B. White and Katharine S. White.

# CHAPTER VII

# Comma Comment

Superfluous Commas; Commas and Adjectives; One-Legged Comma;
False Linkage; Appositives; Restrictive and Nonrestrictive Clauses;
*That* vs. *Which;* Serial Comma; Comma after Conjunctions; Commas
and Colons.

## Superfluous Commas

HOSTILITY toward the comma is rampant these days. This attitude is part of a revolt against Victorian diction that ignores all the changes in the language since 1900. But the usual bald adjuration, "Use the comma sparingly," is about as good advice by itself as "Use the letter *s* sparingly," which might lead to *succes, misive,* and *imposible*. Pick an elderly classic off the shelf, or turn the discolored pages of a fifty-year-old magazine, and you will quickly find what look like superfluous commas to today's eyes. Some of them precede *that*. Others set off adverbs, which we seem to find more assimilable than our forebears did.

Let us lift a couple of examples bodily from *The King's English* (Fowler):
"Yet there, too, we find, that character has its problems to solve." Meredith.

"We know, that, in the individual man, consciousness grows." Huxley.

Some of us would probably be inclined to remove all the commas from both these sentences. An examination of current writing shows that commas are more often omitted when required than used when unnecessary. Thus the comma-haters are seen to be barking up the wrong tree.

Let us consider a couple of instances in which commas *are* used unnecessarily. One of these is in mistaking ordinary adverbs, which do not need to be set off, for parenthetical elements, which do. Here are some examples of this: "The farm laborer could not start his car but, apparently, a car thief could" and "Yesterday, he drove to the city." Writers who use such commas are probably misled by the accepted (but not invariable) practice of setting off such interruptives as *of course, therefore,* and *however*.

## Commas and Adjectives

Another superfluous use of commas is in separation of adjectives that apply cumulatively, rather than separately. Example: "After a hard, second look . . ." This was not a look that was second and, as a separate idea, also hard, but rather a second look that was hard. The mistaken comma after *hard* makes the word apply to *look* alone and not to *second*. The same reasoning fits *balky, old sultan* and *two, short, gloomy acts* (correct: *balky old sultan; two short, gloomy acts*).

A little thought—but not much—is required to differentiate these constructions from *a hot, dusty road* (a road that is hot and also dusty) and *a short, exciting chase* (a chase that is short and also exciting). But how can we tell for certain, especially in doubtful cases, whether to use the comma to separate adjectives? Well, the comma should be easily interchangeable with the word *and*. If not, it is out of place. Compare *hard and second look,* which is impossible, with *hot and dusty road,* which sounds perfectly acceptable, indicating that the comma was called for.

Yet the comma may be omitted from any series of adjectives preceding a noun without causing any damage, and this practice seems to be gaining: *a hot dusty road, a short exciting chase*. At any rate, commas are better left out of such constructions than used where they don't belong.

## One-Legged Comma

Some of us, when confronted with the question whether an element ought to be set off, often seem to want to have it both ways. To be set off, of course, the element must have a comma at both ends—like the parenthetical *of course* in this sentence. (Or, with one comma, the element must be at the beginning or end of the sentence, which amounts to the same thing.) An element that is not set off should have no comma at all.

The cunning wretches I have in mind solve the problem by placing the comma at one end of the clause or phrase and leaving it off the other. This brings about the grammatical infirmity that might be called the one-legged comma. A pathetic offspring of indecision and ignorance, it is limping its way across more and more pages. How are we ever going to trap these guys? They are bound to be half right every time, and if cornered may reasonably blame the missing, or superfluous, comma on a typographical error.

The simplest and most numerous example of the one-legged comma occurs with the prepositional identifying phrase: "Judge George Buck of Erskine County, signed the restraining order." This should be either "Judge George Buck, of Erskine County, signed . . ." or "Judge George Buck of Erskine County signed . . ." The use of commas in this construction is an old-fashioned practice, and generally the no-comma version is considered preferable. The same principle applies to such phrases as "Richard R. Roe of the Foreign Affairs Committee" and "J. David Nelson of the *New York Times.*"

But the commaless version does not sound quite so satisfactory in first-name listings of survivors in an obituary: "Mr. Smith leaves three brothers,

Frank of Ossining, George of New York, and Gerald of Los Angeles." Sometimes it's "a sister, Mary of Italy." Somehow, this usage puts one incongruously in mind of such grandiose designations as "William of Normandy" and "Lawrence of Arabia." A better form for the list of survivors might be "Frank, Ossining; George, New York; and Gerald, Los Angeles." If the *of* must be kept, it had better be preceded by the comma. And as for "Mary of Italy," she should become "Mary, *in* Italy."

Let us look at some cases of one-leggedness where there should be two commas or none. The place where another comma belongs is indicated in each example by a pair of brackets. Either a comma should be placed there, or the existing one should be omitted, as the writer prefers.

"Severe storms [] accompanied by hailstones up to three-quarters of an inch in diameter, pounded western Texas."

"A 47-year-old man [] who had just been released from jail after serving a term for drunkenness, was found burned to death beside a fire."

"This, obviously [] was a planned diversionary movement."

"Committee members [] who had feared White House suppression of the report, were jubilant." This one is not as freely a matter of choice between two commas and none; the decision depends on whether the clause is restrictive or nonrestrictive. With commas (nonrestrictive), the sentence would say all the committee members had feared suppression; without (restrictive), that only those who had feared suppression were jubilant. Probably the nonrestrictive sense was meant.

Now for examples in which two commas, and no less, are necessary:

"All New Orleans schools were closed as a precaution but the storm, bringing winds of 64 miles per hour [] passed the city without causing much damage." A comma is necessary, of course, to mark the other end of the participial modifier. While we're at it, a comma before *but,* to separate coordinate clauses, would do no harm but is not essential.

"Dr. Manlio Brosio, Italian ambassador to Britain [] flew to Rome yesterday." A comma should mark off the other end of the appositive phrase. The same is true of "Joseph Anderson, a carpenter [] of 1843 Weyburn Place."

Finally, a few examples that would be better with no comma at all:

"A corporation, which is unique in the rubber industry has been formed." Placing a comma after *corporation* suggests a nonrestrictive clause, which would mean that corporations hitherto have been unknown in the rubber industry. This writer meant that the corporation he was writing about was unique within the industry, and he would better have expressed this by leaving out *which is* as well as the comma: "A corporation unique in the rubber industry has been formed."

"A gray-haired man in a brown hunting shirt, jumped onto the barricade."

Presumably the comma sets off, or half sets off, the phrase *in a brown hunting shirt,* but such prepositional modifiers do not take commas.

"A few lawgivers, themselves, call it the biggest boondoggle in Washington history." Commas around reflexive pronouns (those ending in *self* or *selves*) are excessive.

To call attention to a word as a word, use italics or quotation marks, not commas. "Magnuson suggested that he had used the word, bottle, a little perversely." The writer of this used commas a little perversely. This sentence should read "the word *bottle* a little perversely" or "the word 'bottle' a little perversely."

## False Linkage

The tendency to spare the comma may well spoil the sentence, as we have noted. Another manifestation of this is what might be (and probably has been) called false linkage. That is, by omission of the comma, elements that should be separated are unintentionally joined.

"No rain is expected for tonight [] and tomorrow the high temperature is expected to be between 70 and 75 degrees." The reader must retrace his steps in the middle of the sentence because at first the prediction of no rain seems to cover tomorrow as well as tonight. The omission of the comma might be defended on the ground that a comma is unnecessary between coordinate clauses. But this principle does not hold unless the sentence is clearly understandable without it. Smooth reading requires "No rain is predicted for tonight, and tomorrow . . ."

Generally, the comma should be used between coordinate clauses unless they are very short. Even then, clarity of sense should govern. "Rain will fall and wind will blow" gets along all right without one, but "He was a man of action [] and deeds interested him more than words" does not. Here are some commaless culls:

"The Democrats are counting on regaining rural votes that went to the Republicans in 1953 [] and the committee is working to that end."

"He said military aid should not be given countries able to provide for their own defense [] and economic aid in the guise of military assistance should be ruled out."

"The weather in Asia was unusually favorable for production [] and growing conditions in India and Pakistan were the best in many years."

False linkage and confused meaning can also result from failure to set off a clause that interrupts: "The guards and prisoners who refused to join in the break were tied and left in the fields." No, Virginia, there were no guards who *consented* to join in the break. What was meant is this: "The guards, and prisoners who refused to join in the break, were tied . . ."

Here's an oddity: "He has two grown daughters and a son at West Point." Co-education has not really been adopted by the military academy. This is really another instance of coordinate clauses needing a comma separation, for ellipsis has squeezed out *he has* after *and*. Try this: "He has two grown daughters, and a son . . ."

## Appositives

There is a marked tendency to drop the commas that we were taught should set off appositives. Whether this is a conscious bent toward a new usage, or merely reflects ignorance, I'll be cussed if I know. I am inclined to set it down to ignorance when I see something like this: "He has been married to his wife Ethel for twenty-six years. Their daughter, Eve, is married to a Harvard man." If this writer was out to do away with the commas around appositives, why drop them from *Ethel* and use them with *Eve*? The constructions are identical. (Eve was, of course, the only daughter.)

Rare appositives are technically restrictive and do not take commas: *My son Barry* (distinguished from my other son, John); an only son would be *My son, Barry*. Others are *Ivan the Terrible, William the Conqueror,* and the like. Omission of commas from other appositives usually occurs in writing that shows other signs of carelessness.

The intrusion of commas and the articles *a* and *an* within certain appositive constructions, however, can raise doubt as to whether one or two persons are being referred to. "The publication will be edited by Dr. Willy Nilly, executive secretary of the conference, and a member of the faculty," is an example of this. Dr. Nilly is both secretary and faculty member, but the sentence may leave the impression that the faculty member is someone else. Omit the comma after *conference* and the *a* before *member*.

## Restrictive and Nonrestrictive Clauses

Lovable Miss Pennypacker, who tried so diligently to pound the difference between restrictive and nonrestrictive clauses into our thick heads, must be ineffably saddened when she reads a good deal of what appears in print, including the polished but sometimes pockmarked prose of the news magazines. The difference between the two kinds of clauses seems more honored in the breach than the observance. Miss Pennypacker might conclude that many of those who write and edit do not even know it exists.

Yet this is not one of those puristic distinctions evident only to those who enjoy separating the flyspecks from the pepper. On the contrary, it is something that directly affects meaning. Thus it is important to every writer interested in exact, unequivocal expression.

The trouble is that words like *restrictive* and *nonrestrictive* (or *defining* and *nondefining,* which mean the same thing) have the ugly smell of formal grammar about them and by themselves are enough to frighten off all but the hardiest seekers after truth. But if you will hold on a minute, we will try to part the grammatical foliage and point a safe and simple path through the wilderness.

The problem arises with relative clauses. You can always recognize a relative clause as one starting with *that* or *which, where* or *when,* or *who, whose,* or *whom.* And the question is whether such clauses should be set off by commas. Consider a sentence like "I waved at the girl who was standing on the corner."

Do we want a comma in front of *who*? It depends on what we mean. As the sentence stands, commaless, the speaker waved to a girl who is identified for the reader by the fact that she was standing on the corner. Let us put a comma in front of *who*. Now the fact that the girl was standing on the corner becomes merely incidental information. The *who* clause no longer identifies her. While it was originally restrictive, or defining, it now has become nonrestrictive, or nondefining, and may be dropped.

The important point to settle is whether the clause is essential to the meaning. If the clause is essential, the comma should not be used; if it is not essential, the comma is required to set it off. This is the law and the prophets on this subject. If you have any doubt whether the clause is essential, try leaving it out. Obviously, you cannot leave out the *who* clause in the commaless version of our example without changing the intended sense. The girl would no longer be identified.

"No woman, whose attire makes her conspicuous, is well dressed." Preposterous, of course, with the commas. For if we leave out the *whose* clause, as the commas indicate we may, we get "No woman is well dressed."

"Every high-school district in the county, which called for a bond issue this year, has won voter support." This was intended to mean that bond issues carried in every district where they were proposed; not, as might be concluded, that every district in the county proposed bond issues and won approval of them. You cannot leave out the *which* clause without changing the intended sense; thus the commas are erroneous.

"The rule exempts commercial lots where there is no restriction on all-night parking." The writer wanted to indicate that commercial lots are unaffected because they do not restrict all-night parking, but what he did, by leaving out the comma before *where,* was to say confusingly that the rule affects some commercial lots and not others. A period could have been placed after *lots*; the rest is merely explanatory.

There are borderline cases in which the comma may be dropped. These generally are instances in which the relative clause bears on a proper name, as in "I feel sorry for Miss Pennypacker who tried so hard." But careful writers still use the comma here.

### That vs. Which

The question of nonrestrictive vs. restrictive elements inescapably involves the question of *that* vs. *which,* though to discuss it is to tread upon quicksand. The easiest way to dispose of the problem is to bid those worried about it to keep their eyes peeled for the usage of good writers and then try to develop a feeling for what seems to be acceptable.

If it is hard—and it is—to make a straightforward approach, let's try backing into this mare's nest. This much is certain: elegance has nothing to do with the choice between *that* and *which*. Those who carefully substitute one for the other on this basis—for opinion differs as to which is the more high-toned—are on a fool's errand.

As a general rule, *that* may refer to either persons or things, but *which* refers only to things. No sooner are these words down on paper than there spring to mind certain other words from that great storehouse of admired English: "Our Father, which art in heaven . . ." You see how it is. But let us flounder on.

Popular usage and grammarians alike seem to be pretty well agreed that *that* (in the sense being considered here) should be used to introduce only restrictive clauses. Nonrestrictive clauses, as we have seen, are set off by commas; restrictive ones are not. Save *that* to introduce restrictive clauses. *Which* is all right with either kind, but is preferred with nonrestrictive clauses.

A rule of thumb may be useful here. If *that* will fit comfortably, it is correct, and furthermore, the clause is restrictive. No one, surely, has such a tin ear that he does not recognize *that* introducing a nonrestrictive clause as a blunder, no matter how little he knows of grammar: "The sun, that had a murky orange color, soon burned off the fog." The writer whose ear does not tell him *which* is required here in place of *that* has no ear. It is true, of course, that this *that* construction was once regarded as correct, but now it is a conspicuous anachronism. In "it was easy to find the house which was on fire," *that* can easily be substituted for *which,* and in accordance with our rule of thumb it is preferable. A corollary to this is that a clause starting with *which* should be set off by commas; one starting with *that* should not.

### Serial Comma

Sometimes it seems as if we are running in circles. Years ago the grammars and the schoolmarms prescribed the comma before the last item in a series: "A press is a maze of gears, shafts, cams, and levers." For a long time newspapers campaigned against the comma in this position, and finally the grammarians and pedagogues gave in.

And now that the battle is won we have a noticeable trend to restore the final comma. The point of the campaign against it, like that of many another prejudice, has always seemed dubious. It is true that usually the meaning is unaffected by the absence of the final comma, but now and then that comma is essential. What happens, of course, after its use has been discouraged, is that it is left out when required as well as when it is not.

This may explain the tendency toward its restoration. Just to show, before going on, that there *are* instances requiring the final comma, consider: "They had brown, green, gray and blue eyes." *Gray eyes and blue eyes* is meant, but *gray-and-blue eyes* is what may be understood without the comma.

Most of the trouble with serial elements grows out of the confusion of one series with another; or, to put it another way, the failure to recognize where one series ends and another begins.

"Voters will go to the polls Tuesday to elect four city councilmen, three school board members, to decide on eight charter amendments and three special propositions." We have here two different groups, and they would be more readably presented as "to elect four city councilmen and three school board members, and to decide on . . ."

When apparently mixed constructions like this are not unconscious, they are probably imitations of the telegraphic style affected by the news magazines, notably *Time,* in sentences like "New construction techniques added strength, durability, sharply reduced costs." Neither this nor the example preceding is either unintelligible or misleading. But a non-*Time* disciple would more probably write "New construction techniques added strength and durability, and sharply reduced costs." To some of us fuddyduddies, the second version seems less rocky and easier to follow. This may have something to do with the fact that the condensed treatment has not caught on widely, and wherever it appears it is conspicuous.

## Comma After Conjunctions

Some of the same writers who neglect the comma when it is needed are fond of slipping it in after conjunctions, especially *and, but, so,* and *or.* At the risk of being cruelly blunt, it must be recorded that there is no sense in this, nor sanction for it. Examples: "They have found it pays, and, we have too"; "Money may not make you happy, but, it will enable you to be miserable in comfort."

Don't be confused by sentences in which a comma legitimately falls after the conjunction because it is setting off a parenthetical element, as in "They have found it pays, and, *I must admit,* we have too." Don't be misled, either, by sentences that start with *and, but,* etc. This construction is common in informal writing, and informal writing ought to be commoner than it is. But a conjunction is still a conjunction, no matter how you slice the sentence. So forget the commas in "And, I took him up on it" or "But, the cork wouldn't come out of the bottle."

## Commas and Colons

"Members of the committee are: Jane Doe, Oscar Zilch, Perry Moore, and Lucinda Knight." Why the colon after *are,* any more than in "I am: Oscar Zilch," since the constructions are identical? It seems likely that the use of the colon in sentences like the first example has grown out of the rule, often loosely understood, that a colon is used to introduce a series—but *not* if the series immediately follows the verb, as in the example. A series, to take a colon, should form an appositive: "Members of the committee are all students: Jane Doe, Oscar Zilch, Perry Moore, and Lucinda Knight." The colon balances off (a) *students,* and (b) the names.

A dash or comma would be possible in place of the colon. One of them surely is necessary to make the sentence understandable. The colon may be removed, on the other hand, from the first example without loss. The simplest rule I can think of to cover this situation will cover many another as well: Don't put in anything you can do without.

# CHAPTER VIII

# Making Numbers Count

Large Numbers; Useless Counting; Figures vs. Words; Fractions;
Figure at Beginning of Sentence; *Some* and *-Odd*.

## Large Numbers

BIG (or astronomical, as the cliché artist would have it) numbers seem here to stay. Everything is out of sight—government budgets, the explosive force of bombs, almost any figure dealing with the atom and its possibilities, and, as always, distances in the heavens, which, like other technical considerations, are appearing increasingly in print.

The least we can do is give the bedeviled, number-stunned reader a break and present these large totals as understandably as possible. Some publications do this, but others apparently have never given the matter a thought.

Large round numbers can easily be simplified. The zeros in 22,000,000 are forbidding enough, but in 22,000,000,000 they have to be counted. What an imposition on the reader! As a matter of fact, he usually refuses to be imposed on in this way, but lets the tails of such numerical comets swoosh past unheeded. How much easier it is to write, as well as to read, *22 million, 22 billion,* or *billion-dollar industry,* rather than *$1,000,000,000 industry*.

The notion that an expression like *$8.6 million* is likely to be read *eight and six-tenths dollars million* rather than *eight and six-tenths million dollars* does not stand up against scientific studies showing that words are comprehended in groups rather than singly. Anyway, we do not read *$8* "dollars eight."

The fact that an expression like *$8 million* may break at the end of a line, momentarily giving the reader the impression of $8, is considered objectionable in some quarters. This objection seems hardly more valid than complaints against the misleading sense that may occur at any line break. Some publications forestall this difficulty, real or imagined, by linking the elements with a hyphen: *$8-million*.

Rounding off is advisable for large figures in most contexts, unless there is some overriding reason against it; *$18,500,000* is preferable to *$18,-478,369*, and *18½ million dollars* (or *$18½ million*) is preferable to either.

## Useless Counting

Many writers not only know how to count, but are unduly proud of it. Of course, they may not be showing off but only trying to be helpful when they add up trifling, meaningless totals. Even so, ungrateful readers have been known to wish they could bite the hand that is feeding them these tasteless tidbits. What can it be about little numbers that holds such fascination? The following will be recognized at once as standard procedure:

"They were joined by their *three* children, John, Ruth, and Mary."

"He was referring to Egypt and Saudi Arabia, *two* nations that control much of the strategic Red Sea coast line."

"This facility and the one in Baltimore are *two* of the finest in the country."

"Sports and music are his *two* hobbies."

The love of little numbers also rears its stupid head in references like *the two, the three, the duo, the trio, the quartet, the quintet,* as used in avoidance of that lovely, simple word, *they.* This quirk is extensively discussed under Problems of Reference in Chapter IX. Words like *duo, trio,* and *quartet* suggest an organization, as of performers; when they are used simply as variants for *two, three,* and *four,* they reflect adversely on the intelligence of the writer.

Sometimes the adding machine gets jammed, probably from overwork. Then we get "Four examination dates have been approved for the positions of fire captain, senior clerk, key-punch operator, and construction foreman." Four each, or one?

"Christmas Day will be observed with two festival services at 9:30 and 11 a. m." Four services or two? A comma after *services* would help, but why not just leave out *two*?

There are other ways to insult the reader's intelligence than by forcing second-grade arithmetic on his attention. One is to labor the obvious with something like "The river reached a peak of 30.7 feet, a little below the predicted crest of 31 feet"; or "Sales for 1954 hit $10.5 million, exceeding the previous year's total of $10 million." More judicious wording would be "The river reached a peak of 30.7 feet, as compared with . . ." and "Sales for 1954 hit $10.5 million, a half-million more than the total for 1953."

## Figures vs. Words

There must be something fundamentally indecent about the use of figures in text, to judge from the way publications generally shy away from it. Some magazines even spell out numbers as large as *six hundred and fifty-three,* thereby demonstrating their scorn for economizing on space, and also their abhorrence of anything so revolting to the sensibilities as *653*. Book publishers tend to spell out numbers under one hundred, round numbers such as one thousand, a million, fifteen hundred, and to use figures for statistics, measurements, and percentages. All other numbers in a paragraph containing *any* number of three digits or more are usually set in figures.

Newspapers usually draw the line at *ten*; that is, numbers under *ten* are spelled out, and figures are used for the rest. A person's age, however, is invariably given in newspapers in figures. *Ten* must have mystical significance as a great divider, for it is generally accepted. Discovering the identity of the man who first fixed on *ten* for this purpose, rather than fifteen, might offer a fitting subject for a Ph. D. thesis in journalism.

The question of which numbers are to be rendered in figures and which are to be spelled out is, of course, a matter of the style of individual publications. And style is a matter of taste or preference, concerning which there ought to be no dispute. It seems that in handling numbers, however, many publications that are concerned about consistency in editorial details often make things unnecessarily difficult.

The rules would be easy enough to follow if it were not for the usual legion of exceptions. Let us sample a few, chosen at random: ages, addresses, percentages, scores, dates, expressions containing mixed figures (*nine* or *ten*), statistical matter (what a bushel basket this one is!) height, time of day, decimals, betting odds, latitude and longitude, temperatures, humidity readings, barometric readings, sums of money, vote totals, page numbers, tables, dimensions, military designations, roll calls, rainfall measurements. These, on one publication or another, are directed to be given in figures, regardless of size.

Some exceptions are freakish: give rain-gauge readings in figures unless they are not taken from the gauge and are under ten (fathom that one, if you can); spell out decades and sums that have been incorporated with words (whatever this latter means); use figures for temperatures except in such expressions as "there was a thirty-degree rise in temperature during the day."

The numerous exceptions, some of them footless and others incomprehensible, cause the copy-editor to stop and ponder when he encounters a number, and then, oftener than should be necessary for such a routine matter, to have recourse to the style manual. Even then he will often not get a conclusive answer, as evidenced by the murky rules cited.

Such considerations as these suggest an earth-shaking reversal: Why not, at the next revision of the style book, or even forthwith, give up the losing fight against the use of figures? Permit the use of figures entirely, and in doubtful instances, let the common sense of the writer or the copy editor govern. The decision to rely on common sense would itself be a gain, for the present welter of arbitrary and conflicting rules certainly is not based on it.

Who would care? Not readers, certainly. Those who have some critical apprehension of the use of language are likely to be nettled by errors and banalities, but not by the difference between *six or eight* and *6 or 8*.

And yet, and yet—the experience of a publication that changed its style to figures entirely for cardinals and ordinals was a sorry one, and the experiment was shortly abandoned. It was bad enough to see things like "Sometimes it walked on *2* legs, sometimes on all *4s*."

But these really turned stomachs:

"He got *1* of those new cookbooks for Christmas."

"Production was a *3rd* more this season."

"The issue was submitted *1st* to the board of directors."

To be sure, none of these latter is really a cardinal or an ordinal, and thus they do not fall under the rule. The *1* is the pronoun *one*, the *3rd* is a fraction, and the *1st* is the adverb *first*. But just try to knock such distinctions into the heads of copyreaders and proofreaders. Once the rule against anything but figures was put out, there was reason to believe they took a diabolical pleasure in changing everything possible to the hideous numerical versions. Things got as bad as *2wice*.

Apart from aberrations, however, it must be admitted that there is indeed something distasteful about the appearance of small figures in text. They give an impression of immature composition, since kids often use them. Cardinals are bad enough, but ordinals are even worse:

"Both Rita and Aly were smiling and happy after their *1st* reunion."

"The man was run over by the scraper and cut in *2*."

"The freshman was the *2nd* who paid tribute to the dean."

The best thing to do, apparently, is to retain a rule. The main complaint against such rules, anyway, is aimed at the confusion created by inconsistent exceptions. But there are more important things than consistency, and no rule should be permitted to flout good taste.

## Fractions

It is well to defer to consistency by shunning such things as *one and ½ feet, two and ¼ miles*. It would be better to make it either *1½ feet, 2¼ miles,* or *one and one-half feet, two and one-quarter miles*. And *.13 of an acre* is preferable to *.13 acres,* as less likely to lend itself to error. Technical publications often place a zero in front of a decimal point: *0.13 of an acre*.

It is easy to give an ambiguous impression in constructions like "The measure would lower the rate from 3 to 2 per cent." Here the reader must decide whether 3 and 2 per cent are the present and proposed rates, or the proportion by which the rate would go down. The intention here would have been unequivocally expressed by "The measure would lower the rate from 3 per cent to 2 per cent."

## Figure at Beginning of Sentence

The rule against starting a sentence with a figure seems defensible enough, because a number coming first *does* look strange. The usual means of avoiding it are to write the number out or to recast the sentence so that something else comes first. The brewers of that intoxicating potion, style, however, have been known to recommend another way out: placing the word *exactly* in front of the figure.

Thus, "Six thousand, five hundred people attended the concert" would become "Exactly 6,500 people . . ." The objection to this ought to be apparent, because a round number like 6,500 obviously is an approximation. But even with figures that are, or are intended to be, precise, as in "Exactly 6,519 persons passed through the turnstile" the intrusion of *exactly* places an emphasis on the accuracy of the figure that sounds strange when such emphasis is unwarranted. Recasting to move the number back is preferable to using a word that may give the sentence a peculiar tone.

The figures 100 and 1,000 are read *one hundred* and *one thousand,* not simply *hundred* and *thousand.* Those who have never taken note of this write "It was a journey of *a* 100 miles" and "He bought *a* 1,000 tankloads of oil." A pox on all such.

## Some and -Odd

*Some* and *-odd,* with numbers, indicate an approximation. They are inept, therefore, with anything but a round number: "Some sixty-nine horsemen" and "Waco is 94-odd miles south of Dallas" have a foolish sound. Naive writers are inordinately fond of *some* with numbers, and the trouble here, as in other cases of fondness, is that they have been impressed by the word as imparting a certain elegance, without finding out what it means. It is absurdly unsuitable as a device to keep from starting a sentence with a figure. "The sailors unloaded some ninety-two cases from the ship" sounded to one critic as if some of the cases were unloaded but not all. When any other indication of inexactness is given, as by *about, approximately, estimated,* and the like, either *some* or *-odd* is superfluous.

# CHAPTER IX

# Clouded Titles

Occupational Titles; Doubled Titles; *Mr.; Mrs.; Miss;* National and Geographical Descriptives; Names of People; *Rev.;* Parochial Titles; *Dr.;* Capitalization; Problems of Reference (Avoidance of Pronouns); *He* or *She; He, She* (——); Leapfrog.

## Occupational Titles

A WANTON bestowal of titles, outdoing even the generosity of fraternal orders, is noticeable in much printed matter. Occupational descriptives, instead of being made appositives, as is customary in less frenetic prose, are often placed in front of names, on the model of true titles like *Dr., Mayor, Health Officer,* and *Dean.* Thus are hatched such characterizations as *Italian soprano Renata Tebaldi, carnival concessionaire Eddie Crews, registered nurse Edith Hampton,* and *Rome tailor Angelo Litrico.*

One problem in the use of such descriptives is: Should they be capitalized? Some authorities think so, on the analogy of true titles. The weight of opinion, however, seems to be that capitalization should be reserved for true titles, such as denote offices, and for established designations like *Dr.* Forms like *Italian Soprano Renata Tebaldi* and *Rome Tailor Angelo Litrico* seem to connote a status that does not exist, and to most people the capitals only look silly.

*Time* magazine appears to have been the fount and wellspring of the false-title foible. In extenuation, *Time* at least has diverted us with inventions like *cinemactress.* Apart from diversions, however, it remains more comfortably intelligible to use full-fledged appositives: *the Italian soprano, Renata Tebaldi;* or, of course, *Renata Tebaldi, the Italian soprano.*

Some writers feel self-conscious, or the word may be guilty, about telescoping what they know in their hearts to be the more readable form. Yet they cannot bring themselves to spurn altogether what they consider the most fashionable form, having seen it so often. And so they compromise, placing the descriptive in front of the name and omitting the article, but retaining the comma of the appositive form, as a compromise to readability. These are typical results: *Italian Soprano, Renata Tebaldi; Nacionalista Party candidate, Carlos P. Garcia; art dealer, Joseph Duveen; Civil War Hero, Gen. William Tecumseh Sherman.*

The followers of this school, like the barefaced false-titlers, cannot agree on capitalization either, as the examples indicate. Compromises are sometimes worse than the evils they would palliate. That is so in this instance, at least. The wedding of the false title and the legitimate appositive is certainly one of the sorriest mismatings journalese has brought forth.

It is a good idea to shun false titles entirely as one of the inventions that tend to make writing sound like the text of a telegram. By omitting what is desirable for clarity, or by distorting natural forms, these devices, however cute, demand unnecessary effort from the reader.

Sometimes there is an attempt to have it both ways, including mixed capitalization, in the same sentence: "Art Dealer Joseph Duveen was once trying to sell a painting to millionaire collector, Samuel H. Kress, whose interest was only lukewarm." If you like it that way, you can have it. Personally, I'll take "Joseph Duveen, the art dealer, was once trying to sell a painting to a millionaire collector, Samuel H. Kress, whose interest was only lukewarm."

## Doubled Titles

It is objectionable to double titles. This is good practice in Germany (*Herr Dr. Kurt Weiss,* the equivalent of *Mr. Dr. Kurt Weiss*) and in England (*General Sir Hugh Borrow*), but not in America. Doubling usually occurs in such instances as *Superintendent of Schools Dr. Gerald Pedant, City Librarian Miss Tillie Bookworm, Councilwoman Mrs. Edna Gleason.* If it is desirable to give both designations, clumsiness may be avoided by writing *Dr. Gerald Pedant, superintendent of schools; Miss Tillie Bookworm, city librarian;* otherwise, simply *Superintendent of Schools Gerald Pedant, Librarian Tillie Bookworm.* Doubled titles are doubly objectionable when there is more than one mention of the name; in such examples the office can be specified on first mention and subsequent mentions will take care of the *Dr., Mrs., Miss,* or whatever.

## Mr.

Whether and when to accord the title *Mr.* is a tricky question on which there is plenty of disagreement. Publications that otherwise bestow it sometimes withhold it from two categories that usually have little in common, although they sometimes coincide: the famous and the infamous, or arrested.

*Mr.* is shorn from the famous on the reasoning, apparently, that they are virtually institutions and that such a commonplace designation would only diminish their stature. Thus we usually do not see *"Mr*. Stevenson," *"Mr*. Hemingway," *"Mr*. Mitropoulos." Many publications *Mr*. only the president of the United States, out of the same special and perhaps overblown respect they show in capitalizing the designations *president* and *chief executive* even when they stand alone. Yet they lower-case *presidency,* which raises a question whether they regard the man as greater than the office.

Criminals and suspects lose their *Misters* in many journals that use the title for men in good repute, on the seeming ground that such undesirables have forfeited their right to the courtesy paid law-abiders. According to American principles of justice, a suspect should be allowed to keep his *Mr*. at least until conviction.

A well-advised exception sometimes is made by *Mister*less papers in handling obituaries. The last name alone gives an unfortunate impression of brusqueness and is capable of injuring the sensibilities of relatives and friends. *Mr*. seems like a small enough tribute to pay at the last opportunity to pay any tribute at all.

Among the things that may be said against the omission of *Mr*. generally is that use of the last name alone tends to suggest subordination. This impression comes from the practice in the military services and also from the style of address used for servants, when there *were* servants. There are men whose hackles rise when they are addressed by their last names alone. There are also those, though this is irrelevant, who are irked by hearing men confer the title on themselves, as for example in identifying themselves over the telephone. For of course *Mr*. is a title of courtesy, and is properly applied only by —and to—others.

In any event, the use of *Mr*. by any publication as a general rule can do no harm. It affords a touch of courtliness in these rude days. Why should we withhold in print the courtesy we would unhesitatingly pay a stranger in a letter or conversation? The omission seems, in borrowed words, not to show a proper respect to the opinions of mankind.

### Mrs.

Strictly speaking, a married woman using the title *Mrs*. should go by her husband's given name, i.e., *Mrs*. John *Doe,* not *Mrs*. Mary *Doe*. Many publications attempt to make this a rule, but it is almost impossible to enforce because many women insist on using their own given names with *Mrs*. in spite of everything. Some organizations even require it within the group. If a married woman uses her given name, the *Mrs*. might well be dropped on first reference, but used thereafter.

## Miss

A curious lapse from chivalry, it seems, is shown sometimes in handling the names of unmarried women who are in trouble with the law. Subsequent references are given as *the Smith woman* instead of *Miss Smith*. This is clearly an aspersion, which conveys in effect the idea that the publication, like a self-righteous old biddy, is drawing her own skirts about her and denying her fallen sister the simple courtesy of a title that merely indicates she is not married. What was that again about casting the first stone?

*Miss* is properly applied to women, married or not, when they are named in connection with their careers, and whether or not, as is often so of actresses, they have professional names that differ from their legal ones.

## National and Geographical Descriptives

The day Ghana was born as an independent nation, I wondered idly what descriptive would be applied to its nationals: *Ghanans,* perhaps, or *Ghanians?* A day or two later I noticed with interest that an Associated Press story referred to them as *Ghanians.* But the same afternoon, in one of those coincidences that keep us from entirely renouncing superstition, I happened to hear two students from Ghana being interviewed on the radio. The interviewer asked them about the proper form, and they told her it was *Ghanis.*

Next, I saw a reference in a news magazine to *the Ghanese economy.* If *Ghani* was the right form for the noun, presumably it was also the right form for the adjective, by analogy with *Israeli* and *Pakistani.* Thus it should have been *the Ghani economy.* That was not the end of the story. I finally learned, from an official pronouncement relayed by the Embassy of Ghana in Washington, that the correct form is really *Ghanaian.*

All this illustrates how beset with pitfalls the formation of descriptives can be and how forms are often arbitrary, showing no regard for analogy. All concerned at least resisted any temptation to call the nationals of Ghana *Ghaners,* which would have seemed to suggest a fate likely to be desired only by an Afrikaner.

Much expostulation results from careless use of the term *Jewish* in connection with Israel. Although Israel is closely identified with the Jewish race and religion, the expressions *Israeli* and *Jewish* are not interchangeable. Israel, like other nations, is composed of peoples of many races and religions, including a substantial number of Arabs and Mohammedans, and Christians of various races, too. *Jew* and *Jewish,* then, in reference to the nationals of Israel, are called for only in the circumstances when those terms would be applied to the nationals of any other country.

Descriptives that come from state names have their peculiarities—at least in the versions sanctioned by Webster. A resident of the Carolinas is properly a *Carolinian,* not a *Carolinan,* and a resident of Indiana, when not a *Hoosier,* is an *Indianian.* Since this is so, why don't we make it *Alaskian, Iowian, Minnesotian, Montanian, Nevadian, Dakotian,* and *Oklahomian?* Of course, we can't and don't. You may have your choice of *Alabaman* or *Alabamian, Arizonan* or *Arizonian, Floridan or Floridian,* and *Louisianan* or *Louisianian.* The versions with the *i*'s sometimes cause a conspicuous shift in accent, as in *Flori*d*ian.*

This field seems to be conducive to whimsy. A resident of Maine wrote me, "We call a person who is unusually vocal in singing the praises of this state a *Maineiac.*" His comment called to mind, antithetically, that *Baltimorean* is sometimes altered by critics of Baltimore's staid traditionalism to *Baltimoron.*

Fred Kerner, executive editor of Crest and Premier Books, New York, was reminded that as a staffer for the Canadian Press he did a piece on Canadian descriptives, which was prompted by a disagreement among the residents of Regina, Sask., as to whether they were *Reginans* or *Reginians.*

"So down the list we went," Mr. Kerner wrote. "Some of the lovely ones are well known: *Haligonians* from Halifax, *Liverpudlians* from Liverpool, N. S., *Québecois* from Quebec City. A tongue twister turned up from the province of Saskatchewan, where the people of Moose Jaw averred they are *Moosechapiskanisippians* (the people from the place where the river looks like a moose's jaw)! But when it came to Head of Chezzetook, N. B., and Bastard, Ont., there were problems."

## Names of People

Names make not only news, but also enemies, unless care is exercised in publishing them. It has been said that few things affront a man more keenly than seeing his name misspelled in print. The only safeguard against misspelled names is actual practice of the care that is incessantly enjoined.

A common impropriety is the identification of a person with only a single initial on first mention in a story: *J. Anderson, R. Thompson.* This is objectionable because it invites confused identity and because many people are likely to feel slighted at having their names truncated. Publications whose standards are high have inflexible rules against the use of names with single initials.

It is in small towns that the most carelessness in the handling of names is to be found. This seems a shame, because in small communities readers are more likely to know each other and to feel offense at any slight. Most of the time a phone call will supply the missing name or initial. If publicity releases contain incomplete names, returning them with an explanation of requirements is likely to bring results.

## Rev.

It is an axiom that clergymen are touchy customers; among the shortcomings that are likely to make them grieve is the misuse of their own descriptive title, *Reverend*. *Reverend* is an adjective meaning *deserving of reverence,* and strictly speaking should never be used with the last name alone, as for example in the locutions *Rev. Jones* or *the Rev. Jones*. The correct form is *the Rev*. Mr. *Jones*.

For the first reference to a preacher, either *the Rev. John Jones* or *Rev. John Jones* is acceptable, although *the Rev.* is considered preferable by sticklers. Thereafter, references should be in the form *the Rev. Mr. Jones,* or, more simply, *Mr. Jones,* which is easier to remember and equally beyond criticism. Just plain *Jones* is acceptable, too, even to ministers themselves, although we are not likely to be so blunt with our spiritual mentors.

Insofar as hatred is consistent with the Christian virtues, many preachers say they hate to be addressed as *Reverend* in the way one addresses a physician as *Doctor*. This is a problem of speech, rather than writing, but the related peccadillo, *Rev. Jones,* turns up in both speech and writing.

This lapse not only inspires righteous indignation, but also causes preachers to break out into verse. My researches have brought me at least three poems that were inspired by it. To be frank, they are pretty painful specimens, whose own infractions of rhyme and meter seem to overshadow the offense they deplore. They also show an alarming lack of restraint at such a venial sin. One of these puristic poets declares the error rends his heart, another hates it like the devil, and a third is ready to punch in the nose the transgressors responsible for it.

In spite of all this, *Rev. Jones* is spreading like repentance at a tent revival. Furthermore, many spiritual leaders are practicing Christian charity toward sinners in this department of usage. I asked the editors of a half-dozen leading church journals for their opinions. The consensus was that they have seen the handwriting on the wall and are ready to defer to it. The nub of the matter is that the layman can see no reason why *Reverend* should differ in its application from *Mr., Senator, Professor,* or *Doctor*; or why, if you can call a senator *Senator* and a doctor *Doctor,* you can't call a preacher *Reverend*.

The layman, in the end, is the one who sits in the seat of judgment on these questions anyway, and the decisions of grammarians, theological and otherwise, are likely to be scattered forth like dust if they run counter to the popular will.

## Parochial Titles

In *Watch Your Language,* Theodore M. Bernstein writes:

". . . Protestant Episcopal clergymen in charge of parishes are always *rectors.* Methodists, Congregationalists, and Unitarians prefer to be called *ministers.* Lutherans are *pastors* as a general rule. Baptists will settle for either *minister* or *pastor.* Roman Catholic parish clergy are always *pastors*; if there is more than one priest in the parish the top man is *pastor* and the others are *priests* on the staff."

## Dr.

We all love the distinction that comes with a title, and some of us love it so much we are willing to enjoy the title without possessing the distinction. That goes especially for those who use honorary degrees. It is well understood that institutions of learning really honor themselves in conferring such degrees. If the recipient has not distinguished himself enough to make this so, the whole affair is even hollower than usual.

No question ordinarily arises concerning the use of the title *Dr.* by doctors of medicine and dentists. Although osteopaths and chiropractors also have a right to the title, generally speaking, people expect them to be identified specifically. A number of states have laws, possibly inspired by M.D.'s, requiring anyone who uses the title *Dr.* professionally on signs, cards, and the like to specify the branch of healing he professes. In England, physicians use the title *Dr.,* but a surgeon or other specialist, particularly one who has made a reputation, is called *Mr.*

Practice is divided among optometrists on styling themselves *Dr.,* and there is resistance by the public, including newspapers, to so designating them. Optometrists hold a degree, however, that gives them the title. The state laws we have noted often also apply here.

For practical purposes, the reader is likely to assume that a medical man whose name is preceded by *Dr.* is an M.D. If he is something else—a dentist, chiropractor, or veterinarian—it is a good idea to say so, and certainly when the context has something to do with his profession.

Now for the Ph.D.'s and other academic doctors. Whether one of this ilk uses the title *Dr.* appears to depend on his modesty. Around great universities, where doctors of philosophy abound, it is generally considered sophomoric to affect the title *Dr.,* although it is often applied by others as an honorific to the heads of departments and the like. Its use otherwise is commoner in small colleges, just as title-happiness generally is endemic in small towns.

But let the Ph.D.'s have their *Dr.*'s. After all, they worked seven or eight years for them, and the title goes naturally with the flaunting of Phi Beta Kappa keys in the nether world of education. Let us save our purplest scorn for those who adopt the title on the strength of honorary degrees. Clergymen (usually D.D.'s) are the chief offenders in this respect.

One worthy was appointed president of a small football college for his promotional zeal, although he had no scholarly background. The trustees were concerned, however, at his lack of a Ph.D., for they considered the title *Dr.* a highly desirable ornament to the office. Arrangements were quickly made to have another small college confer a Litt.D. on the new president, who thereafter dubbed himself *Dr.* and made it stick with the obsequious cooperation of the local press.

The commonest honorary degrees are D.D. (divinity), LL.D. (laws), and Litt.D. (letters, or literature). The commonest earned doctorates outside the medical fields are Ph.D. (technically philosophy, though awarded in many fields), S.T.D. and Th.D. (theology), Ed.D. (education), and Sc.D. (science). On the lower rungs of the scholastic ladder, it has been common in England for the holders of masters' and even bachelors' degrees to so identify themselves, especially on the title pages of their books ("William J. Periwinkle, M.A. Cantab."). But the practice seems to be dying out, and in the United States is possibly even disdained.

## Capitalization

Questions of capitalization are closely involved with problems of names and titles. Apart from its use in those conventions we all agree on, as in starting a sentence, capitalization is mainly a device for conferring status. It is a form of tipping the hat, of shouting "huzza," or, in certain instances, of bending the knee. It has nothing to do with meaning. We know that new york is New York just as certainly with or without the capitals, and that nelson rockefeller is the same scion of wealth we recognize in upper case.

Probably no other mechanical practice shows such divergent and confused treatment as the handling of capitalization. Things are made worse by the fact that some publications, more than others, are possessed by delusions of grandeur concerning matters of opinion about style. Two newspapers in the same town may refer to the *City Hall* and the *city hall*, respectively, but the reader gets the sense as quickly from one as from the other. Furthermore, he does not notice the difference.

Nothing much can be said for or against differing schools of thought on capitalization. Consistency within a given publication is the most that can be hoped for, but even this is made all but impossible by rules that prescribe capitals only part way through a hierarchy. I am referring to the kind of style that calls for *Pope, Cardinal, Archbishop,* but *prothonotary, monsignor, priest; Abbot, Prior,* but *monk, novice, friar;* or, to eschew the ecclesiastical, *Chief of Police, Captain, Lieutenant,* but *sergeant, patrolman;* or even

*Federal, State,* but *city, county.* Inconsistent honorifics of this kind are the sort of thing that makes copyreaders want to bang their heads against the wall.

The capitalization of *president,* in reference to the president of the United States, is almost universal in newspapers, although they do not ordinarily capitalize the word in other connections. The treatment of such references as *king, queen,* and *general* appears to depend on the amount of reverence the editor feels for the offices. It would be unheard of for a British or Canadian newspaper not to capitalize *queen* in reference to the queen of England. They would no more lower-case the word than a public-relations man would lower-case *company* in reference to his own company.

The two great creeds of capitalization are known as the Up Style and the Down Style. The schism is based mainly on a difference in the treatment of generic terms, that is, *Mississippi River* vs. *Mississippi river.* But the creeds manifest themselves in other ways too: *Pope* vs. *pope, Spring* and *Summer* vs. *spring* and *summer, Diesel* vs. *diesel,* and so forth. Idiosyncrasies like the Down Style, especially as it applies to generic terms, are thought to make for breezy, informal readability. This is a commendable goal, but it is questionable whether the Down Style assists it. Addiction to the Down Style often accompanies some of the stuffiest, most turgid writing this side of a government (Government?) report.

Now let me rush in and announce some of my own conclusions on this confused subject:

1. The Up Style is preferable to the Down Style because it is what kids learn in school and is more widely used.

2. But even practitioners of the Up Style should make a stab at some reasonable consistency. This would prevent such divided usage within hierarchies as that noted above.

3. To cut down the style manual to reasonable size, I offer the same prescription as in other stylistic problems: Let Webster, or whatever dictionary you use, be your guide.

## Problems of Reference

Pronouns are among the handiest gadgets in the language, but we often tend to shun them in favor of unnecessarily naming again what we are writing about. Ambiguity, it is true, can result from using pronouns carelessly. But when the reference is unmistakable it seems a shame to forego the terseness, naturalness, and ease of expression that come from writing simply *he* instead of *the official, she* instead of *the housewife,* and *it* instead of *the proposal under discussion.*

Fear of pronouns is related to another idiosyncrasy, love of epithets. This takes the form of a *tour de force,* or something, in which the writer sets out to astound the reader with the number of different names he can think up for the same thing. The reader may be more revolted than astounded by such a shallow trick, but he is, after all, defenseless against it. Thus a game becomes successively a *contest,* an *event,* a *match,* a *set-to,* a *tilt,* an *encounter,* and a *tussle* in the references of as many paragraphs.

Sometimes repetition of a word grates on the ear and is therefore to be avoided. This problem is explored fully, for those interested in its nuances, by Fowler under the headings "Elegant Variation" and "Repetition of Words or Sounds" in his *Modern English Usage.* The gist of it is that a dozen sentences are spoiled by straining to avoid repetition for every one that is spoiled by repetition itself.

Getting back to fear of pronouns, let us retire to the laboratory and dissect a few specimens:

"Three governors planning to attend the conference have stated their intention of turning public schools over to private hands. The three are . . ." Why not *"They* are"?

"A mechanic's helper shot and killed his estranged wife with a shotgun while she slept with one of the couple's three children." When the writer wrote *the couple's* instead of *their,* he not only fled from the smoother construction to the more awkward one, but also ran the risk of raising the question whether the children were those of the mechanic and his wife or of some other couple.

"A spokesman said the group gave a vote of confidence to the negotiation committee and endorsed the latter's stand in refusing a wage increase." Why not *its* instead of the clumsy *the latter's?*

## He or She

Sex rears its head, though not very interestingly, in references that apply to both men and women: "The employee can appeal to the state if he or she feels that he or she is being exploited." *He or she* is not only clumsy but unnecessary. It is a well-established convention that in such instances the masculine pronoun (*he*) is taken as applying to both sexes. The plural pronoun is commonly used, and considered acceptable, in speech, but is questionable in writing: "Every boy and girl had *their* own cup." *His* may be preferable here. A deep thinker once invented a bisexual pronoun, *hir,* for use in such constructions, but it went over like the legendary lead balloon.

## He, She (———)

"Jones said Smith had told him about the affair and that he (Smith) had denied taking part in it." The writer has decided that *he* may be ambiguous. So he put *Smith* in parenthesis beside it, as if to say, "*I* know who I mean, but I must give the dimwitted reader some help." The writer is also trying to indicate that he knows better than to commit the imaginary sin of simply repeating the name, so instead he commits the folly of *he* (*Smith*). *He* (*Smith*) is an example of editing that has been obtruded on the reader. There is no more reason to write *he* (*Smith*) than to let any other mistake, together with its correction, stand in print. One might as justifiably write "Smith (no, Schmidt)." To go back to the original example, sensibly amended: "Jones said Smith had told him about the affair and that Smith had denied taking part in it."

## Leapfrog

Another problem of reference is exemplified by a game we might call leapfrog. It is among the favorites of that fun-loving crew, the gentlemen of the press. In this form of leapfrog, the leaping is done by the reader, whether he likes it or not. The object is to see whether he can make the jump from one to the other of two related references that have been slyly separated by the writer. Here is an example:

"A prominent businessman criticized the city's proposals for off-street parking today as too expensive and poorly planned."

"Rensselaer van Wart spoke at a meeting of the Chamber of Commerce Traffic Committee, of which he is a member."

Is van Wart the prominent businessman? Of course, you fool, the writer might reply. How could it be otherwise? No one else has been mentioned. Yet the link between *prominent businessman* and *Rensselaer van Wart* has to be forged by the reader alone. Depending on a variety of factors, such as the reader's familiarity with the name, more or less hesitation ensues when he encounters such a gap in identification. Neglecting to show the relation between one thing and the next is an offense against the principle of writing that calls for effective transitions. Making the reader guess at, or assume, the connection is a slipshod practice.

In the example, the second paragraph should have been tied to the first by something like "The businessman, Rensselaer van Wart . . ." or "The criticism was expressed today by Rensselaer van Wart at . . ."

Let us go on to what might be called a three-stage example of the same kind of error: "Senator Francis Case, for one, is going to be definitely chary. The South Dakotan has too long a memory. When the newly elected solon heard about the incident, he laughed." There was nothing in what went before to identify Senator Case as either a South Dakotan or newly elected. The reader was expected to jump to the conclusion that all three designations referred to the same man. No doubt the reader did jump to the right conclusion, after a confused moment or two. But why should he have to jump at all?

He may have no stomach for leapfrog. Many readers might have preferred, after the first sentence, something like "The senator, who is newly elected from South Dakota, has too long a memory. When he heard about the incident, he laughed."

Here's another obstacle course: "The judge discharged a juror, after learning that William Roark was related by marriage to the defendant's cousin." Roark was the juror, but even an experienced leapfrogger could not be sure of this without looking for further clues.

Leapfrog appears to grow out of two other foibles—avoiding repetition of a word at all costs, including clarity, and painfully condensing sentence structure. Leapfrog is a game that kids outgrow. Writers might as well outgrow it too.

# PART TWO

# JOURNALESE JUNGLE

# CHAPTER X

# Cherchez le Cliché

Damned by Dogma; Clichés; Journalese; Overwriting; "Clean Copy"; Repetition.

## Damned by Dogma

I F THE job of every newspaperman in the country suddenly depended on his ability to parse a sentence, not a press would roll tomorrow. I don't mean that no newspaperman could do it. I do mean that not enough of them would be left after such a test to put out any papers.

But what of it? There is not necessarily any correlation, after all, between the ability to parse a sentence and the ability to perform acceptably, or even brilliantly, as a reporter. We all know pedagogues who can parse a sentence, all right, but who write all wrong.

Yet I have always wondered whether a solid grasp of the mechanics of language does a newspaperman any harm. The question seems to apply especially to copyreaders, whose job is to exercise some corrective judgment on writing. A reasonable command of the facts of grammar and usage might be worth having just for its own sake. Newspapermen themselves would not place much confidence in a doctor they suspected of being unable to identify the bones in the body, or in an engineer who bragged about never having mastered algebra—as some reporters brag about ignorance of grammar.

It is interesting to note that educators and scientists are placing English at the top of the lists of studies they recommend for stiffening up American education. If scientists and engineers need to know English fundamentals, why not newspapermen?

There is a recurrent yammer about a lack of "professionalism" in newspaper work. No one seems prepared to say exactly what professionalism is, or to tell just how journalism is deficient in it, although a general lack of respect for the average level of competence of its practitioners seems to figure in the deficiency. We know, at least, that professionalism in other fields has something to do with mastery of fundamentals.

But let's not go off on a tangent about professionalism. Let's stick instead to journalistic writing—what it is, what it is not, and what it might be. Sometimes it seems to be aiming at the discarded formality of an earlier day, while unhappily showing no signs of the discrimination and elegance which characterized that day. Stuffiness and pomposity are the sorry results.

The dead hand of stereotyped models is quickly laid on young reporters. If they are to learn a clearer, brighter way to write, they generally must do so by themselves. Intelligent guidance of the inexperienced in matters of composition is a rarity in newspaper offices. This may be asking too much, anyway; the blind cannot lead the blind.

Newswriting is regarded not as something that can never be finally learned, nor as something that would benefit by the continuous application of taste and discrimination. It seems to be regarded instead as a mechanical skill, to be mastered quickly, once and for all, like the operation of a typewriter.

There does seem to be agreement among editors on what the goal of newswriting ought to be; namely, lucid, readable recording of the facts. There are even signs of an awareness that newswriting needs a new approach. The first stirring took place a few years ago, when one of the big wire services hired Rudolf Flesch, who had attracted wide attention with his first book on readability, as a consultant for a year. Viewed from a possibly perverse angle, this development appeared to hold an element of absurdity. Here was a vast organization whose business is the written word calling in an outside specialist to instruct it in the elements of readable communication. It was as if the First National Bank had called in someone to teach its tellers to make change.

The fact is that Dr. Flesch, as he himself made clear in the preface to *The Art of Plain Talk,* was not advancing any particularly novel principles. His approach was novel in that he devised a formula to gauge readability, while at the same time expressing concern lest some readers "wallow in the little rules and computations but lose sight of the principles of plain English."

There really was nothing absurd about the summoning of Dr. Flesch, for it was a long-overdue move in the right direction. But the hardening of the arteries that journalistic writing suffers from is chronic, and cannot be kept in check by calling in an expert temporarily. Every sizable news-gathering organization could use a permanent expert to carry on a continuous campaign against stereotypes, superstitions of grammar and usage, pomposity, and whatnot.

All that is required is a steady program of second-guessing, in writing, conducted by someone who knows what he is doing. Newspapermen are quick to catch on. They can absorb useful ideas about expression as readily as they absorbed the old grammatical hand-me-downs. All they need is someone to point the way. Unfortunately, little is done along these lines, and some of what is done is worthless.

There is an ill-defined feeling in newsdom that grammar and usage are sterile, unduly restrictive considerations, fit only for the attention of pedants. Yet the typical newspaperman is ten times as pedantic about his notions in this field as the typical grammarian. Great changes have come over the approach to language by scholars in the last fifty years. Rules are now regarded as growing out of usage, instead of being forced on it like a straitjacket. Yet no inkling of this principle appears to have penetrated newspaper offices. Although usage is in a perpetual state of flux, the newspaper tendency is to regard it as fixed.

Many newspapers own no reference work on grammar or usage. Many others rely on some archaic or crotchety book that may be worse than nothing (such as Ambrose Bierce's *Write It Right*). It's easy to find newspapermen who have not even heard of Fowler, Flesch, Quiller-Couch, or the contemporary Bergen and Cornelia Evans.

What is the cure for all this? Is there any hope? The only cure seems to be a reversal of misguided and indifferent attitudes toward newswriting. The goal of readability needs more than lip service. A certain elementary taste must be generated in newswriters that will make them shun the cliché and stereotypes of all kinds. A skeptical review of stylebooks and their contents is indicated. Every dictum that cannot be supported by a reason, or that does not conform with modern usage, ought to be junked. Newspapers would be better off if they restricted the use of stylebooks to mechanical matters, and left questions of grammar and usage to reference books by authorities who know what they are talking about.

All is not lost, however, for there are signs, as noted, of an awakening among newspapers to the importance of writing, as against stereotyping. There are even papers whose contents sound like the work of sentient human beings, rather than robots. Among them I would list the *Christian Science Monitor* and the *Wall Street Journal*. It is ironical that an organ of the business world, a world whose prose is generally scorned even by newspapermen, should stand out as strikingly well written.

Newspapers may be coming to see that an exact, unpretentious mode of expression is not only the heart but also the salvation of their business. Perhaps this awakening is prompted by their fear of television as a competitor for attention. For all its shortcomings, the television picture has one great advantage over much printed reportage—it moves.

## Clichés

Q—Why, Mr. Arbuthnot, what on earth are you doing here?

A—I am playing hooky from my mentor, Frank Sullivan, that witty man of letters who made me what I am today. I used to be a newspaperman myself, you know.

Q—Felt impelled to return to the scene of the crime, eh? Does Mr. Sullivan know about your background as a newsman?

A—He considered it my finest qualification when he hired me as a cliché expert.

Q—Ah, yes. Well, to work. Shall we inaugurate the interview?

A—I'd rather you didn't swipe my stuff. But let's launch it.

Q—Theft is a serious charge, Mr. Arbuthnot. And incidentally, charges, in the press, are always . . .

A—Hurled.

Q—To be sure. I would prefer *made,* but then newspaper readers can seldom be choosers. Now, would you tell me . . .

A—Sorry to interrupt, but as a newsman, I never *told*. Always *advised*.

Q—Thank you. I suppose you claimed your sources were authoritative?

A—*Claimed,* yes. Seldom *asserted*. Often *contended,* though.

Q—Indeed. How has your health been?

A—I'm in the pink of condition now, although I suffered a leg fracture in a mishap a year ago.

Q—You mean your leg was broken in an accident?

A—You heard me. I also sustained some lacerations, contusions, and abrasions, but as I said, I'm O.K. now.

Q—Glad to hear it. That you're O.K., I mean. What about the time thieves broke into your apartment?

A—The place was a shambles. The marauders made their getaway with upwards of $500.

Q—Too bad. What do you do for amusement?

A—Oh, I witness a ball game now and then. They hiked the admission charge recently, but attendance has been boosted in spite of it.

Q—Do you expect to get a car when the new models are out?

A—I anticipate that I will secure one, yes. I am anxious to see them unveiled.

Q—I'd like to buy—I mean secure—one myself. But I wish the dealers would slash their prices.

A—You're learning. If you keep at it, you'll be able to turn plain English into journalese promptly.

Q—You mean *on time*?

A—No, I mean *promptly*. At once.

Q—About your job as a cliché expert—does it pay?

A—You mean, is it lucrative? Well, it pays, or lucres, better than newspapering, but then almost anything does.

Q—What did you do before you were a newspaperman?

A—Well, prior to that time I had no visible means of support, although I was a genial host. After I inked the pact with Mr. Sullivan I really hit my stride. Although I am famous, I have been described as quiet and unassuming.

Q—Are you easily embarrassed?

A—Well, I am red-faced when I am beaten to the cliché.

Q—It was very good of you to take this time out for us, Mr. Arbuthnot. Clichés must be the lifeblood and, paradoxically, at the same time the *rigor mortis* of newswriting.

A—You can say *that* again.

The castigation of redundancy and clichés in newswriting often seems like a hopeless exercise. Indeed, faint-hearted critics of those faults regularly conclude that attempts to dislodge them are wasted effort. In the large sense, these defeatists are probably right. There is no reason to hope that the noxiousness of clichés and redundancy can be impressed on any substantial number of the practitioners of journalism. This problem comes down to a matter of taste. Taste can be cultivated, certainly, but it seems unlikely that the capacity for discrimination can be implanted where it does not exist.

There will always be ill-read and dull-witted writers who will be proud of having picked up expressions that the finer-grained despise. Even on the upper levels of ability, opinions will always differ as to whether a particular expression is overworked. George Orwell once fiercely proposed that a writer should rigorously excise from his work every turn of phrase he did not invent himself. This may be going too far. Writing that contained nothing familiar or at least recognizable in this respect might well leave the reader intolerably ill at ease. In any event, no writing exists that does not contain clichés by one standard or another. This state of affairs was once described in verse:

> If you scorn what is trite
> I warn you, go slow,
> For one man's cliché
> Is another's *bon mot*.

## Journalese

What *is* journalese, anyway? Well, Webster, sounding as if he is afraid of offending someone, skates around a definition:

"Journalese. Language of a style considered characteristic of newspaper writing."

Whatever it is, it's not good. The word falls dully on the ear, like its notorious brother, *gobbledygook,* and no one ever seems to have a good word to say for either. Journalese is partly rags and tatters that set much newspaper writing apart from—let's face it—writing that has been more carefully done.

Journalese is full of clichés. Most inferior writing is cliché-ridden, it is true, but newspapering has developed its own characteristic clichés. In the stories of the reportorial cliché expert, a thing is not *kept secret,* but *a lid of secrecy is clamped* on it; rain and snow do not *fall,* but *are dumped;* a river does not *overflow,* but *goes on a rampage*; honors are not *won* or *earned,* in journalese, but *captured*; divisions are too often *crack*; a reverse of any kind does not *threaten,* but *looms;* a development is not *unprecedented,* but *precedent-shattering* (as though precedents were glass, when everyone knows they are rubber); large buildings are not *extensive,* which despite its colorlessness still has more life left in it than the battered *sprawling.*

All such expressions have something in common besides extreme fatigue. If you can shake off, for a moment, the anesthesia they produce, you will see that originally they were dramatic. Even if they were too dramatic to suit the occasion—another characteristic of journalese, not necessarily related to clichés—the first few times they were used they piqued the reader's attention. But that was long ago. How, then, do they come to be used so much? The obvious explanation is laziness. These expressions, and many equally tired ones, have become fixed in the minds of lethargic and unimaginative reporters as the only ones that are suitably descriptive.

When reporters are taxed with the stereotyped flavor of newspaper writing, they sometimes offer as an excuse that much of their work must be done in haste, to meet a deadline. This does not happen to be a good excuse, however, for it would be easier and faster to use the plain language the clichés conceal. Thus if the lazy were even a little lazier, the results would be happier.

Plain language—the words the cliché expert uses himself when he is talking instead of writing—often looks surprisingly fresh in print. It will never wear out, as the clichés have, because it is the natural and inevitable currency of expression.

## Overwriting

You can often tell a news story, if in no other way, by the supercharged effort that has been exerted to make it sound bright and lively. The rawest cub learns at once to strive for this effect. To the old hand, an awareness of that goal, if not its attainment, has become second nature. "Brighten it up" are the words that have accompanied innumerable news stories as they were handed back by the city editor for rewriting. Now, in view of all this, how can we explain the discouraging fact that only the rare news story sounds bright to the reader?

Easy. It's a variation on the old story about the boy who hollered "Wolf!" too often. You remember. People got tired of coming to the rescue just because he liked the excitement. Finally, when a wolf really did appear, they ignored him and he was wolfed. Many newspapermen have yet to learn that you cannot brighten a story by using words whose color or vigor are too much for the occasion. In a given story, this only creates a faintly ridiculous, overstrained effect. When it is done in one story after another, the reader quickly comes to disregard the overwrought verbiage altogether.

We are on difficult ground here, for the exercise of restraint in writing is one of the things that contribute to making it an art. It seems foolish to have any artistic pretensions or aspirations about newswriting, considering the exigent conditions under which it is generally done. About the best that can reasonably be expected is workmanlike communication of facts, leavened as far as possible by felicitous touches of description, bits of humor, and pointed insights.

Obviously, it is easier to tell the story in conversational language than to overwrite. Stories in a conversational tone are easier to read, too. The fact is that readers find overwritten prose tiresome, if not absurd. Reporters know, of course, that the situations they relate seldom live up to the highly charged words they use to relate them. Readers know it, too. Thus the usual state of affairs is that the writer has his tongue in his cheek and the reader has his fingers crossed.

Must I really put forth examples of this kind of thing? Well, all right. Criticism by and of public officials may range from the mild to the severe. Little account seems to be taken of the tone of the criticism, however. It comes out *attacked, blasted, flayed, lashed out at, lambasted,* or *scored.*

"The jury might order him imprisoned for life or flung back into the arms of his family." If the flinging should kill him, as seems likely, he might prefer life imprisonment. The breakup of a three-man stage act could have been reported in those terms, instead of *the trio was shattered. Toss* is a great favorite. Often it is substituted for *throw,* which in fact is stronger, not weaker. But we read of a diplomat tossing a treaty to a conference, of the National Broadcasting Company tossing colors into costumes for TV shows, and of a tax cut tossing a budget into the red.

Is the reader diverted or stimulated by this shrill stuff? Not at all. He's bored stiff, when he is not revolted, and what interest he feels is inspired solely by the factual content. Things are worse when, as is so often true, the attempt to enliven is made with clichés—*hurl* for *make* (an accusation), *smash* or *shatter* for *break* (a record), *soar* for *rise.* Life's not that exciting most of the time, and when it is, the circumstances will speak for themselves.

In a survey of the American press, *The Times* of London commented:

"It is this fundamental striving to attract the attention of, as well as to inform, the normally indifferent citizen which gives modern American journalism some of its most striking characteristics. Notably, it is the cause of its tendency to oversimplify political and diplomatic situations and developments to the point of distortion; to heighten personalities and the part played; to describe complex events in vivid, breathless, exciting prose so that the regular reader must live with a perpetual state of crisis or develop a deliberate indifference as a protection against it."

Jacques Barzun has taken note of the overexcited tone of much journalism by referring to reporters as "writers whose professional neurosis is to despair of being attended to and in whom, therefore, a kind of solemn ritual clowning is inevitable."

## "Clean Copy"

"Clean copy" is the shibboleth of many a newsroom, and no one can reasonably quibble with the general objective. Copy that has been badly messed up with strike-overs and scribbled interlineations is the bane of both the copy desk and the composing room. An absolute ban on strike-overs, as is enforced on many newspapers, is a good idea. So is discouragement of breaking words at the ends of lines in typescript, which can raise unnecessary questions about hyphenation in the composing room. And finally, legibility is the least that can be expected of emendations.

The worship of clean copy, however, has been known to find expression in a reverence for unblemished typescript for its own sake. In this way, mediocre writers who never hit a wrong key, nor change their minds about choice of words or the structure of a sentence, gain a fraudulent stature.

"That guy certainly writes clean copy!" is the admiring verdict. The unspoken implication is that clean copy is, *ipso facto*, good copy. Unfortunately, it may be beautiful stuff to look at but terrible to read. Clean copy, in the sense of unamended typing, ought to be recognized for what it is—a feat of stenography, having nothing to do with the quality of either reporting or writing. The work of the clean-copy artist is likely to be below par, on the general principle that any piece of writing can stand improvement, particularly what is written under the conditions of journalism. The Heywood Brouns who can grind out a couple of thousand words of hard, gemlike prose without any second thoughts are—well, Heywood Brouns.

The self-critical, conscientious reporter who goes over his stuff carefully, substituting better words for worse ones and unsnarling bad constructions, ought to be encouraged in his labors. All too many natively uncritical reporters have been abetted, perhaps unwittingly, in the notion that there is some overriding virtue in clean copy. Clean copy should be knocked off the pedestal it occupies in some newsrooms, and in its place should go well-written copy.

Ben Jonson had something pertinent to say on this subject: "The players have often mentioned it as an honor to Shakespeare, that in his writing he never blotted out a line. My answer hath been, would he had blotted a thousand."

## Repetition

Is it true, as it seems to be, that newswriters do not trust the reader to remember what they have just told him? If not, why can't they be content to allow what they have set down to stand, without repeating or restating it in some obvious way a few lines later? It may be taken for granted that what has been said in the lead paragraph, especially, is likely to stick in the reader's mind, for that is what makes him decide either to read on or to turn to something that interests him more.

Bald repetition of phrases and sentences seems to imply a lack of confidence that they have sunk in. This is no tribute to the reader's intelligence, nor does it reflect any credit on the writer's. Increasingly unfavorable comparisons of newswriting with magazine writing are being made. Footless iteration like the following is rarely encountered in magazines:

"President Eisenhower, smiling broadly, said today that ever since he was five years old his brother Edgar has been criticizing him." O. K. But two paragraphs later, we get this warmed-over dish: "Smiling broadly, the chief executive replied that Edgar had been criticizing him since he was five years old."

As garnish, perhaps, the broad smile has now been moved up front; Mr. Eisenhower is interestingly referred to as the chief executive; and *has been* is changed to *had been,* for some mysterious reason. Do these changes warrant the rehash? Now this:

"The lumber strike is over, and the president of the union calls it 'a draw.'" Passing by the unnecessary quotes around *a draw,* let us proceed to the second paragraph: "'We neither won nor lost the strike. It was a draw,' said George Willard . . ." All right, it was a draw, as the union president saw it. But after having established this in the lead, why not omit it from the next paragraph?

And again: "She's tall, she's tanned, and she says the new Dior 'flat' look 'came just in time to save me.'" Four paragraphs later: "'I think Dior came just in time to save me,' she said." But what will save a story from the flat sound that comes of meaningless repetition?

"He said last night that never before in the history of astronomy have the scientists been able to study a satellite which has traveled as fast as the Russian earth moons.

" 'We've never had this in astronomy before,' said Dr. Whipple." Maybe not in astronomy, but we've had it in print. In fact, we've just plain had it.

You think these are bad? Well, steel yourself. Here's not just duplication, but triplication. Let the press association responsible put on the shoe:

"The White House said today it does not know whether reports of a Russian manned rocket flight are true or not." [There were quotes around *true or not,* but I could not bear to copy them, and to that extent this example is falsified.]

" 'We have no knowledge of the truth of these stories,' Press Secretary James C. Hagerty told reporters.

"Hagerty persisted in his refusal to comment on the reports 'because I don't know whether the story is true or not.' "

And so to bed, to bed, to bed.

# CHAPTER XI

# The Time and the Place

Misused Tenses in Time Elements; Placement of Time Elements; *Today;*
Datelines; Day of the Week.

## Misused Tenses in Time Elements

EXCESSIVE and pointless caution seems to be at the bottom of the use of
the past tense in places where it tarnishes the freshly minted news. This
foible is especially conspicuous in some news magazines, which seem to be
fearful lest the situation at the time of writing may change before the account
is read. It is less prevalent, though not unknown, in newspapers.

"A seaplane with seventeen persons aboard *was* missing south of Japan,
the Navy said today." Conceivably, the plane might have been found before
the newspaper reached the reader. But is it really necessary to pussyfoot like
this, or may the reader be left to assume that the paper is stating the facts of
the time of writing?

Many news stories deal with conditions that will unquestionably persist
between the time of writing and the time of reading. Take, for example, an
account in a news magazine that began: "Connecticut *was* in for a wide-open
and exciting election." Why *was,* since the election was a long way off, and
there was no indication the situation might change? Having started with the
past tense, however, the writer had to stick with it, thus giving a musty flavor
to something that could have been kept fresh by the use of the present tense.
How much more immediate "Connecticut *is* in for a wide-open and exciting
election" sounds!

Writers who insist on using the past tense where the present tense seems
preferable might at least take care not to disconcert the reader by changing
horses in the middle of a stream: "On the drawing boards *are* a physical-
science center, a classroom and office building, a music building, and a student dormitory. It *was* all part of a $48 million building program." The
inexplicable shift from *are* to *was* sounds as if the building program is no
more, although the plans are still on the boards.

"There *was* a machine that *chewed up* old fluorescent tubes, and another
that *keeps* the air in the factory dry." This writer needed help to keep him
on the same time-track.

Here's a general principle that will brighten things up: Avoid the past tense except in narrating completed events. Use the present, as far as possible, to describe conditions in effect at the time of writing. Nothing is lost by saying "A seaplane with seventeen persons aboard *is* [rather than *was*] missing," and something is gained: immediacy. Use the present tense, too, for general statements, and stand clear of such absurdities as "The men who did the most to break the Solid South in the election *were* Democrats and they *intended* to remain Democrats," when in fact they still *are* and still *intend*.

This may be the place to deal with *was a former,* which does not make sense in reference to a living man: "Like Hull and Padrutt, Johnson *was a former* Progressive." The point here is once a former, always a former. *Was a former* (and *was a onetime*) can be properly used only of a dead man to describe a condition that ceased to exist before he died. Even then, the meaning is better expressed with different wording: "The late governor was at one time a Farmer-Laborite."

I once heard about a disagreement between a reporter who wrote, "Officers elected last night *were* . . ." and an editor who thought it should have been *are.* Although, of course, either is correct, an arbiter seriously argued for *were* on the ground that the reporter could justifiably state only the fact as he knew it, and could not assume that the officers would survive until the next morning, when the paper carrying the account of the election would appear!

Antiquarians among newswriters, who are devoted to the past tense at the cost of brightness and clarity, often are not content until they have taken yet another step backward, into the past perfect—also known as the pluperfect. The past perfect (*had gone, had been,* as distinguished from the simple past, *went* and *was*) is useful in establishing a time previous to one already specified. But care should be taken not to confuse the sequence, nor to imply a nonexistent sequence. Often, for no apparent reason, the past perfect is used in place of the past.

When a sentence contains both a past and a past perfect tense, the reader is entitled to assume that the occasion described by the past perfect came first. "A doctor recently *discovered* the nail in a bronchial tube and *had recommended* surgery." *Had discovered* and *recommended* would be more logical, but *discovered* and *recommended* are what come naturally, because the train of events is self-evident.

"Many of the professionals in the audience *had been* in the Center Theater when Ballet Theatre started out on Jan. 11, 1940." The presence of the professionals in the theater did not precede the starting out, but coincided with it; *had been* should be *were.*

Much the same difficulty arises in sentences containing a past time element and a past perfect verb: "He *had been* the youngest member of the College of Cardinals when he was elected in 1946 at the age of forty-six." This is nonsense, for he could not have been the youngest member until he was elected. Instead of *had been, was* or *became* is required.

"Only yesterday Adenauer *had predicted* an accord." *Predicted* would have served better; *had predicted* gives a fuzzy impression the prediction was made sometime before yesterday. "Another futuristic device, a convertiplane, actually *had been flown* in December." *Was flown* is what the circumstances called for.

"She *had been* eighteen when they were married." If so, she had also been seventeen, sixteen, etc. The writer intended "She *was* eighteen when they were married." "In 1899, Joseph Pulitzer Jr., four, sealed a copper box into the cornerstone of a new building. Last week, filled with mementos of nineteenth-century journalism, the box *had* tumbled out of the wreckage." This sounds as if the tumbling out occurred sometime before last week—*tumbled* is what was meant.

Other peculiar pluperfects follow more or less naturally the strange ritual of using the past tense, instead of the present, to report continuing conditions. Biographical sketches are often the habitat of clumsy past perfects where past tenses would read more smoothly.

"In the eighty-two years of his life, Bill Green *had moved* from a poor coal-miner's home . . . His career *had been* anything but meteoric . . . But it *had been* his unspectacular character . . ." Why not the easier "Bill Green *moved* . . . His career *was* . . . But it *was* . . ."? The writer probably set this tense-trap for himself by beginning with something like "Bill Green *was* dead today" (having died the day before). Devotion to the perfect is commendable, but the passion for the past perfect is to be discouraged.

## Placement of Time Elements

Newspaper writers could stay out of some of the grammatical swamps they get into if they would follow the example of Grampaw in "Annie Get Your Gun" and just do what comes naturally. Reporters who would never say "I *today* went downtown" will write in a news story, with the greatest of ease, "The City Council *last night* voted a street-improvement program."

The natural place for the time element is generally after, rather than before, the verb, and often at the very end of the sentence: "I went downtown *today*"; "The City Council voted a street-improvement program *last night*." We don't really need to be told this; everyone, even the illiterate, realizes it instinctively. Why, then, don't we write accordingly?

There are at least two reasons for the misplacement of the time element in newswriting. One is overemphasis on the W's formula—the idea that the lead paragraph should tell when, who, what, where, why, whence, wherefore, which, wherein, and whither—but above all *when,* to impress on the reader what fresh intelligence he is getting. A revolt is now under way, however, on the grounds that all this may be too much to expect the reader to assimilate all at once and that the lead really should be the nub of the story in the simplest and most direct terms. The new gospel is "Damn the W's—full speed ahead."

Another reason for the misplacement of the time element is that a moment of thought may be necessary to select the most suitable place for it. Thinking, as has been said, hurts the head, and to avoid this kind of pain, reporters heedlessly drop the time element in where it breaks the natural flow of the sentence: "The Air Force pressed *tonight* the search for a missing plane." Goofy as it sounds, this kind of disarrangement is nearly standard practice. There seems to be a silent conspiracy, even among those who know better, against putting the time element where it belongs.

When the time element is indispensable (and often it is not, as we shall see) it should be put in a place where it does not stick out like a sore thumb. Let us look at some examples of sheer clumsiness in this respect:

"Ernest Hemingway, who has written powerful novels of violence and death, was awarded *today* the Nobel Prize for literature." (". . . was awarded the Nobel Prize for literature *today*.") Why newswriters should fear to put the time element at the end when it fits there smoothly is a mystery.

"It was his own brother who *last year* spoke out against his political tactics." (". . . who spoke out *last year* . . .")

"Negotiations to end the crippling railway strike reportedly reached *today* their most crucial stage." (". . . reached their most crucial stage *today*.")

The placement of the time element in "World War II veterans *next year* will collect $226 million in dividends on their government life insurance" is defensible if the writer had intended to emphasize *next year,* perhaps in contrast to some other year. But such emphasis was not intended, and if it had been, *next year* should have come first. The writer might have chosen among "will collect $226 million *next year*," or "in dividends *next year*," or "on their government life insurance *next year*." There were so many other places for *next year* that the most awkward one seems to have been chosen deliberately.

Care in placement of the time element is advisable not only to prevent clumsiness, as in the examples, but to keep it from modifying the wrong word or phrase. "The Indian prime minister arrived in Saigon after visiting Communist China today." *Today* belongs after Saigon, because it is intended to fix the time of arrival. As the sentence stands, *today* may be taken as fixing the time of the visit to China.

"Legislators working on the president's blueprint for a revised atomic-energy law today faced two major obstacles." *Today* might be omitted here, and *faced* changed to *face*. If *today* must be kept, it would be better at the end.

Shifting the time element or any other part of a sentence away from its natural position lays emphasis on it. This should only be done intentionally. Newswriters seem to be curiously insensitive to emphasis gained by word order. This is not the place to go into the fine points of this subject, and even if it were, the correct placement of words is the kind of thing that can be learned but not taught.

Possibly I am not giving newswriters enough credit, in that they may be deliberately misplacing the time element to call attention to the freshness of their product. If so, I doubt that it leaves any impression on the reader, except as another irritant. If they really want emphasis, why not put the time element at the beginning of the sentence, which is the most emphatic place for it?

## Today

*Today,* we know, is the magic word of the diurnal press. It sums up the hopes and fears of newspapering—the hope that the reader is getting the news from one's own newspaper first, and the fear of having been scooped. There is a powerful yen to impress on the reader that what he is reading about happened, or at least was first consigned to print, *today,* that no expense or effort has been spared to bring him the news expeditiously, and that nothing could be fresher. This is the reason, no doubt, for the prevalence of *today* in the leads of stories.

Consider wire stories. All are datelined, and few newspapers drop the date. What purpose is served by datelining if the reader must be prodded again with the time element in the form of *today* within a line or two? Even newspapers that drop dates from datelines carry the date of publication in their folio lines. It may be assumed that the reader is surer of few things than of the date of his paper, even without looking.

Often *today* is out of place, dateline or no dateline. It defeats its purpose and detracts from the immediacy of a story dealing with a continuing condition rather than a specific event. The way it is usually used, with verbs in the past tense, gives an old-hat flavor to stories that could be made to sound bright and fresh by omitting *today* and using the present tense.

Instead of "Another month of hot, dry weather *was* in prospect *today* for the already arid Southwest" how about "Another month of hot, dry weather *is* in prospect . . ."? In the second version the subject is kept alive.

"A group of California Democrats *was* lined up *today* against a tax measure being pushed by their Republican colleagues" is improved by making it "A group . . . *is* lined up" since, as the story made clear, the alignment was not just a phenomenon of that day alone.

In summary, *today* is usually unnecessary in any lead that is datelined, and omitting it is the simplest way to solve the problem. Some such leads, however, would be improved by omitting the time element and changing the verb from the past tense to the present perfect. Here is one of them: "A Canadian inventor patented *this week* a way to make the garden grow better." Compare it with "A Canadian inventor has patented a way to make the garden grow better." Not only is it hard to find a comfortable place for *this week,* but the words serve no useful purpose in the lead anyway.

Sometimes the time element would be better left out because it misleads or confuses. "The Soviet Communist chief is in trouble *today*. He is fighting valiantly to hold together the empire left him by his predecessors." *Today* here is not only obtrusive, but ludicrous, because it suggests that a long-continuing situation is of only a day's duration. The same is true of "The competitive athletic program here is on the rocks *today* because of a decision earlier this week to close the school gym" and "An eighty-year-old nun stood firm *today* [is standing firm] against plans to turn her little nation into a Communist state."

## Datelines

The datelines on wire stories in morning papers carry the date of the preceding day, and *today* in those stories is *yesterday* to the reader. This is consistent enough as far as it goes; the reader has the dateline to which he can relate all subsequent time elements in a given story. But let us consider a wire story about an event that will take place "tomorrow"; that is, the day the reader reads the story. What does the headline say? It says the event will happen *today,* for headlines relate to the date of the paper itself, not to the datelines of the stories. The *today* in a local story in the next column, however, is the reader's *today*. It seems as if the sensible cure for this mishmash is to leave the dates out of datelines, thus clearing the way for a consistent treatment of the time elements in both wire stories and local stories.

## Day of the Week

A peculiar effect is created when the day of the week is named: "John Jones *Thursday* shot his mother-in-law." Some newspapers follow this style, instead of saying *yesterday,* on the theory that the time is then more exactly specified, and for other reasons. Certain captious critics have said, however, that the likes of *John Jones Thursday* may leave the impression that *Thursday* is John's last name. At any rate, this construction is still open to the same criticism that applies to misplacement of *today* and *yesterday*—clumsy word order.

I cannot let this subject drop without speculating on what might happen in some hypothetical news story dealing with the cunning Sergeant Friday, or with Robinson Crusoe's famous sidekick, who I believe was just plain Friday. Readers very likely would be favored with something like "Sergeant Friday Friday started a new investigation," or "Friday Saturday helped Robinson Crusoe store provisions."

# CHAPTER XII

# Riding Herd

An Aside to Editors—Editorial Surveillance; Style and Stylebooks;
Use of Dictionaries; By-Lines; Letters to the Editor.

## An Aside to Editors—Editorial Surveillance

ETERNAL vigilance is the price, not only of liberty, but also of readability. It is surprising how little advantage is taken, by many publications, of the opportunity to raise standards by critically reviewing the finished product.

The lack of any systematic surveillance does not merely keep a publication from maintaining as high a standard as it might, but runs the quality of writing and editing into the ground. Close checking of what appears on the printed page is essential to keeping staff members on the *qui vive,* and to giving them a sense of satisfaction in their work and pride in the publication. It is necessary, too, for the good opinion of discerning readers.

When no such checking is practiced, the impression easily gains ground among the staff that nobody cares. On a newspaper, for example, reporters will write haphazardly, and copyreaders will daydream while they hook the paragraphs. A number of staffers may notice some conspicuous error in the first edition, but no one will bother to do anything about it. A new reporter who approaches the copy desk with a suggested correction will quickly desist after he has been greeted a time or two with a scowl or a snarl.

The psychology of newspaper production may be to blame for neglect of post-mortems. The byword is *hurry,* and the habit of haste becomes so ingrained that it persists even when there is time to do the job right. Ignorance on the part of some editors as to what constitutes good expression, and the vain hope of concealing such ignorance, also figure in this situation.

Checking of carbon copies of stories as written by reporters has limited value, because it affords no check on copyreading and headline-writing. Sporadic criticism, as represented by explosive memoranda to all hands from the managing editor, issued on days when he has had a bad breakfast, is all but useless too.

The appearance of the first edition offers a golden opportunity to do a thorough cleanup job. When this opportunity is not seized, the same off-base or wooden headlines, typographical and factual errors, and clumsy constructions go marching steadily through edition after edition.

A better method of keeping a newspaper's columns up to a high standard is to teach the staff to sidestep most errors entirely. This kind of training can easily be accomplished by means of a regular critique. One way of doing it is to post, perhaps once a week, a front page that has been gone over meticulously and marked up. Another way is to put out a two- or three-page bulletin in which mischances are noted and discussed, and in which good work is complimented, too. The leading example of this technique is "Winners & Sinners," the work of Theodore M. Bernstein of the *New York Times*.

It is only human, after all, to be careless when care is not expected or required. The mere fact that second-guessing is practiced thoroughly and consistently is bound to have a salutary effect on the quality of the first-guessing. It will, in fact, prevent a good deal of guesswork entirely.

## Style and Stylebooks

Are stylebooks here to stay? Not necessarily, a perfunctory survey indicates. The shocking fact is that some exceedingly well-edited journals get along without them. In any event, the apparent necessity for a uniform code to govern details of capitalization, spelling, and other mechanical matters on which opinions differ is surely one of the curses of the publications field, especially when the style-mongers grow drunk with the power that corrupts.

Meditation and prayer have convinced me that the best style is the one which governs least. As far as readers are concerned, even the uneducated among them encounter a great variety of practices in what little they read. The variety is so much greater for the educated that inconsistencies of editorial details even within a given publication are likely to pass unnoticed.

Some standardization in style might be expected to have come to prevail among daily newspapers, served as they are in vast numbers by the same wire services and, in lesser but still considerable numbers, by the same syndicates. But in the editing of newspapers we have, among lesser deviations, the Up Style and the Down Style. To a varying extent, from one publication to another, there is what might be denominated the Upside-Down Style. This shows itself in "grammatical" rules that have no basis in grammar, in random off-base spellings and hyphenations, and in weird but prescribed syntactical constructions.

Publications that enforce rules having no standing in accepted practice, either journalistic or linguistic, are setting up obstacle courses for their staffs. In some really style-crazy establishments, it is regularly necessary to take wire stories apart and carpenter them into an unnatural shape to satisfy some such rule. This situation is analogous to that in a washing-machine plant where bolts and nuts would have to be rethreaded, for some mysterious but useless reason, before the machines could be assembled. Such nonsense only adds to the difficulty of the job without affecting the quality of the product.

It is observable that a publication can be far gone in style craziness and still exhibit no intelligent or effective control over what really counts: excising of clichés, fining down of fuzzy expressions, squeezing the water out of redundancies, and tightening of construction. Indeed, there may well be a high correlation between style craziness and poor editing in general. The forest is lost sight of in picking through the leaves, and a pathetic and hopeless reliance is placed on special rules to do a job that can be accomplished only by the continuous application of good judgment.

The attention that stylebooks give to grammar and usage could be all to the good, but many of them also serve to keep alive countless superstitions of usage, many of them peculiar to newswriting. Some favorite stylebook rules were, indeed, once grammar; others never were. Most of them have not enjoyed any reputability among the discerning for the last generation or two.

One such stylebook, used by a newspaper requiring rigid conformity to a farrago of absurd rules, many of them invented by its editor of seventy-five years ago, encourages writers to cultivate "snap and ginger" in their prose. The objective is fine, but how sadly that choice of language dates the thinking behind the book!

Style that goes beyond general principles enabling writers and editors to do their work expeditiously only gratifies someone's idiosyncrasies.

Let us consider some more practical aspects of this question. The stylebook of the *Los Angeles Times* leaves the left-hand pages blank, for notes and addenda, and runs the text only on the right-hand pages. The usual practice, if any blanks are left at all, is to put them at the end of the book. The advantage of interspersing them should be obvious: Notes that can be easily placed opposite the stuff they apply to are more likely to be entered and referred to. It's also a good idea for a stylebook to be loose leaf, like that of the *Chicago Tribune,* and to possess an exhaustive index, like that of the *New York Times*.

Such memoranda as are necessary to supplement the stylebook should not merely be issued in loose sheets. In this form they are quickly mislaid, disregarded, and forgotten. They should be issued in such a form as to facilitate inclusion in an alphabetical file, perhaps on arch boards or in card-file boxes. One such file should be maintained at the copy desk, and at least one more at some central point in the city room. This supplemental material should be incorporated in the stylebook as it is revised.

## Use of Dictionaries

Even the smallest and most impecunious of publications is likely to own an unabridged dictionary; *Webster's New International* has established itself as the favorite. All too often, however, the big book is in a hopeless state—pages folded over, rolled up, and missing to an extent that discourages its use. Sometimes it is an antique that should have been retired long ago.

Publications are, and certainly ought to be, among the first customers for any major revision of the dictionary they use. It ought not to be asking too much that every staff member be supplied with his own copy of a desk dictionary. Words that raise doubts often fail to get looked up because inertia or haste prevents a trip across the room.

If, as is usual, a particular dictionary is designated as the final authority, care should be taken to see that the unabridged and the desk dictionaries are of the same breed. It is well to let the dictionary stand as the authority without exceptions. Short-circuiting it with special spellings, hyphenations, and the like only gets in the way of the job. Such shenanigans load the stylebook with exceptions and set up pointless, artificial hazards to editing. (See Chapter IV for comments on dictionaries and usage.)

Often as not, when an argument about grammar crops up, the editor will haul out and dust off a textbook written in the Victorian era. While their authors have moldered in their graves, the language has gone marching on.

Yet those superannuated texts are better than no grammar at all, which is the lot of some backwoods publications offices. Can you imagine a doctor's office lacking a basic work on anatomy? Every publication not only ought to have a grammar book handy, but should also specify the one it prefers, perhaps in the stylebook, since grammarians do differ on details. Perhaps the most useful grammar for working writers and editors, as distinguished from students, is Perrin's *Writer's Guide and Index to English*.

## By-Lines

Among the more mysterious aspects of the mysterious newspaper business is the rationale of by-lines. The general assumption is that a story is by-lined because of its excellence, and now and then there is something to this. A researcher into the subject, however, would quickly see that by-lines are more often associated with wordage than with excellence.

Further research would show that there are about as many schools of thought on by-lines as there are editors. Some papers use no by-lines at all, on the reasoning that if some other paper learned the names of the writers of its wonderful stories, they would quickly be hired away. Papers at the other extreme are peppered with by-lines. Often this species of fame is substituted for specie.

The natural habitat of the by-line seems to be the sports section. The mangiest sparrow cannot fall to earth in the world of sport but what the chronicler of the episode is identified for an enchanted readership. This state of affairs seems to grow out of the legend that sports-writing, by and large, is more "creative" than the writing of other kinds of news. (See SPORTS-WRITING, in Part Three.)

If a by-line is hanging in the balance, enough wordage will turn the trick. It does not seem to matter whether the story is paralyzingly dull, or composed largely of verbatim extracts from a report or of lists of names. Ever seen a by-line on a one-, two-, or three-paragraph story, no matter how bright or witty? Neither have I. Nowhere does humor have such a low reward as in the newsroom. Yet editors wonder why their pages are so lifeless.

Editors often throw away a powerful incentive by inept decisions on by-lines, or by reserving them, as is so common, for long-winded yarns. Since most reporters aspire to by-lines, this approach is bound to encourage long-windedness. It might be a good idea to allow reporters to make their own decisions on by-lines.

John Gunther, in his fascinating *Inside Africa,* tells about the practice of South African newspapers:

"Some news stories carry not only the signature but the home address of the writer. I have never seen this oddity elsewhere, and never heard a satisfactory explanation for it. Perhaps it gives the writer an added sense of responsibility. At any rate any reader who dislikes a story knows where to find its author after office hours."[1]

## Letters to the Editor

No great savvy is shown by publications that publish letters containing accusations against themselves or challenges of the accuracy of their columns, but neglect to offer any comment or reply. The readers of such letters may be left with any of a variety of impressions, none of them complimentary. One is that the publication, although it condescends to publish the accusation, is too Olympian to take notice of it. Another is that the charge is true, but the editors cannot think of anything to say, or hope no one will notice. Another is that the high command is not aware enough of the publication's contents to realize it is being criticized. And yet another, in the instance of a challenge of the accuracy of reporting, is that the right hand (the editorial-page brain trust) does not know what the left hand (the newsroom) is doing. News magazines generally handle these situations most intelligently.

[1] Gunther, John, *Inside Africa.* New York: Harper & Brothers, 1955.

An attack by a reader, when it impugns a publication's motives and does not merely express a divergent opinion, ought to bring forth a brief statement of the publication's version of those motives. If a reader spots and calls attention in a published letter to an error of fact that has been printed, the publication ought to be big enough to make it clear he is right. Or, if he only thinks he is right, the paper owes it to all its readers to reaffirm the facts, rather than leave them wondering.

Even when the publication's own operations are not in question, an obvious misstatement of fact in a published letter might well be identified for what it is, especially when public issues are concerned.

A series of letters dealing with the same subject might better be grouped under some inclusive heading, rather than mixed among letters dealing with other subjects, all of them carrying separate headings that give no clue to any relationship.

# CHAPTER XIII

# Sez Who?

Needless Attribution; Misleading Attribution; *Said* and Its Variants;
Utterance by Proxy; Excessive Quotation; Wrong Person in Quotation; Misquotation.

## Needless Attribution

ONE of the most pervasive problems of newswriting has to do with the question Harold Ross, the editor of the *New Yorker,* is said to have asked sometimes about cartoons submitted for publication: "Who's talking?" The newsman's word for the problem is *attribution.* Nearly all news stories have this in common, when you come to think about it, because the writer is setting down facts he got from someone else.

Troubles with attribution probably have their root in police and court stories, where there is danger of libel. The young reporter quickly learns that damaging statements must be ascribed to the authorities, or to privileged documents. The danger, both moral and legal, of aspersing someone on the paper's own say-so is impressed on him so unforgettably that he comes to think of attribution as a virtue, rather than as a necessary evil.

Like other principles slavishly followed, that of the need for attribution carries writers overboard, even in police stories. Here is an example: "*Highway patrolmen said* the car skidded 80 feet before striking the truck, which, *they said,* was parked on the shoulder." Can anyone reasonably hold that the first *said* will not alone easily carry the weight of all that follows?

It sounds silly to attribute innocuous bits of general information, but one widely followed school of thought seems to insist on attributing *everything* in police stories. Thus: "The lake is about 20 miles from Podunk and about 12 miles in circumference, *the officers reported.*" What is the net effect of this? Why, it suggests to the reader that the paper has no confidence in any part of the story. Such supercaution might well result in "The sun rose on schedule, *according to the investigator.*"

Stories about crimes in which no arrest has been made hardly need more than one citation of the source, for an unnamed burglar or whatever cannot be libeled. Similarly, the fact of an arrest is a matter of public record, and ought to need no qualification. Consider "*Officers George Hamilton and*

*Walter Schroeder said* the dancer was arrested on a charge of indecent exposure." Another factor enters here: kowtowing by reporters, and even newspapers, to the police. Where this is practiced, the names of the arresting officers are invariably worked into the story, and sometimes the facts of a brief account are overshadowed by unnecessary references to the source of those facts.

The theory is that the publicity makes the officers feel good, and more disposed to cooperate with the press. This is a drain on the self-respect of both sides. An officer can be expected to do his duty, which includes giving the press information that belongs to the public, without being bribed by unwarranted publicity. Newspapers that feed the police with delusions of grandeur in this way are not only cheapening themselves, but also helping to create the situations in which police officials set themselves up as judges of what information shall be given out.

## Misleading Attribution

Attribution has become such a mania that newswriters sometimes end by putting reverse English on what they are trying to say. In this way they unintentionally associate themselves (or their newspapers) with statements they really want to hang exclusively on the speaker. A number of commonly, and carelessly, used expressions imply that what is being quoted, directly or indirectly, is the fact. *Pointed out* is one of them: "The senator has an ugly record of broken promises, his opponent *pointed out*." The effect of this is that the writer, or the newspaper, concurs in the accusation. Even if they do, such acquiescence hardly has a place in the news columns.

Similar impressions are created by *as* with the attributive verb ("*as* he said"), and by *admitted, noted, conceded, explained,* and *cited the fact that.* "A young TV comedian admitted in New York that all funnymen are sick and desperately in need of psychoanalysis." The effect here is not so much that the writer agrees, but that the speaker is conceding a generally accepted fact. There was no occasion for *admitted,* because the point of view being expressed was a novel one, at least at the time.

Other bits of heedlessness can unintentionally convict, as "The couple were indicted as spies by a federal grand jury, but have denied *their* guilt." That hapless *their* assumes the couple are guilty.

There is also such a thing as winking at the reader and saying, by implication, "Take this guy with a grain of salt." That is what the use of *according to* does. When that expression does not cast a shadow on the credibility of the speaker, it may merely sound nonsensical, as in "The Rev. John Jones will ask the invocation, according to the chairman." It is usually preferable to have the speaker *report* or *announce,* instead of using the *according to* formula. *Said he believes,* in place of either *said* or *believes,* also may erect a small BEWARE sign, in that it may imply the speaker is not necessarily to be taken at his word.

*Disclose* and *reveal* are appropriate only in reference to that which has been concealed. It's stupid, when you stop to think about it, to write of the time of a dinner as *disclosed,* or the name of a Rotary Club speaker as *revealed.* I give you, again, *report* and *announce.*

Sometimes attribution, though called for, is doubled. "The secretary and his associates were criticized for what the committees said were 'political and other considerations.' " Either *what the committees said* or the quotation marks should suffice. "Truman told reporters that his memoirs will explain what he said was the part Eisenhower played in the incident." Here *what he said was* indicates unnecessary caution. In giving the substance of reports and the like, it seems superfluous to tack *the report said* or something of the kind onto every sentence, unless the copy is questionable or damaging.

*Advise, contend,* and *claim* are sadly overworked and at the same time inexactly used in attribution. *Advise,* as in "The meeting will be postponed, he advised" is journalese at its worst. *Contend* is suitable only where there is contention or disagreement, and *insist* only where there is insistence. *Claim* may excusably be bent out of shape in headlines in the sense of *say* or *assert,* but in text, where there is no such space problem, it is questionable in that sense. ("The informant claimed he did not know the name of his source.") *Stress* and *emphasize* are suitable only where there is indeed stress or emphasis.

Much hinges on the choice between *as* and *for* in certain attributive constructions. To say that a man was criticized *for* committing perjury is to imply that the perjury was committed, thus aligning the writer with the critic. To say that a man was criticized *as* committing perjury, on the other hand, places the burden of proof on the critic.

## Said and Its Variants

The word *said* and its relations, both rich and poor, pose a problem for every reporter. Not many years ago it was a general custom for reporters to use *said* with the first of a series of quotes. Next came *asserted,* then perhaps *averred, asseverated* (though this word was seldom used, because nobody was sure of it), *declared,* and of course that old stand-by, *stated.* These and perhaps a few others, such as *opined,* were enough to see the writer through a typical interview. If not, it was considered legal to start over again with *said,* the theory being that the reader would not realize by that time that he was getting a warmed-over word. The whole point was not to use *said* or any of the others twice, or anyway, twice in succession. The substitutes were dropped in heedlessly, as if they all meant exactly the same thing. No consideration was given the possibility that one or another might be the most appropriate with a given quotation.

There is abundant evidence that the *said* problem is with us still. A distinguished editor, citing an example of a poor choice of a substitute that resulted in a misleading, not to say damaging, statement, said (or perhaps declared): "There never was a verb better than *said*." This enthusiasm, while understandable under the circumstances, may have been excessive.

The best word is probably different for every quotation. It may be *said,* it may be *roared,* it may be *mumbled.* Whatever it is, it is always the *exact* word. Errors in choice of words are regrettable, but it does not seem likely that the best purpose is going to be served by arbitrarily damming off part of the language and condemning reporters to the use of a single overworked and flavorless expression.

Yet some newspapers, it is, uh, alleged, forbid the use of anything but *said* with quotations. This seems to indicate a lamentable lack of confidence in their staffs. If this lack of confidence is justified, it might be a good idea to hold a seminar in the meanings and proper applications of the fifteen or twenty best-known variants of *said.* Here are some expressions that can stand duty for *said,* when appropriate:

*Admitted, admonished, affirmed, agreed, avowed, barked, begged, bellowed, called, chided, contended, cried, croaked, declaimed, demanded, disclosed, drawled, emphasized, entreated, exclaimed, hinted, implored, insisted, maintained, mumbled, murmured, muttered, pleaded, proclaimed, proposed, rejoined, retorted, roared, scolded, shouted, shrieked, yelled, wailed.*

Some of these words, of course, can lead to trouble if used improperly or indiscreetly. There are others that are unquestionably touchy: *grumbled, insinuated, prated, ranted, spouted, stammered, whined, whimpered.* All these are uncomplimentary to the speaker, but they may be called for in an accurate account.

Even for the timid, however, there are a number of innocuous substitutes that will make for less stodgy writing: *added, announced, answered, asserted, commented, continued, declared, observed, remarked, replied, reported, responded, returned, stated. Stated,* it may be remarked, is overworked, and conveys a tone of formality that is usually unsuitable.

## Utterance by Proxy

The purported utterance of words by smiling, frowning, grimacing, laughing, and similarly impossible methods is frequently criticized:

"Romance seems to be out of fashion these days," he grimaced.

"I'd rather work from the neck up," the actress smiled.

"This equipment is not included in the budget," the auditor frowned.

This is a cute trick, and may be only a fad that will have its day and cease to be. In a way, it appears to be an extension of what Ruskin deplored as "the pathetic fallacy"—ascribing lifelike acts to inanimate things, as in having the sun smile. But Ruskin's criticism is pretty generally regarded as footless carping.

Those who choose to use the device we are discussing must be prepared to defend themselves against the logical, though perhaps hairsplitting and pedantic, complaint that words cannot be formed by smiling, frowning, and the like. In any event, it is a harmless device, since no one is really misled by it, and those who consider it absurd are free to write *he said, grimacing; she said, smiling;* and *he said, frowning.*

## Excessive Quotation

The use of punctuation marks generally is minimized in newswriting, but one of them, the quotation mark, is hopelessly overworked. This probably reflects a morbid anxiety lest the writer appear to be taking the responsibility for opinions or other questionable utterances. Often it will just not do to take a chance that the reader may think the writer is talking.

Quotation marks are often used unnecessarily with what are referred to as fragmentary quotes, when only a word or a phrase is quoted in a sentence that already contains an attribution. The quoted words may have been the ones used by the speaker, but since he has already been credited as the source of the information, there is usually no reason for placing quotation marks around them. The press associations are especially fond of fragmentary quotations. Some wire stories are so peppered with them the writer can hardly call a word his own. Let's look at some examples:

He declined to say what "action" would be taken.

The department said "some" improvement is expected.

The secretary of commerce said the coming year would be one of the "most prosperous" in American history.

That, he said, would "delay" victory.

It is hard to see what is accomplished by the quotation marks in any of these sentences. Perhaps the reporter considered it illegal or immoral to use any word from the direct quotation he was paraphrasing without acknowledging a prior claim, so to speak. Nothing is gained by quoting minor fragments like these, and the quotation marks clutter up the story. They also interfere with readability, for the reader necessarily pauses at a fragmentary quote to decide why the quotation marks are there. If this becomes too confusing, he may give up.

Are all fragmentary quotations, then, undesirable? By no means: "He accused the senator of making 'mean, untrue, and dastardly' statements." No objective account would take the responsibility for such hard words, and even though the statement is cast as an indirect quotation to begin with, the words in quotation marks warrant unmistakable attribution.

In general, however, only especially striking or significant matter should be quoted, and then preferably in complete sentences. Using complete sentences minimizes the danger of giving the wrong impression through quoting fragments out of context. It is the reporter's job to present the meat of things in his own words, and he should not be excessively timid about it. The cure for quote craziness is to try leaving the quotation marks off fragments. Generally this test will show they add nothing.

Another misuse of quotation marks appears occasionally, but it is rarely seen outside the remote backwaters of journalism, and so seems hardly worth mentioning. This is the use of quotation marks around words the writer mistakenly regards as cute, clever, or used in a special sense. Few things are more exasperating to the reader.

When a word is indeed used in some other than its expected sense, *so-called* is superfluous with a term that has been placed in quotation marks: *the so-called "black list."* Either *so-called* or the quotes will suffice. There is no necessity to use quotation marks around a nickname. The usual practice is to introduce a nickname in parentheses: *Meyer (Mike) Berger.* Thereafter, if the writer chooses to use the nickname, it is better simply *Mike,* not *"Mike."* If slang suits the writer's purpose, let him use it forthrightly, and not in quotation marks, which protest too much that he is stooping from another level of diction.

## Wrong Person in Quotation

"Mr. Truman smilingly conceded that he 'feels more kindly toward newspapermen, now that one is about to become a member of his family.' " Obviously the word he used wasn't *feels* unless he said, "Mo'nin' y'all. Ah feels more kindly toward newspapermen."

Writing in "Winners & Sinners," Theodore M. Bernstein thus wittily impaled one of the vices associated with quote craziness, namely, the mishandling of fragmentary quotations so that the speaker appears to be talking about himself in the third person. Quotation marks, until the rules are changed, are supposed to enclose *the exact words* of the speaker. Any change in the form of those words leads to things like the example, and worse.

"In point of fact," the historian remarked, "he couldn't bear to go—he was too immersed in the production of his fourteenth book." This, culled from a leading news magazine, is the worst example of confused quotation I have ever seen. The historian, believe it or not, was intended to be referring to himself. This kind of thing can cause more uncertainty than when the village atheist married the preacher's daughter. "The board acted on the basis of an appeal by Haymes that 'somebody pretty high had made up his mind to get him.' " To get whom? Well, Haymes; but Haymes must really have said "to get *me*."

Some fragmentary quotations are such a mixture of direct and indirect discourse it is a hopeless task to untangle them: "The defendant told the judge he 'didn't allow people to grab his arm,' " and "Stevens said he 'feels in his heart that the responsibility was entirely his.' "

Let us place this question before the house: Why were quotation marks necessary in any of these examples as originally written? The habitual asking of such a question would eliminate perhaps 90 per cent of the quotation marks from news stories. While it might cause unemployment in quotation-mark factories, it would largely cure that loathsome disease, quote craziness.

In American usage, quotation marks go outside periods and commas. This means that when both a single and a double quotation mark fall at the end of a sentence, both go outside the period. Quotation marks go inside the colon and semicolon. There is a tendency to drop, as superfluous, the quotation marks that once were generally used (in lieu of italics) around titles of books, plays, works of music, names of publications, and the like. Such titles are sufficiently identified by their capitalization.

## Misquotation

Most of us were brought up believing that Voltaire wrote, "I disapprove of what you say, but I will defend to the death your right to say it." Chances are that, if resurrected, he would not only disapprove of our saying this, but also decline to defend it. For "I disapprove . . ." is only what S. G. Tallentyre (the *nom de plume* of E. Beatrice Hall, an English writer) thought Voltaire should, or might, have said. She expressed surprise when people regarded the words as a direct quotation, just because she had enclosed them in quotation marks in her book, *The Friends of Voltaire*. Well, what great thinkers omit to express, industrious and imaginative biographers will put into their mouths.

Mark Twain and General John J. Pershing are also entitled to join the legion of those who complain of misquotation. And unlike the politicians who comprise most of that shrill group, they would have a good chance of making their complaints stick. "Everybody talks about the weather, but nobody does anything about it" is usually ascribed to Mark Twain. Charles Dudley Warner, however, when he was editor of the *Hartford Courant,* wrote in an editorial: "A well-known American writer once said that while everyone talked about the weather, nobody seemed to do anything about it." This is not conclusive, of course, for Warner may have been ascribing the remark to Twain, who was his close friend. *Bartlett's Familiar Quotations* says in a footnote that it is often attributed to Twain, though not found in his published works. Burton Stevenson, editor of *The Home Book of Quotations,* has been talked into changing the attribution from Twain to Warner in his book, and some other dictionaries also credit Warner.

Popular fancy has General Pershing striding down the gangplank at the head of the American Expeditionary Force, striking a pose, and declaiming to a throng of bug-eyed Frenchmen, "Lafayette, we are here!" But this *mot* belongs to a ringer, Charles E. Stanton, chief disbursing officer of the AEF, whom Pershing deputed to speak for him at the tomb of Lafayette in Paris on July 4, 1917. Pershing never offered a satisfactory excuse for having omitted to think up this immortal announcement himself. The public's assumption that he was its author, however, may well have taken the edge off the winning of World War I, as far as Pershing was concerned, while at the same time possibly poisoning the life of Stanton.

"Baldness may not be pretty, but it's neat. ANON." I saw this in a magazine advertisement. Now, for one thing, the wording is not quite right, and for another, Anon did not say it. The original version is "There's one thing about baldness—it's neat," and the author was that wit and baldhead, Don Herold. Other approximations of this witticism turn up from time to time, but usually without a mention of Herold, even in most dictionaries of quotations. These words are unquestionably destined for the ages, and I am glad to say that they are properly credited to Herold in at least one book, Evan Esar's *Dictionary of Humorous Quotations*.

Often as not, the name *Frankenstein* is applied to a monster. Frankenstein was not the monster, however, but the scientist who created it, as set forth in the novel of that name by Mary Shelley. The misapplication is so prevalent it is recognized as a secondary meaning of *Frankenstein* in at least two reputable dictionaries. Even so, the revival of old Frankenstein movies on TV may be tending to correct this mistake. In much the same way, Horatio Alger is sometimes referred to as the hero of his rags-to-riches stories.

The expressions *pinch hitter* and *front runner* are so often debased from their original senses it seems hardly worthwhile to attempt to rehabilitate them. In baseball, where *pinch hitter* originated and still holds its original sense, it means a replacement sent to bat with the expectation he will do better than the man he is substituting for. In other connections, alas, it now means merely a replacement, sometimes an inferior one. *Front runner* originally had the sense of a fast starter who soon falls behind. Now, mostly, it is used to mean just he who is in the lead. Similarly, *leading question,* an expression from the courts of law, is strictly one that suggests its answer, and not just a prominent question. *Corpus delicti,* often used in reference to the body of a victim of a murder, does not really mean that at all, but rather the evidence necessary to establish that a crime—not necessarily murder—has been committed.

"God rest ye, merry gentlemen" is the way we often see it, but not without an uneasy feeling that we have also seen it "God rest ye merry, gentlemen." This latter version does not quite seem to make sense, and *Bartlett's* puts the comma after *ye*. But all things come to him who waits, and while I waited there came to me something by Charles D. Rice in *This Week*. "The comma should be placed after *merry*," he wrote. *"God rest ye merry* was a common greeting in early England." The *Oxford Dictionary of Quotations* concurs in the late comma.

Lord Acton is usually quoted as having said, "All power corrupts . . ." but the uncorrupted version is "Power *tends to* corrupt, and absolute power corrupts absolutely." Consistency is often flatly called the hobgoblin of little minds, but it was qualified in Emerson's original to "A *foolish* consistency . . ."

Emily Kimbrough, in entitling a book *How Dear to My Heart,* did nothing to curb the prevalent misquotation of "How dear to *this* heart are the scenes of my childhood" (Samuel Woodworth). Thomas Hardy and Ernest Hemingway used more care in borrowing *Far from the Madding Crowd* and *For Whom the Bell Tolls,* respectively. Yet Thomas Gray is frequently supposed to have written it "Far from the *maddening* crowd," and John Donne's line is often pluralized to "For whom the *bells toll."*

Rudolf Flesch points out, in *The Art of Plain Talk,* that Churchill's famous wartime offer to the British nation, which is generally remembered as "blood, sweat and tears" was in fact "blood, toil, tears and sweat." Flesch notes that Churchill's intention was to encourage people in the war effort, and that the popular distortion of what he said not only damages the original rhythm, but ends on a defeatist note, *tears.*

Topsy is often invoked as a comparison with something or someone that "jest growed." Topsy's remark on this subject, however, was void of *jest*: "I 'spect I grow'd." Don Quixote's avocation of mixing it with windmills is the basis for a popular metaphor signifying quixotic (if the adjective is permissible) effort. This is generally rendered "tilting with windmills." Should be "tilting *at."* The tilting here is the military exercise of charging with a lance; it has nothing to do with pinball. Cervantes said "Let the worst come to the worst," not "If worse comes to worst." It was a savage *breast,* not *beast,* that Congreve said music hath charms to soothe.

The cloud "no bigger than a man's hand" that has become the standard reference to a small but menacing omen was pristinely "There ariseth a little cloud out of the sea, like a man's hand." This is from the Bible, as are some other warped quotations. The "prophet without honor in his own country" is, more precisely, *"not* without honor *except* in his own country." Money is unduly berated as the root of all evil, but it is *the love of money* that the Bible warns against. This at least gives the rich more comfort than the pronouncement that it is easier for a camel to go through the eye of a needle than for a rich man to enter into the kingdom of God. "The voice crying in the wilderness" is more exactly "the voice *of one*." And it is not a fall, finally, that pride goeth before, as in the popular misconception; rather, "Pride goeth before *destruction,* and an haughty spirit before a fall."

Shakespeare, inevitably, has also been the victim of inexact quotation, sometimes involving the choice of prepositions: "Such stuff as dreams are made *on*" (not *of*); "Hoist *with* (not *by*) his own petard." Shakespeare *painted,* rather than *gilded,* the lily: "To gild refined gold, to paint the lily."

"Alas, poor Yorick," we hear it declaimed; "I knew him *well.*" But the lines run "I knew him, Horatio; a fellow of infinite jest, of most excellent fancy." It was not "a *poor* thing but my own," but rather "An *ill-favored* thing, sir, but mine own." If somewhere Shakespeare's spirit is aware of what is happening, it may be muttering, in company with some others, "An ill-quoted thing, sir, but mine own."

Did it ever strike you that the idea of Cinderella wearing a glass slipper is an unhappy one? The story is fantasy, of course, but even fantasy must have a basis in reality. Poor Cinderella apparently danced the evening away in slippers made of one of the hardest and most unyielding of materials, since her day antedated fiber glass. And if that were not enough, attempts were made to force one of the slippers on hapless but hopeful maidens throughout the kingdom, when the prince set out to find her.

Originally, that slipper was not glass at all. The idea of a glass slipper resulted from a mistake in translation, according to the *Encyclopaedia Britannica.* The English version of the story comes from the French tale, *Cendrillon,* by Perrault. Perrault wrote of *pantoufle en vair* (a slipper of fur), but the translator confused *en vair* with *en verre* (of glass). The idea of a glass slipper is too firmly associated with Cinderella now, however, to hope for any change. She'll just have to suffer.

# CHAPTER XIV

# Doing Something About It

## Weather Stories

"EVERYBODY talks about the weather, but nobody does anything about it." Anyone who has not seen this witticism quoted in the press at least 500 times must be an illiterate. It is only fair to warn that legislation is being contemplated in several states to forbid its further use. The backers plan to get around the Constitutional prohibition of abridgment of freedom of the press by classifying it with intolerable public nuisances. Indeed, there is even talk of making its use a federal offense, on the ground that the weather is an article in interstate commerce.

Whether nothing can be done about the weather has become a questionable proposition anyway since the development of cloud-seeding. There is no question, however, that something can be done about weather stories in the newspapers. First, let's sacrifice all that impressive but unintelligible mumbo jumbo about high- and low-pressure areas, well-defined frontal systems, and other technicalities of the forecasting business. That stuff may be all right for the detailed report in the back pages, for it undoubtedly is interesting to a certain group, like every other specialty. But such complexities seem out of place in the general weather story, because the average reader does not understand them. There may be some question whether even the forecasters understand them, when you compare the forecasts with the weather.

Temperatures are commonly spoken of in weather stories as *cooler* or *warmer,* although a temperature, being a reading, can only be *higher* or *lower*. An *increase* (rather than a *rise*) or a *decrease* (rather than a *drop*) are no better.

Weather writing, like all newsdom, has its clichés. You might expect that anything as changeable as the weather would inspire some variety in the terms used to describe it, but this seems to be a vain hope. Newspaper readers, especially in a wet season, must be unnecessarily depressed to read without variation day after day that the rainfall total has been *boosted;* that rivers are on a *rampage;* and that rain and snow are being *dumped*—like garbage, presumably. Rain is also often spoken of delicately as *dampening* (never *wetting*), but a rain that merely dampens hardly qualifies as a rain. Typhoons usually *pack* winds of such-and-such velocity. *Twenty-five-mile-an-hour winds* could be more neatly disposed of as *twenty-five-mile winds*.

The temperature, when high, gets where it is in only one way: it *soars*. On the other hand, when it drops quickly, it must *plummet*. The fog always seems to *roll in*. This sounds as if it's on wheels, instead of cat feet, as Carl Sandburg had it. The weather writers' gods, of course, are Jupiter Pluvius and Old Sol.

A faithful stand-by in stories related to wet weather is the comment that the rain *failed to dampen the spirits* of some person, group, or occasion. Maybe so, but where the rain fails, banalities like this one are likely to succeed.

## Obituaries

It has been predicted, I believe by Saul Pett of the Associated Press, that the next war will be between reporters and copyreaders. Perhaps the one after that will be between those who hold that a man is survived by his *wife,* and those who insist that he is survived by his *widow*. Stylebooks favor both sides of this disagreement. Nothing very grievous hangs from the choice between one word and the other, probably. Those who prefer *widow* argue that, once a man dies, a widow is what his wife incontrovertibly becomes.

My own preference in this morbid struggle inclines toward *wife,* perhaps because I was exposed at an impressionable age to some editor's predilection for it. The choice of *wife,* however, can be supported by an examination of the word *survive,* which means *to remain alive*. She who remains alive was, at least at the outset, the wife rather than the widow.

But debates over points like this are useless. No one who has ever thought about the matter enough to have formed an opinion in favor of either *wife* or *widow* is likely to be budged an inch. Even so, the use of *wife* can be justified from another direction. A woman is likely to see herself called a widow for the first time in her husband's obituary, and she can easily be spared this shock.

To press things a bit further, if a man is survived by his widow, why does one not speak of women as being survived by their widowers? Or of parents being survived by their orphans? Quite obviously those words, apart from other considerations, would seem to be laboring the fact of bereavement. Thus also with widow?

William J. Foote, managing editor of the *Hartford Courant,* brought to my attention a new slant on the matter. "Except when both husband and wife are exposed to some peril to which he succumbed and which she survived, I won't agree that the wife survives, almost universal newspaper practice to the contrary notwithstanding," he wrote. The effect of this view is to exclude the use of *survive* from the ordinary obituary, in favor of *leave* (*He leaves his wife*). Nevertheless, the basic question remains: which stays behind—the wife or the widow?

Unreasonably squeamish relatives sometimes seek to withhold from publication the age of a deceased woman. Reporters should press for it, however, because if an obituary is worth printing at all, it should surely give the age of the subject. One's age, it has been well said, is the fullest possible description in the smallest possible space. Withholding the age of a living woman may be an act of chivalry, but after she is dead her sensibilities can hardly be affected. There seems no way this can hurt relatives, either.

The omission of any information about what the subject did for a living is a conspicuous fault of many short obituaries. This is the most interesting fact about a man.

The use of a nickname is an indignity, except in instances when a man is widely and publicly known by it. Even then, it should be used parenthetically with the full, formal version of his name.

This may be quibbling, but the line *funeral arrangements are pending* seems to be a useless statement of what the reader can assume, especially when the practice is to publish those arrangements once they have been made. It is growing common to speak of the subject of an obituary as having been *preceded in death* by some other member of his family, but this expression smacks of the unctuous mortician. Like such euphemisms as *passed away* and *departed this life,* it is a fit subject for interment. And while we're at it, let's exhume that plain old word *undertaker*.

## Military Publicity

Those whose connection with the armed forces ended with World War II will be dismayed to hear that the situation is still normal, if not more so. Or so one might conclude from a review of so-called home-town publicity, now a large but apparently bumbling industry. An editor of my acquaintance kept tabs for awhile on the quality of military press releases reaching his desk, and came up with a tale sad enough to elicit sympathy from a Regular Army doctor.

Some such material is a month old by the time it gets to the newspaper, and when it concerns maneuvers, leaves, and other matters having time value, this delay kills it. Mailings are often duplicated, and a good deal of carelessness is evident in factual details. A consistent error has a certain virtue (at least it may look right to the unknowing), but as many as three versions of the same name sometimes appear in a single handout.

Too many releases of the fill-in variety use the name of the person the paper is interested in as a hook to hang a long and useless disquisition on the glorious history of the unit of which that person is a transient member, or to introduce a rhapsodic description of the facilities of the station at which he may be spending six weeks for training.

One such release was put out to report completion of basic training by women at a WAC training center. It ran to 303 words. Of this total, 60 pertained properly to the person who was the subject, and were all that any paper would be likely to use. The remaining 243 words (80 per cent of the total) went off on an ecstatic tangent dealing with the beauty of the center, its resemblance to a college campus, the fact that another training command is headquartered at the same fort, structural details of the buildings, air-circulation and heating arrangements, apportionment of rooms to various functions (including laundry and drying), and the existence of a band and an explanation of its mission (34 words for this, no kidding).

But the worst vice of military publicity is its shameless spotlighting of officers generally, and of commanding officers in particular. All you can see in many pictures of the home-town hero is what shows from behind some general or admiral who is pinning the medal on him. In other instances, the picture or story is hogged by some gold-braided buffoon "inspecting" or "giving a 'well done' " to a project whose existence he was ignorant of until the press arrived.

Those few commanding officers who have sense enough to retire to the background are often pushed to the fore by their sycophantic press agents. Papers in towns where there are permanent military establishments must continually edit back into perspective the commanding officers, who have only a technical connection with much of the news those establishments produce.

Most military releases would be the better if, like Caesar's Gaul, they were divided into three parts, and two of those parts were thrown away.

## Pictures

One picture, says the Chinese aphorism, is worth more than 10,000 words (or 1,000, or 100,000, depending on the state of the rate of exchange). This notion, if nothing else, may justify the 500-odd words expended herewith on some random observations about pictures and related matters.

It seems to be standard practice to describe any woman in the news, particularly a crime story, as *pretty, attractive,* or even *beautiful.* This device, employed not as reportage but to titillate the reader, regardless of the truth, is certainly effective in bringing to life an otherwise moribund account. But it may be one of those tricks that should have gone into the ash can in view of the increasing maturity shown generally by the press in recent years.

On more than one paper the editors have grown so conscious of, and nettled by, the unremitting parade of beauties in the news that standing orders have been given to delete all appraisals of women's looks. The reason is that when women who are described as beautiful in one edition are pictured in the next, they often turn out to be dismal crows. The use of such descriptives as *pretty* or *beautiful* in cutlines or in a story accompanying a picture seems simpleminded. Judgments in such matters vary, and when the evidence is at hand for the reader to decide for himself, why not let him do so?

Then there is the old-maidishness practiced by some newspapers in banning cheesecake from their columns. The logic offered is that newspapers are essentially family mediums and do not want to hasten the initiation of their young readers into the mysteries of life. Assuming that there is something shameful about the exhibition of shapeliness and that prudery is helpful in the education of the young, such explanations might have more force if those papers did not carry movie and other ads containing pictures far more revelatory and provocative than what they reject as news photos.

Cutlines present some hazards. (It may be appropriate to comment on the tendency to apply the word *caption* to the explanatory matter beneath pictures. Properly speaking, a caption is a heading, not a legend.) Pictures, which show something in the process of happening, seem to demand the utmost immediacy in the accompanying text. But need we be jolted by the recurrent absurdity of coupling the present tense with a past time element? It comes out this way:

"General Douglas MacArthur and Japanese Prime Minister Shigeru Yoshida *meet* for a private chat in the general's hotel suite *yesterday*"; or "William Willis *stands* aboard his balsa raft as it *moves* off the Peruvian coast late *last month*." How much more sensible it would sound to say "General MacArthur and Prime Minister Shigeru Yoshida *met* (or *are shown as they met*)" and "William Willis *stood* (or *is pictured standing*)."

Then we have the tiresome occupations of *looking on* or *standing by,* assigned to supernumeraries who happen to be in a picture and, since they cannot be cropped out, must be identified. The truth might be diverting: "Those other two guys just muscled into the picture."

## Meeting Notices

Meeting notices, unfortunately, constitute a large part of the content of many newspapers. I say unfortunately because this stuff often is of no interest to anyone but the members of the organizations concerned, who already know what it says. Much depends, of course, on the size of the town. In little places where everyone knows everyone else and every reader goes through the local news line by line looking for names, there is probably no way out but to announce and report meetings in sickening detail.

In larger places, however, just as slavish a policy is often followed. Editors in those places might well re-evaluate a practice that robs a large amount of space from the presentation of information of general interest. Any such re-evaluation is likely to be agonizing, however, because usually the editors and publishers themselves are members of one or more organizations.

True, people like to see their names in print, no matter how flimsy the excuse, and there is probably no arguing with any editor who uses this principle uncritically as a criterion of news. Sometimes it seems as if such editors might as well publish a page a day out of the city directory or the telephone book.

Still, meeting notices could be rid of some current excrescences, such as references to *guest* (or *featured*, or *principal*) speakers, *special* guests, *noon* luncheons, and dinner *meetings*. There is rarely more than one speaker at a club meeting, and he is almost always a guest. A luncheon, by definition, is at noon, and guests are special by virtue of their guesthood. I have never heard, at any rate, of nonspecial, or routine, guests. A dinner at which members will gather is perforce a meeting.

"The Customs Service will be discussed *in a talk* by . . ." and "presided *at the meeting*" would be just as good, if not better, without the italicized words. The announcement that someone *will be the speaker at* can be tightened to *will speak at* or *will address. Elected to the board of directors* may as well be *elected to the board* or *elected a director*. Why lovingly list officers when elected, and again when installed? *Is affiliated with* is just a pretentious way of saying *belongs to,* although this phrase is most often a vice of the society pages. And since co-chairmen are equals, how is it justifiable to speak of one of them as being assisted by the other? A dismaying characteristic of meeting stories is some such revelation as this: "Herman Aardvark, president, presided." Disregarding the unhappy repetition of sound, why should the president's name be dragged into story after story? Even when someone presides in his place, the fact is hardly worth noting.

Where to draw the line on announcements of no interest outside the membership of a group may be difficult to decide. But the *Schenectady Union-Star* drew it several years ago in front of *Refreshments will be served,* and suffered no shock.

## Labor Disputes

The standard formula in reporting labor disputes is to tell only the size or percentage of the increase sought or gained. Seldom do stories tell what the unionists' total wages are (or would be). Yet total pay is the most interesting and meaningful fact to the reader. It enables him to relate the wages in dispute to his own income and to incomes generally. True, wage scales are often complicated, but it is not too difficult to give at least sample ranges for the most typical or numerous categories of employees.

# PART THREE

# WAYWARD WORDS

# A Glossary of Usage

## A

**a, an.** Omitted, p. 28; before words beginning with *h,* p. 29; before words beginning with *y* sounds, p. 30; before figures, initials, etc., p. 30; wrongly used with numbers, p. 30.

**abbreviations.** Of state names, p. 81; of names of agencies and organizations, p. 81; of proper names, p. 80.

**about.** Pp. 48-49.

**abrasion.** P. 53.

**accents.** See *diacritical marks; typewriter tricks.*

**acceptable.** Sometimes misused for *receptive.* "The natives of this area are acceptable to Christianity" does not say what the writer intended. He wanted to describe them as ready to sign up, but instead gave the impression they had passed some kind of entrance examination.

**accidents.** The use of technical terms in reports of accidents is explained on p. 53.

**act, action.** *Action* often appears in places where it seems the word should be *act* or something else. The consensus of various authorities is that the choice between *act* and *action* is based less on rule than on what sounds right in the context. Of course, any writer accused of misuse of one or the other will say that his choice sounded right to *him.* A sentence involving some kids who had emptied their piggy bank to pay their father's traffic fine read "The judge dug into his pocket and reimbursed the children after learning of their *action.*"

This may go against no one else's grain, but I feel the word should have been *act*; or, less stiltedly, the sentence might have read *after learning what they had done.* But after pondering the authorities' pronouncements, I must admit being unable to find any satisfactory distinction in the usage of *act* and *action* that clearly tips the scales either way in this instance. Generally, however, *action* refers to the doing, and *act* to the thing done; beyond this, an act is usually something single, whereas an action may be

**157**

made up of more than one part. I decline to lead anyone into the ramifications of the usage of these words, because I got lost there myself.

**actual, actually.**   Writers often seem thunderstruck by their own perspicuity. This, or something like it, may account for the presence of *actual* and *actually* where they give an uncalled-for impression of "You won't believe this, but that's what happened." For example "No sooner had the Reds appeared than they were actually pelted with tomatoes." *Actually* is required only to point out the contrast between actuality and something else. When there is no such contrast, there need be no *actually*.

The following examples are all open to criticism on this basis:

"This week *actually* marks the anniversary of Sikorsky's first flight." Yes? Well, it felt as much like a Sikorsky week as it did like any other.

"The President has become so concerned over leaks from the National Security Council and the Cabinet that he has *actually* cut down on the number of officials attending the meetings." You mean he wasn't merely pretending to cut down on them?

"The stocks were sold at prices above *actual* market prices." Better: "above the market."

"Economic activity for March might be up a point when the figures are in. *Actually,* this is the encouragement economists have been waiting for." Maybe those economists were suspected of waiting for some other kind of encouragement, but the context gave no such indication.

"Only two of the persons present *actually* spoke." What were the others —ventriloquists' dummies?

Actually (it must be contagious) the word is being used as an unnecessary intensive, and like all such, it plays the writer false by taking away, instead of adding, force. Porter G. Perrin writes that intensives "may be used for a just emphasis, but they usually suggest an oral stress and are often out of place in writing. Too many of them suggest the schoolgirl style."

**A.D.**   Lint-pickers of the world, attention! It's wrong to write of *the tenth* (or any other) *century* A.D., even if it is done all the time. The reason is that A.D. stands for *anno domini* (the year of our Lord), and any jackass knows a century is not a year. The tendency to regard A.D. as the opposite, for all practical purposes, of B.C. may prove irresistible, however. The really large view, incidentally, has been achieved by the historian, Arnold Toynbee, whose scope spans so many centuries he feels constrained to designate events of his own life as having taken place in "A.D. 1907" and "A.D. 1903." As indicated by Mr. Toynbee's usage, A.D. properly precedes the year; B.C. follows it.

**added fillip.** In such constructions as "He gave the investigation an *added* fillip," *added* is redundant.

**adhere.** My risibility is touched, perhaps farfetchedly, when I read that someone *adheres* to a style of presentation, a plan of study, or whatever. Such a plan of study, it seems, would be printed on flypaper. This is not an out-and-out bastardization of the word, however. As Fowler points out, the British speak of *giving in adhesion to* (i.e., backing) a political party, for example, but he frowns on the form *adhere to* in this sense. To avoid a suggestion of the ludicrous while losing nothing, it may be well to write of *following* a plan of study, *supporting* a party, and *obeying* the rules.

**adjacent, adjoining.** See *contiguous*.

**adjectives.** Piled-up adjectives, p. 21; limiting adjectives, p. 22; nouns as adjectives, p. 27; repetition of defining adjectives, pp. 55-56; commas and adjectives, pp. 86-87; articles omitted, p. 28; false possessives, pp. 26-27. See also *modifiers*.

**adjust, readjust.** *Adjust* means bring into position, or into a proper relation. The necessary shift may be in any direction. *Readjustment* is in great favor as a euphemism for *pay raise*. Pay rates can indeed be adjusted, to bring them in line with those for comparable work elsewhere, for example, but only if the change may be in either direction. If only increases (or cuts) are under consideration, it is more explicit and thus better to say so. In another connection, the writer who told of a readjustment of milk-inspection areas might better have said *realignment* or *rearrangement*.

**admit to.** P. 47.

**adopt a wait-and-see attitude.** An overblown way of saying *wait and see*, as is *adopt a hands-off policy* for *keep hands off*. Both are journalese clichés.

**advance plans, planning.** See *future plans*.

**adverbs.** Wrongly hyphenated, p. 76.

**advise.** Objectionable and inexact when *say* or *tell* will serve; journalese as used in those senses.

**adviser, -or.** Insistence on *adviser* in preference to *advisor* is one of the more fanatical prescriptions in many style manuals. Webster, it is true, cites *adviser* first, indicating it is the preferred form, probably because the verb from which the noun comes is *advise*. Nevertheless, Perrin points out that *adviser* is now changing to *advisor* by analogy with *advisory,* and it seems likely that *advisor* is now the predominant form.

**affect, effect.** The confusion of these words is so common they might be expected to have become interchangeable, but there is no sign of this. To *affect* is to have influence upon, as "the moon *affects* lovers"; to *effect* is to accomplish, as "A merger was *effected.*"

**affirmative, negative.** "He replied in the *affirmative*" and "Her answer was *negative*" are generally merely pompous ways of writing "He said yes" and "She said no." *Affirmative* and *negative* are favorite pretensions among the military, especially.

**affray.** This word has a technical legal sense, but it is used indiscriminately, in sports and other news stories, for *fight, contest, game,* and the like.

**Afrikaner, Afrikander.** *Afrikaner* is the term applied to a South African of Boer descent. *Afrikander,* sometimes described as the British term, is said by John Gunther in *Inside Africa* to be an old-fashioned form applied now only to a breed of cattle.

**after.** See *following.*

**aggravate, annoy.** *Aggravate* means *make worse,* and not, except in dialectal usage, *annoy*: "The president is completely satisfied with his new house, except for one *aggravation*—the pigeons." *Annoyance* was meant. The word is correctly used in "Continual questioning *aggravated* his impatience."

**ah, aw.** The time has come, the walrus said, to strike a blow against the confusion in the lands of *ahs* and *aws.* Agreement seems pretty general that *ah* denotes relish or approval, or sometimes comprehension, and *aw* indicates remonstrance, disgruntlement, or protest. Webster seems to have goofed on this one, because both meanings are assigned to *ah,* while *aw* is not even listed. To me, at least, something like " *'Ah,* shucks,' said the boy," seems to represent a baffling conflict of emotions.

While we are dealing with the subarticulate, let us consider *uh-huh* (meaning *yes*) and *huh-uh* or *uh-uh* (meaning *no*). The use of these expressions in writing is small, to be sure. But there seems to be confusion here, too. *Webster's New International Dictionary* lists *uh-huh* but omits the converse, *huh-uh,* though of course it is just as prevalent. The occasional renderings *hunh-unh, unh-unh,* and the like seem open to the objection that they are not phonetic, if indeed they are pronounceable at all. *Unh-unh,* especially, seems liable to interpretation as either *yes* or *no.*

**ain't.**  Do you look down your nose at people who say *ain't?* You may feel you have good reason to, considering how that word was impressed on us in school as the leading example of bad English. *Ain't* is a contraction for *am not,* strictly speaking, and no doubt owes its popularity to the fact that it is easier to say. It developed from another contraction, *an't,* which went out of circulation a long time ago, in the unaccountable way words have.

If *ain't* had continued to be used only for *am not,* it might never have fallen into disrepute, for some authorities today consider it acceptable in that sense. In one construction, there is no substitute for *ain't* that does not seem equally objectionable. That construction is the question *"Ain't I?"* The strictly grammatical way of expressing this is "Am I not?" but that sounds a little too stilted to most of us. Some say, instead, "Aren't I?" but this has a distinctly feminine overtone, and most men and many women will reject it as too cute.

*Ain't* is at its worst when it replaces *isn't* or *hasn't,* as in "He *ain't,"* or *aren't* or *haven't,* as in "We *ain't."* In such uses *ain't* is unquestionably one of the marks of the uneducated, like such errors as "He don't" and "We wasn't." The fate of *ain't,* which at least has a small claim to respectability as a contraction for *am not,* seems to be hanging in the balance. Time and again reports come from conventions of linguists to the effect that *ain't* is gaining ground. The news is always reported in a startled tone, however.

**all-around, all-round.**  In the sense of *generally capable* or *versatile, all-round* is the preferable form: *an all-round athlete.*

**all right, alright.**  *Alright* may some day establish itself as acceptable, but the correct form still is *all right.*

**all together, altogether.**  *All together* means *in a group,* as "We will go *all together";* altogether means *entirely,* as "The idea is *altogether* ridiculous." *In the altogether,* a colloquialism meaning *naked,* is sometimes ludicrously rendered *in the all-together*: "The article described a scandalous Hollywood party at which the actor cavorted in the *all-together."*

**allude, refer.**  To *allude* to is to suggest without naming the thing specifically; to *refer* to is to name specifically.

**allusive, elusive, illusive.**  *Allusive* (usually with *to*) means *in reference*: "The remark was *allusive* to the Bible." *Elusive* means *hard to catch*: "The rabbit is *elusive." Illusive* means *illusory* (the more common word) or *deceptive*: "Mirages are *illusive."*

**also.**  As a conjunction ("The automobile needs repair; *also,* it must be repainted") *also* is not in good odor. Usually the trouble can be corrected by adding *and*, substituting *moreover, in addition, besides,* or by shifting the position of *also* to make it function as the adverb it is. "A typical picnic menu includes wieners, buns, beer, *also* potato salad." (*and* or *and also*.) "*Also* the general situation needs to be re-evaluated." ("The general situation *also* needs to be re-evaluated" or "*In addition* [or *besides*], the general situation . . .") "*Also,* the plans by officials to be helpful were often frustrated." (*In addition, Besides,* or "The plans . . . *also* were often frustrated.") It may be taken as a rule of thumb that *also* at the beginning of a sentence or clause is probably wrong, except in such constructions as "*Also* on the agenda are . . ." where *also* is used as an adverb but has been taken out of its normal position: ". . . are *also* on the agenda."

**alphabetical agencies.**   Pp. 81-82.

**alternate, alternately—alternative, alternatively.**   *Alternate,* as an adjective, means *in turns; first one and then the other. Alternative,* on the other hand, involves a choice. An alternate course of action is interchanged with another; an alternative course is a substitute.

The idea that *alternative,* as a noun, is a choice between two things and no more is pedantry. "Several alternatives confronted the diplomat" is perfectly acceptable.

*Alternate* as a noun applied to a person means *substitute.*

**amass.**   This word is best used in reference to a great quantity; in the sense of *accumulate* or *score points,* it is a dearly beloved counter word of sportswriters.

**ameliorate.**   "Kennan set himself the job of *ameliorating* the single-minded fascination that the Soviet problem holds for Americans." Mrs. Malaprop rides again. *Ameliorate* means *improve,* and anyway, it's a bookish word. What this writer really meant is a question; *mitigating* or *counteracting,* possibly.

**among.**   See *between, among.*

**amuck, amok, berserk.**   *Amuck* is the spelling generally preferred to *amok.* The word comes from the Malayan *amoq,* meaning *furious. Amuck* is stronger than *berserk; amuck* connotes murderousness, *berserk* (from Berserkers, wild Norse warriors of mythology) means merely *enraged.*

**and.**   At beginning of sentence, p. 94; followed by comma, pp. 93-94.

**and (but) which, and (but) who.**   The consensus appears to be that *and which* and *and who* (as well as *but which* and *but who*) are permissible only after *which* or *who* respectively, a principle that can be defended as desirably emphasizing parallel construction. Fowler cited exceptions that he considered permissible, but his reasoning is tortuous, and his general conclusion favors the principle stated here. Partridge agrees with this principle, and it is observable that careful writing follows it. Often, however, *and which* and *and who* are used where a single *which,* or *who,* or *and* alone would be smoother.

"Life has two strikes on children deserted by their parents *and who* never experience the love and home life adoptive parents can give them." *who have been deserted by their parents and never experience* or *who have been deserted . . . and who.*

"Most Italians believe that the loot, known as the Dongo Treasure, *and which* has been valued at $32 million . . ." *Dongo Treasure, which has been valued* or *which is known as . . . and which is.*

"Production of European-type grapes, which are grown almost exclusively in California and Arizona, *and which* account for most of this year's crop . . ." This conforms with our rule but *and account for* is simpler.

"Most men entering their eighty-ninth year *and who* have won wealth and fame might be content to sit back at ease." *who are entering . . . and have.*

"Fritz Weaver, who played Hamlet last summer, *and who* is one of the most versatile actors in the American theater, is shockingly believable as the haunted weakling." Make it ". . . summer and is one . . ."

In summary, it may be said that nearly all Fowler's examples are disagreeably involved or quaint to the modern ear, and would likely be stated today in ways that would not cause the *and which* problem to arise.

**and/or.**   This expression is objectionable to many, who regard it as appropriate only in a legal document. As recommended in *Watch Your Language* (Theodore M. Bernstein), "The law allows a fine up to $25 *and/or* thirty days in jail" would better be "a $25 fine *or* thirty days in jail or both."

**anno domini.**   See *A.D.*

**annoy.**   See *aggravate.*

**another.**   The use of *another* with an additional number is sometimes criticized: "Eighteen persons were summoned as witnesses, and *another* six were interrogated." The reason given for the criticism is that *another* means *one more of the same kind*; thus it would be correct only if the second figure were the same as the first. This does not stand up against dictionary definitions of *another,* however, one of which is "distinct, or different, from the one considered." In any event, *another* in *another six* modifies the omitted but understood *persons.* Yet it must be conceded that *another* in the example could easily be dispensed with, or that the sentence could as well be written *and six more were interrogated.*

**antagonist.**   See *protagonist.*

**anticipate.**   *Expect* is not a dirty word, but many of us have washed it right out of our vocabularies and substituted the more orotund *anticipate.* The absence of *expect* and its displacement by *anticipate* is, in fact, one of the most conspicuous earmarks of journalese. *Anticipate* does not mean the same thing as *expect,* however, and alert writers distinguish between them. To expect is simply to look ahead to, but *to anticipate* has the sense of seizing time by the forelock, of preparing or being prepared in some way for what is to come.

In "Agricultural officials *anticipate* production will be about the same as last year" we have the work of some pretentious ass who could not settle for a simple *expect,* which is what the sentence calls for.

"The principal *anticipated* normal attendance" is wrong or right, depending on whether he did something in expectation of it. Probably he *expected.*

This writer made the right choice: "The collection date was set a week earlier this year in *anticipation* of an increased workload." *Expectation* might have passed muster, but *anticipation* is precise.

"The woman said she was pregnant and *anticipating* a child within two months." Madam, leave those calculations to your doctor.

The ad that ballyhooed a film as "The most *anticipated* motion picture of our time" was an unintentional example of truth—the awful truth, that is—in advertising.

If you're too tired to decide which you need, use *expect. Anticipate* is seldom required, and with *expect* you'll seldom be wrong.

Some hold that *anticipate* is appropriate for something that is awaited eagerly. But alas, this is only a delusion that grows out of misuse. Although a recent compendium of usage condones this sense, it is supported neither by dictionary definition, derivation, nor the observable practice of careful writers.

**antidisestablishmentarianism.**   This word now seems to have been disestablished as the longest one in the language, and let's be glad of it. Millions must have grown sick of hearing it announced as such by those who are enchanted with useless information. But even if the king is dead, the customary cry, "Long live the king!" sticks in the throat. The reason for this is that the new king is *pneumonoultramicroscopicsilicovolcanokoniosis.* Forty-five letters, as against twenty-eight in the old one. It's a disease— like going around telling people about *antidisestablishmentarianism.*

The dubious tidings about the new longest word appeared in *Word Study,* a publication of the G. & C. Merriam Co., the dictionary people, for teachers of English, linguists, and other harmless drudges, like the author of this book. Other candidates, however, have been announced by other dictionary-makers.

**any more.** Critics of the use of *any more* in a positive sense may be drawing too hard a line. Literary idiom allows it in heightening a contrast, and not merely with an explicit negative. A writer in *Word Study* cited as an example of dialectal use the sentence: "*Any more,* it's hard to find a good glass of beer." The only exceptionable thing about this is the word order; not even a purist would boggle at it if it were put: "It's hard to find a good glass of beer *any more.*" Both versions imply a contrast with times when a good glass of beer was easy to find. The following, on the other hand, are examples of truly dialectal, and thus objectionable, use: "They certainly have good television programs *any more*" and "One can get terribly discouraged just by reading the newspapers *any more.*" It may be that a contrast was intended here, but *any more* cannot indicate it unassisted; the presence of some such modifier as *hard* in the sentence about the beer, or *hardly,* as in "We *hardly* see her *any more,*" or *seldom,* as in "Wells are *seldom* dug *any more*" is required. In other words, *any more* cannot be used in an unqualifiedly positive statement.

**apostrophe.** In possessives, pp. 67-68; in plurals, p. 72; omitted in names, pp. 26-27.

**appear.** *Appear* with an infinitive can easily cause ambiguity. It is to be avoided in sentences like "The budget was approved after no one *appeared* to protest," which can be taken to mean either that no protesters appeared, or that statements made about the budget apparently were not protests. See also the discussion of infinitives of purpose, pp. 34-35.

**appositive.** Misrelated, pp. 24-25; commas with appositives, p. 90.

**appraise, apprise.** *Appraise* means *set a value on,* as "*appraise* a house"; *apprise* (usually with *of*) is a highfalutin way of saying *inform, tell* or *notify,* as "*apprise* him of danger" and "*apprise* us of the circumstances."

**approximately.** P. 99.

**apt, liable, likely.** *Apt* and *likely* are so often used interchangeably in the sense of *prone to* that it may seem like quibbling to draw a distinction: "It's *apt* [likely] to be cold on the pier." Quibblers, however, tend to preserve *likely* for this sense and to use *apt* to mean *fit, suited,* or *to the point*: "His reply was sarcastic, but it was *apt.*" *Liable* is often used loosely for *likely*: "At this rate, we are *liable* to win the award." Discriminating use, however, generally applies *liable* only to what is undesirable: "An over-heated radiator is *liable* to explode." *Liable* is also used in the sense of *exposed to legal action*: "If a stair is broken, the householder may be *liable*."

**arc, arced, arcing.**    Something needs to be done about the verb forms *arced* and *arcing,* but it's hard to say what. The verb *arc,* from which they come ("The power will *arc* across the lines"; "The demented assassin tried to *arc* his grenade close to the low ceiling, toward the ministers' bench"), is pronounced *ark,* but the conventions of pronunciation would ordinarily soften the *c* in *arced* and *arcing.* This makes it seem as if the pronunciation should be *arsed* and *arsing,* which, of course, is not merely wrong but unseemly. Dictionaries give *arcking,* which solves the problem, as a variant spelling, but this form is never used. By attempting to discourage the use of *arc* as a verb in this technological age, one would only be making an arce of himself.

**around, round.**    See *all-around, all-round.*

**arrest.**    *Arrest* is best used to mean "take into custody." Some assume that an arrest consists in the mere act of being halted by an officer of the law. This assumption apparently results from confusion of differing senses of *arrest.* One of those senses is simply *to stop,* as when we say "The hurtling boulder *was arrested* by a crevasse." The legal sense is something else again; it is "to take or keep in custody." In law violations, of course, the legal definition is the one that must apply.

In the popular mind, the word *arrest* produces an image of some unfortunate being marched off to the jug. This does not happen in the mere issuance of a ticket, and when that act is described as an arrest the suspect suffers an undeserved indignity. It is just as easy, more accurate, and not unjustly derogatory to say that the suspect was given a summons or a ticket, or was cited. *Cited,* though perfectly proper both legally and linguistically, seems more favored in the West.

**artful, artistic.**    *Artful* means *devious* or *crafty,* like Dickens' Artful Dodger. *Artistic* means *possessing the quality of art,* as "an *artistic* arrangement of flowers" and "*artistic* ability."

**articles.**    (*the, a, an*) omitted, p. 28; in appositive constructions, p. 90; *a, an* before *h,* p. 29; with figures, initials, etc., p. 30.

**as.**    Vs. *like,* pp. 41-43; vs. *since, because,* p. 43; as a preposition, p. 48; omitted, p. 48; vs. *for* in attribution, p. 140.

**as . . . as; not so (as) . . . as.**    P. 44.

**as if.** P. 42.

**as of.** *As of* is properly used in a more or less technical sense to indicate the state of affairs at a particular time: "*As of* the first of the month, your bank balance was $137.45"; "He will rank as major *as of* January 15." It is, however, a legalism, and easily sidestepped, by those who object to it, with other prepositions: "*On* the first of the month . . ."; "He will rank as major *from* January 15." *As of now* is undesirable as an intensification of *now*; *right now* or *at present* is preferable: "*Right now* his chief interest is philately."

**as regards.** See *regard*.

**assure.** *Assure* takes an object; no ifs, ands, or buts. Thus "The United States, the president *assured,* will always be willing to discuss the question" sounds off-balance because it flouts idiom. The president was assuring *somebody*, not just doing it in thin air. See also *remind*.

**as to.** See *whether or not*.

**as with.** Used for *like*, p. 42.

**at, in.** P. 47.

**athletic-s.** P. 26.

**at present.** See *presently*.

**attacked.** In the sense of *sexually assaulted*, a newspaper euphemism. Reports like this are not uncommon: "The woman's arm was broken, her ear cut off, and her cheek slashed, but she had not been *attacked*."

**attorney.** Strictly speaking, an attorney is not necessarily a lawyer, but merely someone who has been authorized to act for another; that is, who has been given power of attorney. As noted in the *Dictionary of Contemporary American Usage,* however, in this country *attorney* is all but synonymous with *lawyer*. More than that, any close observer will notice that *attorney* has become the genteel word for *lawyer*. Thus most lawyers prefer to be referred to as attorneys, and newspapers, almost always sedulously deferential in these matters, cater to this preference. There are lawyers who unpretentiously advertise themselves as such on their shingles, however, and there are also newspapers that shun on principle any word intended to confer a specious dignity.

**attractive.** What has happened to beautiful women? There really are still plenty of them around, of course, and maybe even more than ever. But most of us don't call them that. The usual word for a looker seems to have become *attractive.* "What an attractive girl!" is now the standard tribute. Not *beautiful, lovely, handsome, pretty, bonny, comely, fair, beauteous, pulchritudinous,* or *good-looking.* Words often change in sense and force, and this seems to be happening, at least for the time being, to *attractive.* Strictly speaking, an attractive girl is not necessarily a pretty one at all, but one who attracts. It cannot be denied, however, that there is a connection between beauty and attraction. It seems questionable whether *attractive* as a synonym for *beautiful* or *pretty* is more than a fad. People who choose their words carefully, at any rate, still appear to be reserving *attractive* for the idea of attraction, which may not include beauty.

*Attractive,* in fact, is rather tame as a substitute for *pretty* or *beautiful.* Women, who seem fondest of using it, may be choosing the word subconsciously as a means of giving credit where due with one hand, and at the same time watering it down with the other. *Beautiful, pretty, lovely,* and *good-looking* are still holding on, however. *Handsome* can be properly applied to a woman as well as to a man, contrary to the ideas held in some quarters, but it suggests elegance rather than beauty.

*Comely* and *fair* now have an old-fashioned sound. (*Comely* is pronounced *come-ly,* not *coam-ly,* a version sometimes heard.)

**attribution.**   Pp. 138-140; needless, pp. 138-139; misleading, pp. 139-140; *said* and its variants, pp. 140-141; excessive quotation, pp. 142-143; utterance by proxy, pp. 141-142.

**au naturel.**   It is hardly necessary to resort to French to say *naked,* but if it must be, at least it should not be misspelled *au natural.* See also *all together, altogether.*

**author.**   As a verb ("The book *was authored* by an expert in the field") *author* is not in the best standing. The consensus is still, despite some opinions to the contrary, that books are *written,* not *authored.*

**avoid.**   *Avoid* frequently usurps the place of *prevent.* To avoid is to keep away from, as in "The horse veered to *avoid* the tree," while to prevent is to keep from happening, as in "The dam *prevents* the snow-melt from escaping." One company headed its interoffice communication blanks with the advice, "Avoid Verbal Orders." Any employee who took this literally, however, was asking to be fired. Another example: "The firemen fought *to avoid* flying sparks setting fire to neighboring roofs." Properly, ". . . fought to *prevent* flying sparks from . . ."

**aw.**   See *ah, aw.*

**aweigh.**   See *under way.*

**awful.** *Awful* no longer means only *awe-inspiring*; in common parlance it means *terrible* (itself something of a perversion) or *dreadful.* It may yet be necessary, however, to spell it *aweful* to restore it to its original sense, as one writer did in referring to "The *aweful* powers of the presidency." Thus does the wheel of corruption come full circle.

**awhile, a while.** Strictly speaking, *while* is a noun (as considered here) and *awhile* is an adverb. This means that *for a while* is the equivalent of *awhile,* and that "We loafed for *a while*" and "We loafed *awhile*" are correct, but "We loafed for *awhile*" is incorrect. This distinction is often disregarded, however, with the practical effect that *awhile* seems well on its way to recognition as a noun, with no irreparable damage to the language.

**ax, axe.** Axe is the British preference in spelling.

## B

**back yard.** The question whether an expression should be rendered in one rather than two words (*airbase* vs. *air base, payroll* vs. *pay roll*) is on the whole an academic and useless one, fit only for the deliberations of those who have nothing better to do than compile lists of exceptions for style manuals. Decisions on such matters usually reflect only opinions, often wrongheaded ones insofar as they resist dictionaries, on how far the evolution from two words to one has progressed in specific cases.

But it seems that something valid may be said against the frequent amalgamation of *back yard* into one word. When this happens, the convention appears to dictate that the pronunciation should be *back*yard. But, as everyone knows, the accepted pronunciation lays equal stress on both parts; this would seem to call for the preservation of *back yard* as two words. The defense, if any, of *backyard* ought to justify *frontyard,* but *frontyard* is unknown.

The same logic, if this *is* logic, applies to *home town* vs. *hometown.* A case can be made out, however, for both *backyard* and *hometown* when they are used as modifiers (*a backyard incinerator, a hometown hero*) because here the stress shifts to *back* and *home.*

**bail, bale.** *Bail* means dip water out of, or post a bond; *bale* means tie in a bundle. Boats and prisoners are *bailed*; hay is *baled* (made into bales).

**balance.** In the sense of *rest* or *remainder,* this word is best left to the accountants. One style manual, however, curiously discourages the use of *rest,* as well as *balance,* in this sense. This would make of Shakespeare's poignant line, "The remainder is silence."

**balding.**   Some critics say there is no such word, but if not, how does it find its way into print, and in reputable surroundings? These critics appear to reason that *bald* is an adjective, and that to make a verb form such as *balding* from it is illegitimate. There is a verb *balden*, however, meaning to grow bald, although it is little used. Presumably *baldening* is a legal form of *balden,* and so *balding* may be merely a contraction of *baldening*. In any event, *balding* (*Bald and balding politicians usually keep their hats on when their pictures are taken*) fills a need.

**banquet.**   *Banquet* is unduly sumptuous for *dinner,* as used to describe most such gatherings today, and the word has been discouraged to the extent that it is now generally avoided as pretentious, together with *repast* and *collation.*

**barbiturate.**   Thus spelled; not *barbituate.*

**bar, saloon.**   The changes in American drinking habits and attitudes have been accompanied by changes in the words used for the places where drinking is done. Before Prohibition, which took effect in October, 1919, the place for public drinking was a saloon and nothing else. Its chief identifying characteristics were swinging doors, a free lunch, and a clientele that was almost exclusively male. Those were the days when you could send a boy out with a bucket to fetch some beer.

The word *saloon,* just a colorless designation at one time, was successfully associated by the dry, or pro-Prohibition, interests with disreputability, low-lifes, "Father, dear Father, come home with me now," and all that sort of thing. Perhaps because of this propaganda, *saloon* is now all but a dirty word, and there are states where its use to designate a place of business is prohibited by law. On the other hand, its revival by the legal gambling resorts of Nevada, though prompted by its Old West flavor, has a refreshing effect.

In spite of its low estate at present, *saloon* has a more or less distinguished ancestry. It developed from the French *salon,* meaning a reception room or hall, especially in a palace or great house. Later the term was applied to the gatherings of literati and other intellectuals conducted by French ladies of fashion in such rooms.

*Saloon* at one time had other applications than to a drinking place. People once spoke of the *dining saloon* aboard a ship, for example (it is now *salon*). By the time Prohibition was repealed in 1933, *saloon* had such a bad connotation that its general revival was out of the question, especially from the standpoint of businessmen who opened bars. A great effort was made to popularize the term *tavern* for this purpose, but it never really caught on, except in names of establishments. When used otherwise, it seems to be equated with *beer joint*.

*Cocktail lounge* is rather specialized, calling to mind a somewhat tony place, more likely to be frequented by women. But the word-of-all-work for a drinking establishment today seems to have become *bar*, which is equally and neutrally applicable up and down the scale.

**because.** Vs. *as*, p. 43; see also *reason is because*.

**behalf.** The question sometimes arises whether *on* or *in* is correct with *behalf* (*on my behalf*; *in my behalf*). Partridge, following the *Oxford English Dictionary*, holds that confusion here leads to the loss of a useful distinction. *On behalf*, strictly, means *as the agent*, or *instead of*: "Since I was unable to appear, he reported *on my behalf*" [that is, *in my place*]. *In behalf* means in the interest, or for the benefit, of: "She put in a good word *in my behalf*" [that is, *to my credit*]. It may as well be conceded, however, that the loss of which Partridge complains is irretrievable. *On* and *in* are used indiscriminately with *behalf*, and *on* or *in behalf* are used invariably to mean *in the interest of*. Different wording is used for *as the agent*, or *instead of*, because *on* or *in behalf* no longer convey this sense explicitly.

**belabor.** A curious defiance of idiom appears in the expression *belabor a point*. The generally accepted and correct version is *labor a point*. *Labor* in this connection means to work out with effort or in detail, or to elaborate. *Belabor*, on the other hand, means to strike blows upon. Belaboring is what one would use a shillelagh for. So it is plain that one could only blunt a point by belaboring, rather than laboring, it. Those who speak of belaboring a point, however, do have history on their side, for *belabor* once meant to work carefully at. Yet the dictionaries agree that idiom now calls for *laboring* a point or question.

**believe.** See *feel*.

**bells.** Writers who essay to give a salty flavor to things by saying *six bells* instead of *six o'clock* are drifting off course. Bells formerly were sounded on shipboard to divide four-hour watches into half-hour intervals, so six bells would be eleven o'clock, three o'clock, etc.

**belly.** P. 62.

**benedict.** *Benedict*, for *newly married man*, is society-page lingo, like *just-weds*. (Strictly, it would be *Benedick*, from the character in *Much Ado About Nothing*.)

**berserk.** See *amuck, amok*.

**beside, besides.**   *Beside* means at the side of; "We stood *beside* the canyon."
*Besides* means in addition to: "*Besides* the lecture, there was a concert."

**between, among.**   The question here is whether *between* (rather than
*among*) can be correctly used of more than two things ("a war *between*
six nations"); the answer is yes, despite the quibbles sometimes raised in
objection. Some would restrict the use of *between* to instances when the
things are considered in pairs, but no such limitation is supported by dictionaries or usage. The *Oxford English Dictionary* specifies that *between*
may be used of relations between two or more things. See also p. 46.

**bi-.**   In such expressions as *biennial -ly,* and more especially *bimonthly*
and *biweekly, bi-* has become ambiguous, no matter what the dictionaries
say. It is safer to make it *every two years* (*months, weeks*) or *twice a year*
(*month, week*), or *semiannual, semimonthly, semiweekly,* as appropriate.

**birthday anniversary.**   There is a dimwitted school of thought that insists
one can have only one birthday—the day on which he is born—and that
recurrences of the date must be his *birthday anniversary.* This notion is
unsupported by either dictionaries or usage, but it does illustrate what
often goes on in the heads of the compilers of style manuals. When they
raise their voices in congratulatory song, it is presumably with "Happy
birthdayanniversary to you."

**boast.**   In statements like "Such clubs now number more than a thousand
and *boast* assets in the millions," *boast* is nothing to brag about. The impu-
tation of boasting is no compliment, and the writer usually makes it
undeservedly. Journalese.

**boat.**   The idea that *boat* cannot be applied to a seagoing vessel, but only
to a small open craft, is a naval fetish. In the technical sense, *ship,* as a
large vessel, is opposed to *boat. Boat,* however, is acceptably established
in casual references to ocean liners and otherwise.

**boatswain.**   Readers of tales of the deep are familiar with the rendering
*bosun* for *boatswain,* but in the Navy, at least, the favored pronunciation
is *boatson.* Yet *forecastle* is said the way the fictioneers have it (*fo'c'sle*).

**boost.**   Overblown and journalese for *increase, raise.*

**bosom, breast.**   It was a sad thing to see a loathsome nice-Nellyism employed by a nationally known theater critic, a man whose prose is usually
notable for unflinching directness. He reported an episode in a play in
which, as he revoltingly put it, the "false bosoms" were torn from the

dress of an actress. *False bosoms* is certainly going the long way around to avoid *falsies*. Everyone knows what falsies are, and there seems to be no other reason than prissiness for sidestepping such a popular and well-established term.

*Bosom* itself, for *breasts*, is a genteelism that seems to have emanated from the world of brassière advertising. *Bosom* is, indeed, the equivalent of *breast* (in distinction to *breasts*), but both *bosom* and *breast* are applicable equally to men and women in designating what is otherwise known as the chest. We have all read of children being pressed to the bosom, and of a dagger being plunged into the breast. *Bosom* and *breast*, however, in these strict senses, tend to be literary, if not poetic. In any event, they are asexual.

*Breasts* may be too explicitly anatomical for many purposes, and it is likely that *bosom* will continue to be widely used in that sense. The word *bust* once was popular, though never reputable, in this connection, but now seems to have fallen into disuse. *Busts,* of course, is beyond the pale. It is only to be expected that the powerful urge to cover up the thing itself should extend to the language chosen to describe it. The Balinese may be the only people in the world forthright enough to call a breast a breast without equivocation. We have falsies, which are probably unknown in Bali.

**both.**   *Both* is often redundantly used with such words as *equal, alike, agree, together. Both* indicates duality, or twoness; duality is already established by such words as those cited. "They are *both* equally deadly" and "*Both* are equally liberal" should be "They are equally deadly" and "They are equally liberal." "*Both* appeared together in a new Broadway show" should be "They appeared together . . ." *Both agreed* is unsuitable if the agreement is reciprocal; it should be *they agreed*. "*Both* looked alike" is illogical; "They looked alike." Fowler noted that *both* with *as well as* is ungrammatical. The exegesis is not simple, but the construction offends the ear; "*Both* students *as well as* teachers protested the ruling" should be "Students *as well as* teachers" or "*Both* students and teachers." *Both* in constructions of this kind should always be paired with *and*, never with *but*. "The story prompted *both* a slow but methodical investigation" is impossible; "The story prompted a slow but methodical investigation."

**brackets.**   Formed on typewriter, see *typewriter tricks*.

**breach, breech.**   Like *affect* and *effect,* often confused. In their commonest senses as nouns, a *breach* is a place that has been broken open (*a breach* *in the dike*), and a *breech* is the back end of a gun. As a verb, *breach* means break open (*breach* a cask). *Breech* as a verb has no current sense, though it was once used to mean put pants (breeches) on.

**break, broke.** It has been seriously argued that "Mrs. Jones *broke* her leg" is improper and absurd unless she did so deliberately. This is good, unmistakable idiom, however, and he who impugns it is only playing the fussbudget. See also *suffer, sustain, receive;* and *had.*

**breast.**   See *bosom, breast.*

**bring, take.**   These words are opposites in the sense that *bring* indicates motion toward the speaker or agent, and *take* motion away from him. *Webster's Dictionary of Synonyms* cites as illustrations of their use: "a mother asks a boy setting out for school to *take* a note to the teacher and to *bring* home a reply; a farmer *takes* his cattle to the market and *brings* back a supply of sugar, flour, and fresh meat." The indifferent use of *bring* and *take* is so prevalent, however, that the distinction may be on the way out.

**bugger.**   *Bugger* is widely enough known in the sense of *sodomite* as to be offensive in its alternate sense as a term of affection, "a cute little *bugger*." The word in this sense, although it will be understood as it is meant (without a sexual connotation), is not merely slang but exceedingly coarse slang, and such an expression coming from a woman may mark her as either raffish or ignorant. *Bugger* as a verb (*bugger the works*) suffers from the unsavory associations of *bugger* in its sexual sense.

**(the) bulk of.**   A bootless variant of *most of.*

**burglary.**   The word means breaking and entering. Writers should distinguish between it and *robbery,* taking away by force or threat; *theft,* taking what belongs to someone else; and *holdup,* which is essentially the same as robbery but involves the use of a weapon.

**bust, busts.**   See *bosom, breast.*

**but.**   At beginning of sentence, p. 94.

**but that.**   P. 45.

**but which, but who.**   See *and (but) which.*

**buy.**   The aspersion of *buy* as a noun ("This car was a good *buy*") as not standard is the work of those remarkably out of touch with the facts of usage. It is recognized by Webster, the *American College Dictionary,* and the *Oxford Universal Dictionary*.

**by-lines.** Pp. 135-136.

## C

**cable, cabling.** See *steam shovel.*

**caesarian.** Those who exercise themselves over capitalization will find of interest a bit of lore contributed by Dr. Peter C. Pulvang of Plattsburg, N. Y., to the *Saturday Review*:

> ". . . the first written use of the term *caesarian section* was by Crooke in 1615. In actual fact the term does not relate to Julius Caesar but rather to the Latin *caesus,* which in turn derives from the verb *caedere,* to cut."

The conclusion is that it should be *caesarian,* not *Caesarian.* Dr. Pulvang did not question the legend that Caesar, like Macduff,

> was from his mother's womb
> Untimely ripp'd,

however, and he reported that caesarian sections are recorded as having been performed successfully as early as 500 B.C.

**campus.** Years ago it was unheard of to apply this word to anything but a college, or institution of similar rank, having more than one building. More recently, however, high schools, especially in the West, where one-story construction is common, have developed similar layouts, and the word *campus* has been inevitably applied to them. To resist this on the ground that they are only secondary schools is surely a form of snobbery, even if it does set the college graduate's teeth on edge and the old school tie aflutter.

**can, may.** The old rule was that *can* should be used for the possible, and *may* to ask permission: "*Can* he beat the record?"; "*May* I look at your watch?" But the feeling for this distinction is being lost, for *can* is being used to ask permission with no lack of politeness.

**canvas, canvass.** *Canvas* is heavy cloth; *canvass* means, usually, to go from door to door soliciting.

**capital, capitol.** The *capital* is the city and the *capitol* is the building.

**capitalization.** Pp. 107-108.

**captions.** P. 152.

**capture.**   In connection with sports events, especially, a sadly bruised variant of *win.*

**cardiac.**   See *heart attack.*

**case.**   In redundancies, p. 55.

**caused from.**   This is a common example of the offenses against idiom that spring from a wrong choice of preposition; correctly, *caused by.*

**cedilla.**   Formed on typewriter, see *typewriter tricks.*

**celebrant, celebrator.**   Strictly, a *celebrant* is one who performs a religious ceremony, such as a priest who conducts a mass, and a *celebrator* is one who celebrates, as on New Year's Eve. The distinction is tenuous, however, and of dubious value. It may already have been done to death by the widespread, if heedless, preference for *celebrant* in both senses.

**cement, concrete.**   Technically, *cement* is the powder that, together with water and sand or gravel, is used to make *concrete.* Like many technical terms that have gone into common use, however, *cement* has lost its distinctiveness. *Cement sidewalks* is commonplace, and so are similar uses. The context always shows, anyway, whether the reference is to the powder or the finished product ("eighteen sacks of *cement*"; "a *cement* bird bath").

**center, centre.**   *Centre* is the British preference in spelling.

**chain reaction.**   This expression, a gift from the atomic physicists, is what Fowler would have called a popularized technicality. As pointed out by Bernstein in *Watch Your Language,* "*Chain reaction* does not mean a great quantity; it means a process in which a cause produces an effect that in turn becomes a cause, and so on." Thus a flood of telephone calls to the police, prompted by an explosion, would not be a chain reaction unless the calls were self-multiplying.

**chair.**   *Chair* as a verb meaning serve as chairman is not fully acceptable, in spite of its popularity on the society pages, where some other questionable verbs, such as *host,* find a haven. "Mrs. Adams *chaired* the meeting" carries an alarming suggestion of *attacked with a chair.* If this is too farfetched, in any event *chaired* accomplishes nothing that *presided at, led,* or *directed* does not.

**chaise longue.**   *Chaise longue* (pronounced *shaz long,* and meaning, in French, *long chair*) seems in great danger of becoming *chaise,* or *chase,* *lounge,* perhaps on the assumption that this piece of furniture commemorates a lounger named Chase.

**character.** In general, this word is most appropriately applied to people. Its use concerning things, in the sense of *quality, kind, sort,* and the like is a species of personification and at the same time often an exhibition of pomposity. A well-known company has for some time been advertising itself as a "maker of watches of the highest character." What is meant is *quality. Character* sometimes turns up in phrases where it merely serves to give a mushy effect to the writing: *the delicate character of the music* (delicacy), *activities of a public-spirited character* (public-spirited activities), and *concentration of an intermittent character* (intermittent concentration). Such expressions are characteristic, these days, of fusty prose. "The residential *character* of the neighborhood" might better be *nature* or *status,* but the difficulty of settling on a satisfactory substitute suggests that this may be one of those exceptions in which *character* is acceptable. "It is regrettable that an incident of this *character* has occurred" would be better, however, with *kind.*

**chat.** See *informal.*

**cheap.** *Cheap* means low in value or in price, not simply *low.* Goods may be *cheap,* but prices must necessarily be *low.*

**cheesecake.** P. 152.

**Chinaman, Chinese.** *Chinaman* is considered demeaning; the preferred form is *Chinese*: "Four *Chinese* and one American were detained in customs."

**choice.** See *pick, choice.*

**chord, cord.** Although these words have the same ancestor and both can mean *string, chord* in its commonest use means a group of musical tones sounded together in a pattern. The folds in the throat that produce the sound of the voice are vocal *cords,* not *chords.*

**Christmas tree.** A courtly bow to a Captain Donahue of the New York Police Department, who, as quoted in the *Reporter,* described a switchboard as lighting up like Luna Park, instead of like a Christmas tree. Christmas trees may get a bad name from their association with this battered simile.

**cite.** See *arrest.*

**citizen.**   Since this word has the meaning, among others, of one who owes allegiance to a state and is entitled to protection from it, it should be used with care, to prevent the ambiguity that often arises when *inhabitant* or *resident* would be a better choice. People were citizens of cities in the days when cities were states; it may be better now to speak of them as inhabitants, or residents, of their cities. "A citizen met the bus that delivers the papers." Since this was merely a resident, and not a citizen as distinguished from an alien, *resident* would have been the happier word. "The county now has 221,900 citizens, a record." This sentence, from a population report, referred to inhabitants, and could be genuinely misleading as distinguishing between citizens and aliens. Yet it is not wrong to speak of "a citizen of Chicago" or "a citizen of Utah." And *citizen* sometimes is unavoidable, as in *citizens' advisory committee.*

**civilian.**   A civilian is one not in military service; use of the word to differentiate those not in any kind of uniform, as for example nonpolicemen, is questionable. Next we will be offered some such distinction as *mailmen and civilians.*

**claim.**   Not in the best odor in the sense of *say* or *assert;* journalese. Properly, *claim* carries the idea of asserting a right, or ownership, and its use for a simple declaration grates on the ear: "Some grammarians claim the construction is incorrect."

**clarify.**   *Clarify* means *clear* or *clear up,* and is wrong in the sense of *answer*: "He spoke to clarify questions farmers may have about tractors." Only the asker, if a question is obscure, can clarify it; this speaker's intention was to *answer* the farmers' questions. Apart from this, *clarify* is too great a favorite in official prose, where things are always supposedly being clarified. Sad to state, they are rarely *cleared up,* either by the use of *clarify* or in fact.

**clean copy.**   Pp. 122-123.

**clerical designations.**   Pp. 105-106.

**clichés.**   The dictionary definition of cliché is "a trite phrase; a hackneyed expression." This leaves wide open the question, trite or hackneyed to whom? Language is full of stock phrases, many of which are indispensable, or at least not replaceable without going the long way around. The expressions that draw scorn as clichés, however, are generally those that attempt a special effect—usually dramatic or humorous. Whether a particular expression is regarded as a cliché depends upon the discrimination of the regarder. A good way to acquire an acute and extensive awareness of clichés is to read Frank Sullivan's reports from his cliché expert, Magnus Arbuthnot, as set down in such books as *A Pearl in Every Oyster, A Rock in Every Snowball,* and *The Night the Old Nostalgia Burned Down.* The subject is explored in Chapter X of this book.

**climactic, climatic.** *Climactic* refers to *climax, climatic* to *climate.* "*Climatic* conditions are ideal in California"; "That is the *climactic* scene in the play."

**close to.** *Close to* is a gaucherie for *nearly* or *almost*: "*Close to* 750 delegates are expected to attend the convention"; "They seek to lure *close to* a million people."

**co-.** P. 78.

**coal oil.** See *kerosene.*

**coed.** Just as *campus* (which see) is now applied to high schools, so *coed* is applied to high-school girls.

**cohort.** *Cohort* enjoys considerable vogue as a synonym for *colleague, associate,* or *companion.* But careful writers do not use it in this sense. In the Roman army a cohort was one of the ten divisions of a legion, and in modern usage the word means a large band of people. The *Dictionary of Contemporary American Usage* speculates that the misuse in application to a single person is based on a false analogy with *co-worker.*

**collation.** See *banquet.*

**collective.** *Collective,* in the sense under consideration here, is what Fowler might have stigmatized as a vogue word: "The people at this haberdashery keep their *collective* ear tuned to what men want to wear." The users of it apparently are eager to flaunt their learning, for they are dimly aware that *collective* is a technicality of grammar, applied to words that denote a group: *jury, crowd.* From there they go on to fashion a literary trick they hope is cute. The examples to be cited should show that the use of the word in this way is unnecessary, absurd, or both.

"The New York Housing Authority is no doubt laughing up its *collective* sleeve." Meaningless. The members of the authority may be laughing up their several sleeves, but it is hard to imagine a sleeve that sleeves them all.

"The 389 men of the customs staff resigned themselves *collectively* last week to days loud with questioning." Superfluous and meaningless.

"An unprepared American public and a government almost equally bewildered rubbed their *collective* eyes." Superfluous and meaningless.

"Local experts merely cocked their *collective* eyebrow at the prediction." Preposterous.

"Then they had to defend their ideas before the committee, which seemed to have its tongue in its *collective* cheek." How a collective cheek without a collective tongue?

"In the auditorium we could hear the audience whistling and stamping its *collective* feet." The collect for today is: Abstain from such sleazy tricks as using *collective* in the ways illustrated.

**collectives.** Pp. 70-71.

**colloquialisms.** Pp. 51-52.

**colon.** Introducing a series, p. 94.

**colored.** See *Negro*.

**comma.** After conjunctions, pp. 93-94; with parenthetical elements, p. 86; with adjectives, pp. 86-87; one-legged comma, pp. 87-89; with *of* phrases, pp. 87-88; serial comma, pp. 92-93; with reflexive pronouns, p. 89; with coordinate clauses, pp. 89-90; with appositives, p. 90; with restrictive, nonrestrictive clauses, pp. 90-92.

**commandments, sequence of.** A towel-company ad that appeared in a number of national magazines read: "Friend of ours in the hotel business received a conscience note enclosing a five-dollar bill the other day. 'I am an old lady with a Christian upbringing . . . don't know what possessed me, but when I left your nice hotel last week I broke the Seventh Commandment. Now I can't sleep of nights. Please forgive me . . .' "

A critic of this ad commented: "O. K., lady. Far be it from me to cast the first stone."

His assumption that the Seventh Commandment is the one forbidding adultery was probably shared by millions. But this lady, whose title to ladyhood was clearer than may appear at first glance, evidently was reared in a faith in which the Seventh Commandment forbids stealing. The old girl had made off with a towel she admired, and was sending the money in to pay for it (it says here).

For reasons clear only to a theologian, different faiths use different numbers for some of the commandments. To Catholics and Lutherans, the Sixth prohibits adultery and the Seventh theft, while to most other denominations the Seventh deals with adultery and the Eighth with theft, corresponding to the sequence in the King James Version of the Bible. There are other differences among various creeds, both in numbering and in apportionment of the text. Those who essay to quote scripture for their purposes are warned that reference to a commandment by number alone may not be enough, and may indeed be the broad road to perdition.

The different methods of numbering were commented on in the May, 1957, issue of *Changing Times* as follows:

"There are two ways of dividing Exodus 20:2-17 (and Deuteronomy 5:6-21) into a set of ten commandments. There is no doctrinal difference between these, and both cover precisely the same material—it's a matter of practice in the arrangement of that material.

"The original Jewish arrangement, also used by almost all Protestant denominations, considers the First Commandment to be verses 2 and 3, '. . . Thou shalt have no other Gods . . .'; the Second to be verses 4 through 6, 'Thou shalt not make unto thee any graven image . . .'; and the Tenth to be verse 17 in its entirety. In Roman Catholic and Lutheran practice, the injunction against idolatry is considered part of the First Commandment. This advances the numbering of the subsequent commandments . . . Then the number ten is preserved by dividing verse 17 into a commandment against coveting thy neighbor's wife and one against coveting his worldly goods."

**commence.** *Commence*, where *begin* or *start* will serve, has taken on an old-fashioned sound, and harks back to more leisurely, spacious days.

**Commie.** *Commie* for *Communist* sounds ridiculously palsy-walsy, especially when used, as it often is, by people who could not be more bitterly opposed to Communism. Why should *Commie* sound palsy-walsy? Perhaps because the endings *y* and *ie* are characteristic of expressions that connote affection, and also of baby talk. Compare *dog* and *doggie*, *Bill* and *Billy*. Oddly, it seems that the same people who use *Commie* often mispronounce *Communist* as *Commonist,* rather than *Commyoonist.*

**compare to, with; contrast.** *Compare to* means liken to or place in the same class; "He *compared* me to a thief" means "He *likened* me to a thief." *Compare with* means examine in relation to: "He *compared* me with a thief" means "He set my qualities beside those of a thief, to show either similarities or differences." This distinction is even more useless than some others that are fancied by purists, however, because the senses overlap. As Perrin notes, in the common construction with the past tense, *with* and *to* are used indiscriminately, and it may as well be recognized that *compare with* and *compare to* no longer convey any reliably distinctive meanings. For practical purposes, it may be assumed that both *compare with* and *compare to* will be taken to mean *note differences, similarities,* or both. When unlikeness is pointed out, *contrast* is generally used: "The paintings were contrasted with those of an amateur." See also p. 47.

**complected.** *Complected* for *complexioned* is dialectal and not good usage: "A dark-*complexioned* [not *complected*] man."

**complement, compliment.** *To complement* is to complete or fill out; *to compliment* is to praise. "The jacket *complements* her ensemble"; "She was often *complimented* on her taste in clothes."

**compose, comprise, consist of.** These expressions cause hesitation by some writers, who wonder which suits their purpose. In the sense at hand, namely, *be made up of*, there is nothing much to choose from among them. *Comprised of* is a mistake by analogy with *composed of. Comprise* means include or embrace, and does not take *of. Webster's Dictionary of Synonyms* offers as an example of correct use "The district *comprises* three counties and part of a fourth." The temptation to write "The district *is comprised of* . . ." should be resisted, for the whole comprises the parts, and not the reverse. Many will consider "The district *is made up of, consists of,* or *is formed by*" plainer language, and thus more desirable, than *comprises*.

**compound modifiers.** Hyphenation of, pp. 75-76.

**compound nouns.** Plurals of, p. 72.

**compound verbs.** Divided, pp. 36-37.

**conclave.** This word, though a favorite variant of *convention,* properly means a secret, or private, meeting.

**concrete.** See *cement, concrete.*

**condition.** *Condition* in *heart condition, lung condition* is a faceless euphemism for *disease* or *ailment.* Every heart has some condition, healthy or otherwise.

**confess to.** P. 47.

**congratulate.** *Congratulate* is so unanimously mispronounced *congradulate* over the air, even by Groucho Marx, who really ought to know better, that the bastard version may be expected to creep into print, as indeed it does.

**congress.** *The congress,* p. 28.

**congressman.** The ways of words are indeed mysterious. There is every reason why *congressman* should mean either *senator* or *representative,* and some insist that it does. A senator is so rarely referred to in this manner, however, that it may as well be conceded that usage has attached *congressman* irrevocably to representatives.

**conjunctions.**   *As* vs. *like,* pp. 41-43; *while,* p. 43; comma after *and, but, or,* pp. 93-94.

**consensus of opinion.**   *Of opinion* is redundant with *consensus,* which, incidentally, is often misspelled *concensus.*

**consider.**   Let us consider *consider,* the breeder of a whole nest of peccadilloes. First, *as* after *consider* is not idiomatic. "He was *considered as* a coward" should be "He was *considered* a coward." This also applies to *termed.* The error probably comes from a mistaken analogy with *regard,* which properly takes *as*: "He was *regarded as* a bum."

"Unfortunately, too many editors and reporters nowadays consider official handouts *as* news" is ambiguous in a wry way. The utterer of the complaint meant that what is not news is being treated as if it were, instead of being rejected. But he may be understood as regretting merely that handouts are getting consideration. *For* may be more explicit than *as* when *consider as* is used in the sense of *give consideration to*: "Steam was *considered as* the source of power" [but electricity was used]. *For* in the place of *as* will prevent misunderstanding of *considered as* in the sense of *regarded as.*

*Consider* is often sloppily used in place of *deem, believe, think, feel, decide,* and the like, and it sometimes usurps the place of *regard as.* "The official imposed the ban because he *considers* the art work is obscure" and "The general *considers* the Russians will not provoke a showdown" really call for *believes* or *thinks.* (But *considers the art work obscure,* omitting *is,* is another cure.)

"My mother's family was opposed to her marriage with my father, *considering that* he was not good enough for her." *Considering that* may easily be read in the sense of *because,* but the writer meant ". . . *regarding* him as not good enough for her." See *regard.*

**consist in, of.**   To consist *in* is to inhere or reside in: "The value of the advice *consists in* its honesty"; to consist *of* is to be made up, or composed, of: "The cake *consists of* flour, milk, eggs, and other ingredients." See also *compose, comprise.*

**contact.**   The fight against *contact* both as a verb ("I'll *contact* him") and as a noun ("George has some good *contacts* in that town") is unquestionably a losing one. Some years ago, when it first appeared, *contact* as a verb was complained of as abominably overworked. It is a nice question whether its use has now subsided, or whether we are so used to seeing it we no longer particularly notice it. *Contact,* strictly speaking, means *touch,* and in the sense at hand it is used to mean *get in touch with.* As the shortest distance between two points, *contact* in this sense will hardly be pushed aside. It has an inclusive meaning that none of the substitutes sometimes proposed can offer.

"In this event, the family physician is *contacted.*" *Called?* This is ambiguous for *telephoned* or *summoned,* and neither may fit. *Consulted* is possible, but not likely.

"Eleanor said her mother has not tried to *contact* her since her arrest." *Call?* This does not include *visit,* which *contact* does. *See* does not include *call. Reach* does not include *visit. Get in touch with* is always possible as a substitute. *Contact* as a verb can be avoided, and it is up to the writer to decide whether it is worthwhile. In deciding, he may as well keep in mind that *contact* as a verb has not fully emerged into the sunshine of complete acceptance, and is still partly in the shadow of its commercial origin. *Contact* as a noun ("He made a number of useful *contacts* on the trip") is hardly open to aspersion any longer.

**contend.**   An unexplainable variant for *say, assert,* and the like, when used, as it often is, of statements with which no disagreement is indicated.

**contiguous.**   Although this word is sometimes admitted in a looser sense, it might be restricted to what *touches*: "California and Nevada are *contiguous.*" *Adjacent* and *adjoining* are suitable in the senses *near to one another* or *side by side.*

**continual, continuous.**   Let us shed a tear for the erstwhile distinction between these words, which has all but faded into nothingness, despite the agonized efforts of purists to keep it alive. Generally speaking, distinctions are a good thing, because they make for exactness. But first, the writer must intend the distinction, and next, the great body of readers must be aware of it.

Some methods of making distinctions appear to have lost out because the words that once made them are so similar people have trouble telling them apart. There was a time—and some insist it is still here—when *continuous* was regarded as meaning *uninterrupted,* and *continual* as meaning what we now usually express by the word *intermittent.* The similarity of *continual* and *continuous* is probably what did them in, and now they are used interchangeably in the sense of "going on indefinitely, with or without interruption." The fact that Webster now cites each as the synonym of the other looks like proof that they have reached the end of their careers as words of usefully different meanings.

To convey the precise original sense of *continuous,* we are now likely to write *incessant;* and to convey the original sense of *continual,* as noted, we are likely to write *intermittent. Incessant* and *intermittent* are unmistakably recognizable for what they are intended to mean, which is more than can be said of *continual* and *continuous*, even if the writer has made his selection knowingly.

For the assistance of those who want to preserve the distinction, there is a mnemonic device, invented by Theodore M. Bernstein of the *New York Times*: the *ous* of *continuous* may be regarded as standing for *one uninterrupted sequence*. It may be, however, that the mere need for such a device is a final damnation. Curiously, instinct leads us to the right choice in tangible connections: we naturally say *a continuous rope, a continuous electrical conductor*. This may help in making the choice for what is intangible.

If any more need be said, let it be this: Margaret M. Bryant of Brooklyn College, writing in *Word Study,* cited statistics leading to the conclusion that *continual* and *continuous* "are now being employed interchangeably by even the literary writers."

**contractual.** Often misspelled *contractural*.

**contrast.** See *compare to, with*.

**controversial issue.** See *noncontroversial issue*.

**contusions.** P. 53.

**convince.** See *persuade, convince*.

**cop.** One of the many anguished campaigns against the use of the word *cop* has been kept in motion by no less a personage than J. Edgar Hoover, director of the Federal Bureau of Investigation. His idea is that more respect than is conveyed by *cop* should be shown to officers of the law. Newspapers, especially, have been enjoined to eschew the expression. Some do so, but even the rest are aware, certainly, that the term is not a reverential one. As far as most newspapers are concerned, *cop* is just too handy a headline word to be resisted.

Many people are likely to boggle at the idea of giving any special respect to police officers, to the extent of banning a useful and generally accepted word. While *cop* may be objected to as not showing respect, it does not show any particular disrespect, either. It does show familiarity, perhaps of a kind that many policemen like to think of as existing between themselves and the public. *Cop,* which of course is slang, but prevalent enough so that it may become good usage, is traced by Simeon Potter in *Our Language* to "copper, one who *cops* or *caps* (Latin *capere,* 'to take')."

John Lardner, writing in the *New Yorker,* drew a distinction between *cop* and *copper.* The latter, he said, is invariably disparaging, and he speculated that objectors to *cop* are confusing it with *copper.* Some critics of *cop* hold that the term is the equivalent of *shyster* as applied to a lawyer, or of *quack* as applied to a doctor. This view has no real basis, however, for no question of competence is implied by its use.

Commenting on Mr. Hoover's campaign, Hal Boyle of the Associated Press wrote in part:

> "Cops don't like the average citizen to call them cops. But what do they call themselves when talking to other members of their profession? Cops! . . . What man in the long blue line doesn't take pride in being called 'a good cop'? What policeman can resent a big-eyed kid who looks up at him and says, 'When I grow up I want to be a cop just like you'? Any word can be good or bad, depending on the way it is said. People can be policed, but nobody can police a language."

**cope.** "Every company sent one girl representative. They all managed to cope without blushing." Idiom requires that *cope* be accompanied by *with,* and that *with* be followed by an object, as for example, "*cope* with the exhibit of pornography in the courtroom." This brings to mind the man who was asked whether he liked Kipling. "I don't know," he replied. "How do you kipple?"

**cord.** See *chord, cord.*

**coronary.** See *heart attack.*

**corps, corp.** *Corps* (pronounced *core*) as in *Corps of Army Engineers, corps of cadets* is often illiterately rendered *corp,* an expression that does not exist, except with a period as an abbreviation for *corporation.*

**corpus delicti.** Pp. 145-146.

**counting.** Unnecessary, p. 96.

**count noses.** As a means of ascertaining or reporting attendance, this method has its limitations, for it does not allow for the two-headed. Anyway, for a change it might be more interesting to count ears and divide by two.

**couple.** P. 71.

**court litigation.** Redundant. Litigation is inevitably associated with a court.

**coveted.** In writing of the Pulitzer prizes or any other award, writers should be enjoined, "Thou shalt not *covet*."

**crack.** Overdone as an adjective applied to a train, regiment, division, or what you will. As a clipped form of *wisecrack,* see *quip*.

**crack down on.** The frequency with which this expression is used in connection with enforcement of laws or rules is enough to make the thin-skinned crack up.

**critical.** As used of those who are laid up, *critical* ("The patient is in *critical* condition") should be handled with care. It does not mean simply seriously ill, but in a state of crisis, or hovering between life and death. Criticisms of the word as often used in headlines (" 'Auto Victim Critical' —and he has a right to be") are captious.

**criticise, criticize.** *Criticise* is the British preference in spelling, and its use in this country may seem affected.

**crumby, crummy.** The correct spelling of this slang term, meaning *shoddy,* is *crummy*. Inconsistently, a fellow held in low esteem is a *crumb*.

**cum.** The persistence of this Latin preposition, which means *with,* in phrases like "The vagaries of want-*cum*-debt creation" and "education-*cum*-football" is nothing less than intellectual ostentation; indeed, such phrases have taken on an overtone of facetiousness. Those who know no Latin may be confused by *cum,* and the rest enjoy no advantage from its use. Even to those who know what *cum* means, "The vagaries of want *accompanied by* debt creation" is worth consideration. The use of foreign expressions in writing aimed at a wide audience is excusable only if the expressions convey something that has no exact equivalent in English.

**currently.** Like *presently* (which see), *at present,* and *now, currently* is unnecessary except to contrast the present with some other time.

**custom, custom-built.** The debasement of *custom-built* can be blamed on the advertising gentry. It once meant "built to the specifications of the buyer," and still does, unless you read it in an ad, where everyone now realizes it dishonestly means "mass-produced, but having some pretensions, not necessarily justified, to quality." *Custom-built* and *custom* are generally misapplied in this way to automobiles and houses. See *estate*.

**cutlines.** P. 152.

# D

**dame.**  The *New York Times* critique, "Winners & Sinners," notes:

> "In British usage *Dame* is equivalent to *Sir*. Therefore to speak of *Dame Pankhurst* is as ridiculous as to speak of *Sir Churchill* or *Sir Raleigh*. Neither title is ever coupled with the family name, but only with the full name or the first name alone. Moreover, the wife of a *sir* (a knight) is *Lady* plus the surname."

**dangling participles.**  Pp. 22-23.

**dash.**  Formed on typewriter, see *typewriter tricks*.

**data, datum.**  *Data* is technically the plural of *datum,* but this remains of interest only to Latinists. *Data* is almost invariably used as a collective with a singular verb: "The data is interesting but unreliable." Its use with a plural verb is still correct, of course, but unusual: "The data are mostly in the form of percentages." *Datum* is all but extinct.

**datelines.**  P. 130.

**day of the week.**  Used in time elements in news stories, pp. 129-130.

**deadline.**  See *newspaper terms*.

**debut.**  *Debut* as a verb has a slangy sound, but its usefulness may win it a respectable place yet: "The automobile industry debuts its new models in the fall"; "Prohibition debuted last week south of the border."

**decimate.**  The primary meaning of this word is a comparatively weak one; the Latinist knows that it means to strike down one in ten (men), and he is shocked to see it used in the sense of *destroy a large part of*. *Decimate,* like *mediocre,* however, has grown muscles, and the stronger sense is recognized. The restricted, original meaning is so specialized that the word is all but useless today in that sense. Allowing the extended meaning, however, *decimate* is often used absurdly, as in "Some classrooms were nearly decimated by the student strike." The writer meant *emptied*.

**defence, defense.**  *Defence* is the British preference in spelling.

**defi.**  What ever happened to *defi*? No front page used to be complete unless it had one being hurled. Looks as if there are fashions in headlinese, and as if some bromides wear out, only to be replaced by others. Or is it defiance itself that has gone out of style in an age of conformity?

**definitely.** In the sense *certainly, indeed* ("The program has *definitely* been canceled") as opposed to its precise sense of *in a well-defined way* ("The boundary was *definitely* established on the final map"), this word retains a slangy tone, but may graduate into full acceptance. *Definitely* and *but definitely* for *yes* or *of course,* in reply to a question, are fads.

**definitions.** In dictionaries, pp. 62-63.

**degrees.** Academic, pp. 106-107.

**Democrat, -ic.** In recent years leaders of the Republican Party have drummed up a crusade to encourage the use of *Democrat* as an adjective, rather than *Democratic*; for example, *Democrat senators.* The object is primarily political, rather than linguistic. The sponsors of the crusade have explained that they fear *Democratic* suggests Democrats have a monopoly on the concept of democracy. There is reason to believe that the usage is a manifestation of illiteracy, since it was first noticeably employed by a senator whose handling of language exhibited other peculiarities.

This foible was delicately pinpointed in a *New Yorker* piece by Richard H. Rovere, who described how the writer of a letter being read before a Congressional committee, "employing a well-known mannerism, had written of *Democrat senators.*" The man reading the letter, Mr. Rovere recorded, "paused after *Democrat,* coughed a polite little cough, and said 'ick senators.'"

I hope nobody reads any political pleading into this little lecture, because it seems to me that literateness ought to be as bipartisan as foreign policy. *Democrat* senators is no better English than *Republic* senators would be, and it is likely to leave the reader feeling a mixture of distaste and puzzlement.

As to general acceptance, even by Republicans, this crusade has gone about as far as a snowball in hell. The reason has nothing to do with political implications, but is based rather on the rocklike public resistance that always meets attempts to monkey with entrenched forms, regardless of motive.

Let us save our sympathy for the poor editor. Now, on top of all his other woes, he must decide whether quoted matter full of expressions like *Democrat Party,* planted there by Republicans, should be allowed to stand. If he does let them stand, he may incur the disdain of linguistically sensitive readers who have not heard of the crusade and will set them down to sloppy editing. But if he changes *Democrat* to *Democratic,* he may run the risk of meddling in editorial policy.

**demolished.**  See *totally destroyed*.

**denier.**  Some terms that are freely used by advertisers are understood by practically nobody. Take *denier,* for example, as applied to women's stockings. The average woman has a fuzzy idea *denier* has something to do with fineness, but I could not find one who could say even approximately what *denier* is. Webster defines *denier* as "a unit expressing the fineness of silk, rayon, or nylon yarns in terms of weights in grams per 9,000 meters of length." So the smaller the *denier* number, the greater the fineness.

**deprecate, depreciate.**  *To deprecate* is to disapprove of; *to depreciate* is to belittle. A remark, for example, may be either *deprecatory* or *depreciatory,* and since these words are often confused, it behooves the writer to make his choice with care.

**descriptives.**  Geographical and national, pp. 103-104.

**designed.**  Vastly overworked in the sense of *intended* or *planned*; in this sense it has become journalese. "The rose bushes are *designed* to act as a net to catch cars hurtling off the road." *Intended.* "The new fire engine is *designed* for protection of the entire county." *Intended.* "The demonstration is *designed* for a lay audience." *Intended* or *planned*. Sometimes, before an infinitive, the word could be omitted altogether: "Theater officials announced a new program [*designed*] to appeal to service clubs"; "Permission has been granted for filing of a complaint [*designed*] to block the payment."

**destroyed.**  See *totally destroyed*.

**device, devise.**  A *device* is a contrivance, to put it briefly, and *to devise* is to contrive. In nontechnical usage, *device* is always a noun, *devise* always a verb.

**diacritical marks.**  Marks such as the umlaut (as in *schön*, German for *beautiful*) and French accents (as in *fiancé, cliché*) sometimes create a problem for the writer who wants to preserve them, because the typesetting equipment of many publications, particularly newspapers, does not contain accented letters. (For their formation on the typewriter, see *typewriter tricks.*) Words that have been taken over from French into English, such as *fiancé, protégé,* and *cliché,* are tending to lose their accents. Diacritical marks occur rarely in English words, and many users of adopted words either are unaware that they require accents in strict usage or are willing to dispense with them. A handful of newspapers, however, and most books and magazines carefully retain accents; there is no question of the favorable impression this makes on the critical reader, together with the discriminating use of italics and of capitals and small capitals. Some words that possess accents in French have come into good English usage unaccented; one of them is *employee,* now sometimes spelled *employe.* It was once possible to distinguish between male and female by employé and employée, but now both spellings, unaccented, refer indiscriminately to workers of both sexes. The careful writer can only be referred to Webster for the decision on the use of accent marks in particular cases (Webster retains them on *fiancée, fiancé, cliché, protégé,* and *protégée,* for example). Oddly, even when the accents are ignored, standard usage maintains the sex distinction in the spellings *fiance* and *fiancee,* unlike what has happened to *employe* and *employee.*

The German umlaut usually creates problems only with foreign titles and names, such as Götterdämmerung and Lübeck. The accepted convention is to render the umlauted a, o, or u as ae, oe, ue: Goetterdaemmerung, Luebeck. Often, however, the problem will be ignored, as in Gotterdammerung.

The dieresis (as in coöperate) is about the only native diacritical mark. It indicates, of course, that the *o* beneath is given the short sound. But coöperate is nearly always rendered *co-operate* or *cooperate*; the dieresis is being flung to the winds, like French accents in Anglicized words.

**dictionaries.**   Pp. 62-63; use in newsrooms, p. 135.

**die from.**   P. 47.

**diet on.**   This expression is rare, though legitimate, in the sense of *eat* or *subsist on,* and likely to be misunderstood: "This pet owl *diets on* mice and chicken." What one *diets on* is likely to be thought of as restricted diet: "On my doctor's orders, I am *dieting on* nonfat foods."

**different than; different, various.**   The idea that there is anything wrong with *different than* is a superstition; the phrase is idiomatic when it introduces a clause. The usual forms are illustrated by "The rich are different *from* you and me" and "The weather is no different *than* it was yesterday." *Different to* is excoriated by British pundits on usage, but this form is unknown in the United States. *Different* is often used unnecessarily: "We called on twelve *different* people." The word is excess baggage unless there is some occasion to stress differences; if *unlike* cannot be substituted for *different,* it is better left out. *Various* is preferable to *different* merely to indicate diversity without emphasizing unlikeness: "*Various* [not *different*] actors have performed the role."

**dilemma.**   A dilemma is not merely a problem or predicament, but one that presents a choice between *evils;* this is made evident by the phrase *horns of a dilemma.* The problem of a choice between the love of two beautiful women is not a dilemma, for neither alternative is distasteful; nor is a choice between what is desirable and what is undesirable.

**disassociate.**   See dissociate.

**discomfit, -ure.**   Observable usage, for better or worse, has toned these words down from their precise and original meanings. Perhaps because of their resemblance to *discomfort,* they are commonly used in much the same sense. The *American College Dictionary,* recognizing this trend, admits *disconcert* as one meaning, but Webster has not yet budged from *put to rout, frustrate.* Fowler noted a tendency to use *discomfit* in too weak or indefinite a sense, and it may be said that the tendency has gone full speed downhill since. He who wants to preserve *discomfit* and *discomfiture* in their pristine senses (*overwhelm* or *utterly defeat*) is free to do so, if he is willing to chance being misapprehended. "The guest was *discomfited* by the lack of a salad fork" is a typical example of how *discomfit* has fallen these days.

**discover, invent.**   Often confused. To discover is to find what already exists, as for example a new element. To invent is to devise or create. Machines are invented. It appears, however, that it is possible to create new elements that do not exist in nature.

**disinterest, uninterest.**   Disinterest is impartiality; uninterest is lack of interest. An umpire, ideally, is disinterested; one who does not care about the game is uninterested.

**dismiss against.**   P. 47.

**dissociate, disassociate.**   Both are correct, but *dissociate* is to be encouraged on the principle that what is simpler is preferable.

**distaff.**   Everyone knows that *distaff,* dearly beloved of newsmen, is used to mean *pertaining to women,* but who knows exactly what a distaff *is,* anyway? Well, a distaff turns out to be a gadget used in hand spinning, an operation few can now remember. When a figure of speech grows so old that its basis is no longer common knowledge, it may be time to drop it.

**divorce.**   *Divorce* as a verb, for better or worse, is irrevocably transitive. "They divorced after two years" is therefore impossible; correctly, "They were divorced after two years."

**dock, pier, wharf.**   The use of *dock* to mean only the waterway beside or between piers or wharves is nautical cant, and not in accordance with general usage. *Dock* is properly interchangeable with *pier* or *wharf*. *Dock workers* exemplifies this, for the reference is almost invariably to longshoremen, and not to workers in drydocks.

**double in brass.**   This expression is probably open to criticism as a cliché when used as a figure of speech, but apart from this its point is often blunted. A photographer for a newspaper, for example, was described as doubling in brass because he also took pictures for a magazine. *Double in brass* is applied in the world of music to a player whose primary instrument is a string or one of the wood winds, but who is capable of playing a brass, such as a trumpet or trombone, when necessary. The term has also been used in vaudeville and circuses concerning performers who doubled as musicians. A reporter who was also a photographer might be described figuratively as *doubling in brass,* but the expression is no more suitably applicable to one who does the same thing in different places than to a musician who plays the violin in two orchestras.

**dove.**   *Dove,* as the past tense of *dive,* is a particular target of scorn in style manuals. Why this should be is a mystery, for not only is *dove* acceptable, but it is in commoner use than *dived,* which is becoming all but literary. It is true that dictionaries designate *dove* as colloquial, but contrary to a widespread misconception, this is no stigma. *Colloquial* just refers to plain talk, something that everyone should strive for. In England, *dove* is dialectal, but this is not England.

**Down Style.**   P. 108.

**Dr.**   Pp. 106-107.

**dramatic, -s.**   Pp. 25-26.

**drouth, drought.**   Writers vex themselves over which of these forms to settle on. They are equally correct, and although Webster gives preference to *drought, drouth* seems in greater favor, perhaps by analogy with the process by which *draft* has supplanted *draught* in most senses.

**drowned, was drowned.**   *Drowned* is preferable to describe an accident: "He *drowned* last year in the channel." "He *was drowned*" suggests murder, although this form is often carelessly used when no such suggestion is intended.

**drug.** The shunning of this word as a noun in the sense of *narcotic,* as is sometimes done for fear of offending druggists, is a silly concession to commercial influence. It is akin to refusing to print requests that no flowers be sent to a funeral, lest it hurt the business of florists.

**drunk, drunken.** *Drunken* is the preferred form of the adjective for attributive use; that is, in front of the noun modified: *a drunken driver. Drunk* is preferable as a predicate adjective: "The policeman himself was drunk." This principle is borne out by Webster and by observation of careful usage. Nevertheless, it may be that *drunk* as an attributive (*drunk driver*) is verging into acceptance.

**due to.** *Due to* falls into the category of expressions that are much used but faintly suspect. Anyone who is at all attentive to usage has an idea, at least, that *due to* is supposedly sinful in certain constructions. Usage has washed its blemishes away, however, and it may now be freely used as one chooses.

A review of the grounds on which *due to* was once aspersed may be of some interest, especially to lint-pickers. The old idea, as set forth by Fowler, was that *due to* could not stand in the place of *owing to* or *because of.* According to this reasoning, in other words, *due to* could not be used as a preposition introducing an adverbial modifier. This discussion is getting loathsomely grammatical, so let us try to illuminate it with some examples. The old idea was that "Asian flu is *due to* an imported virus" is acceptable, because here *due* serves as an adjective modifying *flu,* but that "*Due to* Asian flu, he missed three days of school" is no good, because here *due to,* as a preposition, introduces a phrase that modifies the verb *missed.*

All this is hair-splitting, as our age views these matters. Either *owing to* or *due to* will sound acceptable in these constructions. Anyway, it has been demonstrated that *owing to* and *due to* are identical in origin, and if *owing to* can grow up and become a preposition, why arbitrarily bar the path of opportunity to *due to*?

For the benefit of those who insist on hewing to the old prejudice, there is an easy way to tell whether a doubtful *due to* conforms. The idiomatic line between *due to* and *owing to* is pretty blurry, but not the one between *due to* and *because of.* If *because of* can be substituted for *due to,* then *due to* is wrong—according to the old rule. "Asian flu is because of an imported virus" is clearly impossible, and thus *due to* is acceptable. But "Because of Asian flu, he missed three days of school" is fine, and so *due to* is not. All this, let me make clear again, is balderdash in the view of modern authorities, who permit us to scatter *due to*'s where we like.

*Due to the fact that,* a popular locution, is objectionable not because it uses *due to* as a preposition, but because it is the long way around for *because*.

**duo.**   P. 96.

**during the course of.**   Redundant for *during*.

### E

**each other's.**   Doubt is sometimes felt whether *each other's* is a proper form. It is indeed: "They mistakenly took each other's hats."

**Easter Sunday.**   Technically redundant, but so well established that criticism of this expression is quibbling.

**economic, -al.**   Although *economic* may mean either *pertaining to the science of economics,* or *money-saving,* usage generally favors *economical* in the sense of *money-saving:* "*Economic,* as well as social, factors were considered"; "The use of dried milk is economical."

**editorial we.**   Pp. 72-74.

**-ee.**   It has been useless for some time to insist that the termination *-ee* denotes the person (or thing) to which something is done, rather than the doer. True, the *lessor* is the one who grants the lease, and the *lessee* is the one to whom it is granted. The *draftee* is the one who is drafted. The *addressee* is the one to whom something is addressed. The *appointee* is the one who is appointed. The *employee* is the one who is employed.

But this pattern is far from invariable. The *refugee* is not the one who is given refuge, necessarily, but the one who seeks it. The *standee* is not the one who is stood (up?), but the one who stands. Similarly, *escapee* has Webster's recognition as one who escapes.

Nevertheless, it is usual for *-ee* to denote the doee, rather than the doer to. There is a tendency to coin words, often with the intention of humorous effect, by adding *-ee: handshakee, nicknamee.* A surprising number of such expressions have found their way into Webster, among others *civilizee, counselee, interviewee, permittee, quizzee.*

**effect.**   See *affect, effect.*

**egghead.**   At worst, this is a disparaging, and at best, a patronizing, term for *intellectual,* though why intellectuals should be either disparaged or patronized is a sad question. *Egghead* was said to have been first applied to the followers of Adlai Stevenson by a Connecticut Republican, John

Alsop, whose brother, Stewart, used it in a nationally syndicated newspaper column on Sept. 26, 1952, *Newsweek* reported. Warwick Deeping,
however, wrote of "a little eggheaded pedant" in *Second Youth* in 1920.
Those who enjoy demeaning intellectuals as eggheads might ponder these
words of Ken Purdy as they appeared in the *Democratic Digest*:

> "Whatever illusions to the contrary they are currently entertaining in Wash-
> ington, the fact of the matter is that the world, when it is a place worth living
> in, is run by eggheads. It was an egghead, not a practical man, who found fire,
> an egghead cut the first wheel and wrote the first law. The bow and arrow was
> invented by an egghead, and the atomic bomb was made possible by an egg-
> head—a long-haired egghead at that—who sat for a long time staring at some
> funny symbols on a blackboard. The practical men—characters with the talents
> of bricklayers who wear signs on their chests saying 'I am a Production Genius'
> —are apt to forget that they owe their very reasons for existence, always and
> in every case, to an intellectual."

**egoist, egotist.**   The egoist places his own interest first as a principle of
conduct; the egotist is a braggart. The distinction, however, is being
blurred by careless interchange, and in any event seems to be of little
value, since the one is likely to be the other.

**elderly.**   The word means *getting on in years,* and efforts, especially by
newspaper editors, to fix a starting point, say at sixty or seventy years of
age, for the application of the term constitute one of their more harmless
follies in the field of language. It is noticeable that, as they themselves
grow older, their starting point tends to rise. Elderliness, like many other
qualities, often resides in the eye of the beholder. To a teenager, her
parents of forty are likely to qualify for this descriptive. To a more lenient
judge, elderliness is beyond middle age. *Elderly,* unless applied conspicuously too soon, is a gentler term than *aged* or *old,* and as such has its uses.

**electronic, -s.**   P. 26.

**elegant variation.**   P. 109.

**elevated.**   As a substitute for *high* ("Elevated temperatures are a symptom
of disease"), *elevated* is pretentious. This is true also to some extent of its
use in place of *promoted*: "He was *elevated* to his present position last
January."

**ellipsis.**   General, pp. 56-57; of verb forms, p. 57; of pronoun plus *to be,*
p. 57; to avoid repetition, p. 56; with numerical comparisons, p. 58; indication of, p. 58.

**else's.**   Forms like *everyone's else* and *nobody's else* are technically correct and were once in common use, but now they sound like gaucheries. The accepted forms are *somebody else's* and *nobody else's*. "His fan mail outruns *everyone's else*" should be "His fan mail outruns *everyone else's*."

**elusive.**   See *allusive, elusive, illusive*.

**emigrate, immigrate.**   The choice here is a matter of viewpoint. One who leaves a country *emigrates* from it, one who comes in *immigrates*. Thus someone in the United States may speak of a person emigrating from another country, or immigrating into this one. The same principle holds for *emigrant* and *immigrant*.

   *Out-migration* and *in-migration* are illegitimate substitutes born, apparently, of a combination of ignorance and desperation.

**eminently, imminently.**   It is a terrible reflection on the state of the language that any such distinction as this should have to be explained, but there it is. *Eminently* means *notably* or *conspicuously*: "The settlement was considered *eminently* fair." *Imminently* means *in a short time* or *very soon,* and is usually said of something that threatens: "The attack was expected *imminently*." Then there's *immanent,* which means *existing within*: "The god was regarded as being *immanent* in the stone image." *Immanently,* a rarity in its proper sense, sometimes turns up in the place of *imminently*.

**endearment, terms of.**   *Dear, darling, honey, sweetheart,* and the like, as habitually employed between husbands and wives, are good examples of words that have been squeezed dry of their meanings. All of us have heard *dear* uttered in a tone that could only be described as a snarl. The effect would be laughable if any consciousness of the meaning of the term remained. Used over and over as terms of address, such endearments quickly lose all their warmth. It may be that no love is great enough to sustain the continuous use, with any sincerity, of endearments as terms of address. Thus, when you come right down to it, the habit of using them is really stupid.

   Couples who have a genuine respect for the meanings of words are likely to address each other by their given names, except on occasions that call for something else. Given names are neutral to begin with, and it is easier to invest them with a snarl or a caress than it is to put reverse English on *dear*, or even to put the juice back into it.

   While we are on this subject, someone ought to do a survey on whether the practice of husbands and wives calling each other *Mama* and *Daddy* after the arrival of the first offspring is dying out, as it appears to be. By adopting the terms properly applicable to them by their children, parents

are really sacrificing their adulthood, in a sense, and identifying themselves with their children. When a child hears his father calling his mother
*Mama,* he may get the impression that they both have the same relation
to her.

**ended, ending.**   *Ended* is preferably used of what is past, *ending* of what is
to come. "The report covers the decade *ended* (not *ending*) in 1950."
"He is enrolled in a course *ending* next year." *Ended* never displaces
*ending,* though the reverse often happens. See p. 24 for more discussion
of the tenses of participles.

**endorse, indorse.**   *Endorse,* it was once held, meant to write one's name
upon, and *indorse* to approve or vouch for. Thus, strictly, one would
*endorse* a check and *indorse* a product. But this distinction has gone the
way of *continuous* vs. *continual. Indorse* and *endorse* are cited by Webster
as synonyms. Both words are now freely used in both senses, except that
*endorse* seems to be putting *indorse* out of business altogether. There is
no loss here, really, for the context always shows which of the original
senses is meant.

**engine, motor.**   The occasional efforts to pretend there is a distinction
between *engine* and *motor* that can be consistently applied are wasted.
Idiom holds sway here. Machines run by steam are always *engines*; those
run by gasoline are indifferently *engines* or *motors*; those run by electricity
are nearly always *motors.* Derivation is no help; a *motor* is that which
imparts motion, and an *engine* is that which has been produced by in-
genuity. The word *engine* is sometimes applied to machines run by electricity but having a reciprocal action. In rocketry, *engine* is applied to
rockets that use liquid fuels, and *motor* to those that use solid fuels.

**engineer, scientist.**   With the ever-enlarging role of science, scientists have
expressed annoyance at the use of their designation for others. The general
distinction is that a scientist is concerned with the creation of knowledge,
and an engineer with its application. Others who apply technical knowledge but do not originate it may be properly referred to as *technicians,*
in the absence of some more explicit designation. The term *scientist* is so
general, even if properly used, that it is hardly satisfactory these days.
Some more explicit designation, such as *biologist, astronomer,* or *physicist,*
is desirable.

**enigmatic.**   The word means *puzzling* or *mysterious,* but is often misused
in the sense of *dubious* or *questionable.* "The success of the new system
is *enigmatic*" was intended to mean, not that the success was inscrutable,
but that it was in doubt.

**enormity, enormousness.** The fight against *enormity* (which strictly means wickedness on a large scale) in the sense of *enormousness* is probably all but lost. Webster defines *enormity* as "State or quality of being enormous, esp., exceeding wickedness . . ." *Enormity* is used far oftener in this sense, disregarding the *esp.,* than otherwise, and no one misunderstands. The difficulty seems to be that a noun derived from *enormous* is needed, and *enormousness* is clumsy. The *Oxford English Dictionary* defines *enormity* in the sense of "excess in magnitude" as an incorrect use, but it also notes that this error dates from 1846. Since the context unmistakably shows the sense, there seems no reasonable objection to acceptance of *hugeness* as a meaning of *enormity*.

**ensure, insure.** *Ensure* and *insure* are interchangeable in the sense *make certain*: "Hard work will not *ensure* success"; "Careful workmanship *insures* quality," but *ensure* has a noticeable edge. *Insure* is predominant in the sense *guarantee against loss*.

**enthuse.** *Enthuse,* meaning to express enthusiasm, has made its way into the dictionaries, though it is designated a colloquialism. That designation is nothing against it, but *enthuse* remains under a shadow cast by the contexts in which it is found.

**equally as.** P. 55.

**ere.** See *poesy*.

**espantoon.** Remember the adage to the effect that it is the shoemaker's children who go barefoot? Well, on the one hand there was H. L. Mencken, who was more prominently identified with Baltimore than any other man of letters, with the possible exception of Edgar Allan Poe. He lived there all his seventy-five years. One of his leading works is *The American Language,* which contains thousands of fascinating histories of American expressions. On the other hand we have *espantoon,* a word that apparently began in Baltimore, and whose use seems to have been pretty well confined to that city. It means *a policeman's night stick,* or *truncheon*.

You might expect that Mencken, who combed the continent for his scholarly and interesting etymologies, would have given the full treatment to *espantoon,* a curious expression on his own doorstep. But although he used the word, both in the basic volume and in the first supplement, he did not deal with its origin. According to Webster, *espantoon* is a variant of *spontoon,* which comes from the Italian *spontone*. A spontoon is described as "a kind of half-pike formerly borne by officers of infantry; hence, a policeman's club . . ."

But the story of just how *espantoon* was born and came to be the exclusive property of Baltimore apparently remains to be told.

**estate.**   *Estate* has had a damaging comedown, at least in real-estate promotion. No one is surprised or even amused any more to find ordinary subdivisions ballyhooed as "estates"; the term has even been applied to trailer parks. It's almost enough to make a man wish he weren't rich.

**estimated.**   P. 99.

**-eth.**   The unavoidable demand on the writer who gets cute is that he know what he is doing. He makes an unnecessary ass of himself, for example, by using foreign words or phrases in the wrong sense, or by misspelling them. After having gone out of his way to exhibit his erudition, he is surely in a ridiculous position when he shows that his grip on it is shaky. By the same token, if he finds it desirable to revert to Middle English for special effect, he ought to keep in mind that the termination *-eth* goes only with the third person singular (*he, she, it*) : *He thinketh, she smileth, "The Iceman Cometh."* Most of us pick this principle up by osmosis, from the Bible and other ancient readings: "I will lift up mine eyes unto the hills, from whence *cometh* my help." It invites derision to write things like *I cometh, you smileth.* The second-person form is *-st,* and it calls for *thou* as a subject. (Quaker usage is specialized, and invariably calls for *thee.*)

**euphemisms.**   Pp. 61-62.

**evacuate.**   In the sense of *remove people from a place, evacuate* is standard, accepted usage, superstition to the contrary.

**evince.**   *Evince,* though good English, has tended to become a newspaper variant for *show*.

**ex-.**   P. 79.

**except, excepting.**   *Excepting* where *except* will serve is not only exceptionable but disagreeable. It may reflect the justly scorned love of the long word. At any rate, no one who knows *excepting* can be unaware of *except*. *Excepting* has its own uses, and ringing a change on *except* is not among them. An example: "Everything about the new cars is easier to handle *excepting* the payments." *Excepting* as a preposition is acceptable only if it follows *not* (*not excepting the payments*).

**exclamation point.**   Formed on typewriter, see *typewriter tricks*.

**ex-convict.**   P. 79.

**ex-felon.**   P. 79.

**exhaust.**   This is a transitive verb, which means it must take an object. "She *exhausted* easily" should have been "She *became exhausted* easily."

**exist, existing.**   The notion that only what is alive exists is a superstition. *Exist* means *be* as well as *live,* and is properly applied to inanimate things and even insubstantial ones, such as ideas. See also *presently.*

**expect.**   See *anticipate.*

**expensive.**   *Expensive* means high priced. "The average man finds the prices pretty *expensive*" is an absurdity. He found the *goods* expensive, the *prices* high. See also *cheap.*

**extended.**   Unnecessary, inexact, and pretentious as a variant of *long,* as in *an extended illness.* What is extended is that which has been given greater extent, and thus an extended illness is not simply a long one, but one that has gained a new grip on its victim after signs of remitting.

# F

**facts.**   A good, solid word, as satisfyingly reliable as what it means, but you would never know this from the mealymouthed way it is often used. For example, "The true *facts,* on the other hand, are . . ." A fact is either true or not a fact. The frequent remark, "He has his *facts* wrong," is nonsense. If what he has are wrong, they are not facts. The same thing applies to *actual facts, real facts.*

**fail.**   This word carries a strong implication of falling short in an attempt, but it is often used where there is no question of an attempt: "Buckingham Palace *failed* to confirm the story"; "The burning bed *failed* to disturb the sleeper"; "The weekend of rain *failed* to affect the river level." If there is any virtue in direct statement, *did not confirm, did not disturb,* and *did not affect* are preferable.

**fair-trade laws.**   A political euphemism. Fair-trade laws have nothing to do with fair trade from the consumer's viewpoint; their purpose is to force retailers to maintain a price structure fixed by the manufacturer, a device that the bargain-hunter, at least, considers highly unfair, as does the cut-rate merchant. Many publications, unwilling to fall into the trap of mis-representation that is set by this term, preface it by *so-called.* See also *right-to-work laws.*

**false comparison.**   Pp. 59-60.

**false linkage.**   By omission of commas, pp. 89-90.

**false possessive.**   P. 68.

**false titles.**   P. 107.

**falsies.**   See *bosom, breast.*

**farther, further.**   Some lost souls worry about the applications of these words. The purist holds that *farther* applies to distance and *further* to anything else, e. g., *a farther journey, a further consideration.* Few writers appear to be aware of this distinction, however, and some who are ignore it. This may be the kind of choice best governed by ear. Fowler hazarded that *further* would drive out *farther,* since *further* may be used both to indicate distance and in the figurative sense (*a further* [*farther*] *journey*), whereas *farther* will not do in the figurative sense: *a further* (never *farther*) *consideration. Further* and *farther* are both still actively in use, however. The use of *farther,* as we have seen, is naturally restricted by idiom; attempts to place limits on *further* serve no purpose.

**faze, phase.**   *Faze* means *disconcert* or *daunt,* and it is usually used with a negative: "We were not *fazed* by the setback." *Phase,* often wrongly used in that sense, is a noun meaning *aspect*: "The lecturer described the *phases* of the moon." With *in* or *out, phase* is a verb, usually found in military contexts, with the meaning *place in* (or *take out of*) *operation,* both by stages: "This program will be *phased in* by Christmas." This use may have caused the confusion of *phase* with *faze.*

**feature.**   As a verb meaning "exhibit as a prominent aspect," this word is in good standing but often overworked: "Yankee Stadium usually *features* bases 90 feet apart"; "The new church will *feature* a large sanctuary." In instances like this, it would be better to use simply *has* and *will have,* or to give a more unmistakable emphasis to what is being pointed out as a feature.

**feel.**   Alice Hamilton, M.D., gave good usage a shot in the arm with an article, "Words Lost, Strayed, or Stolen," in the September, 1954, *Atlantic.* Her needle touched a nerve in me when she found amusing "the increasing rejection of *believe* and *think* in favor of *feel.*" The prejudice against *feel* in this sense has long seemed to be a superstition, especially in its rabid form, to the effect that nothing is felt that is not apprehended by the sense of touch. True, the good doctor did not go to that extreme. But then all cats are gray at night, and disapprovers of *feel* in any other than the tactile sense will quote such diagnoses as hers to their purpose. The virus must be isolated before it spreads.

To the extent that no word is the exact equivalent of another, *feel* is not the exact equivalent of *think* or *believe*. Its use, however, does not necessarily imply reliance on the feelings or emotions. In the general meaning of *have a notion, be more or less convinced,* or *sense,* it is well enough established to be beyond cavil. Shakespeare used the word in that way: "Garlands, Griffith, which I feel I am not worthy yet to wear" ("Henry VIII"); so did Trollope—"She felt that she might yet recover her lost ground" (*Barchester Towers*); Thomas Hardy—". . . we feel our rout is imminent . . ." (*An Ancient to Ancients*); and Abraham Lincoln— "It is difficult to make a man miserable while he feels he is worthy of himself."

*Feel* has numerous extensions, and some lexicographers, it is true, do not divorce it from emotion. Webster counterpoises "to believe, esp. on vague or indefinite grounds" (score one for our side) with "to be convinced of emotionally rather than intellectually" (game tied, 1-1, at end of first inning). The *Oxford English Dictionary* gives one sense as "to apprehend or recognize the truth of something on grounds not distinctly perceived." It is not easy to perceive distinctly what the learned dons are driving at here, but look at an example they cite: "The proposed legislation was felt to be expedient." Substitute *believed* or *thought* for *felt,* and if the result makes you queasy, call Dr. Hamilton.

Oddly, a sense the OED specifies as "to believe, think, hold as an opinion" is designated obsolete. Examples are cited from writings going back as far as 1382, however, which indicates at least that the modern and apparently growing use springs from an ancient and possibly noble line. We may ignore the fact that many such lines have produced bastards, because people who make their way in the world establish their own reputability. So do words.

A revival seems afoot, however, because the *American College Dictionary* defines *feel* as "to have a general or thorough conviction of"; the *General Basic English Dictionary* as "have idea that"; and *Webster's New World Dictionary of the American Language* as "to think; believe; consider." At least two synonymies can be mustered for our cause. *Laird's Promptory* gives *to believe* as one sense of *feel,* and offers as equivalents "consider, hold, sense; see THINK, BELIEVE." Allen's *Synonyms and Antonyms* gives *believe* as a synonym of *feel.*

*Feel,* then, does not appear to be such bad medicine after all. If they are not too bitter a pill, these lines, spoken by the Prince of Wales in "Henry IV," Part II, may be prescribed for all who would impugn useful words on shaky grounds:

> "I feel me much to blame,
> So idly to profane the precious time."

**feel bad, badly.** There is a widespread notion that *feel badly* is the correct form, *feel bad* an error. It may be based on the fairly tenable assumption that *bad* is not a reputable adverb. Usage has pretty well established *feel badly* as describing remorse or regret; *feel bad* is limited to describing physical discomfort. One who says he feels badly when he is sick is likely to be misleading.

**feminine forms.** Many of these, such as *ancestress, aviatrix, authoress, poetess, postmistress,* have fallen into disuse, perhaps proving that equality of the sexes is truly here. *Postmistress* is not recognized by the federal government, which designates all postmasters *postmasters*.

**fewer, less.** The rule is that *fewer* applies to individually distinguishable units (*fewer people, ships, houses*), and *less* to what is not (*less sugar, less time*). It is conspicuously apparent, however, as Perrin notes, that "*Fewer* seems to be declining in use and *less* commonly takes its place." *Less people* is so common as not to attract the attention even of purists. Perrin cites *less hands* and *three less seats*.

**fictitious.** Often misspelled *ficticious*. The word has a favorite application to checks written with intent to defraud. *Fraudulent* seems a better choice here, for, as Webster points out, "*fictitious* implies fabrication and, so, more often suggests artificiality or contrivance than intent to deceive or deliberate falsification." The word distinctly connotes fiction rather than fraud.

**fight with, against.** *Fight with* is ambiguous: "He fought with the Spaniards" fairly prompts the question, "Which side was he on?" The context usually explains. Nevertheless, *fight against* or recasting are worth consideration.

**figures.** Vs. words in text, pp. 96-98; starting a sentence, p. 99; see also *numbers*.

**finalize.** *Finalize,* like *implement* as a verb, is hopelessly associated with gobbledygook, and the user can only expect to bring scorn on himself.

**fine.** The idea that *fine* may not be used to denote superior quality, as in *a fine man, a fine day,* but must be reserved for the idea of physical fineness (*fine-grained*) is a superstition. It is true, however, as noted by the Evanses, that *fine* is not in the best standing in the sense of *well,* as in "He is doing fine."

**finishing touch.** Sentences employing this phrase are often subjected to some painful twists. A finishing touch sounds like something that would be *given* a building, plan, or whatever. But frequently we see that finishing touches are being *made to, made on,* or *put to.* For example: "He put a personal touch *to* his story"—surely a saucerie for "He gave his story a personal touch." There does exist, of course, the touch that is *put on,* the touch for a fin before pay day, which is just as painful but in a different way.

**firm.**    This word has the technical meaning of *a partnership.* In the general sense of *a business establishment,* however, it is so widely accepted that the more restrictive sense is now useful only to lawyers and in legal documents.

**first and foremost.**    May be left to the political orators, together with *view with pride* and *point with alarm.*

**flag.**    See *newspaper terms.*

**flagship.**    "The PRESIDENT JACKSON was the first American flagship to enter the canal." Unhappy compression is at the root of the trouble. The writer meant "the first ship flying an American flag," but by condensing it, presumably to "the first American-flag ship," set the stage for "the first American flagship." Now, this is totally confusing and erroneous, for a flagship, as every old salt knows, is a naval vessel carrying the commander of a force, or occasionally, a merchantman designated as foremost in a fleet.

**flaming inferno.**    Redundant. An inferno is a hell, and the use of the word for something that is burning permits no doubt as to the variety of hell.

**flammable, inflammable.**    Fire underwriters and others interested in safety have promoted the use of *flammable* in preference to *inflammable,* on the assumption that *inflammable* may be misunderstood to mean *noncombustible.* This reasoning may have some merit, and there is a noticeable increase in the use of *flammable,* though *inflammable* has by no means been driven to the wall. As to usage, the words are equally reputable.

**flatter, flattery.**    Flattery, as we all know, is insincere praise, but the ad writers have found a new, and in their idiom, sincere, use for the word in applying it to articles of clothing, as in saying a girdle *flatters* the figure. The word may be left to the hucksters in this sense, together with their concept of sincerity.

**flaunt, flout.**    Often confused. *Flaunt* means to display in an ostentatious or boastful manner: "The faction *flaunted* its superior strength." *Flout* means *mock*: "A speeding motorist *flouts* the law."

**following.** In the sense of *after* ("*Following* the movie, they had some ice cream"), *following* is sometimes damned, but the worst that can fairly be said of it is that *after* is shorter, plainer, and more natural.

**for.** Vs. *as* in attribution, p. 140.

**force, -d.** Often used inappropriately, conveying a stronger sense of compulsion than is warranted. "Pupils through the third grade at the Roosevelt School will be *forced* to attend half-day sessions this term." This conjures up an image of the wretched kids manacled together and marching to their half-sessions in lock step. It would be more in key with the circumstances to say "Half-day sessions *will be necessary*" or that the pupils *will have to attend* half-day sessions. "If the county cannot make up its mind, the city will be *forced* to make other plans." *Will have to.* "Some of the sixteen squad cars were *forced* to go bouncing over bumpy roads to catch the elusive hot rods." *Had to go.*

**former, latter.** Strictly correct usage requires that *former,* even when used without *latter,* may refer only to the first of two. In the light of this rule, a mistake is made in writing "He spotted a man and a woman and two children, all obviously hurt, the *former* most seriously." The right words here would be *the first* or *the man.* Although *former* and *latter* are correctly used in denoting each of two, one school of thought regards this device as merely a puzzle that makes the hapless reader look back and figure out which is which.

Samuel Johnson, if we can trust Boswell, belonged to this school:

> "He disapproved of parentheses; and I believe in all his voluminous writings, not half a dozen of them will be found. He never used the phrases *the former* and *the latter,* having observed, that they often occasioned obscurity; he therefore contrived to construct his sentences so as not to have occasion for them, and would even rather repeat the same words, in order to avoid them."

**for the purpose of.** Unnecessary verbiage in place of an infinitive construction. *For the purpose of circumventing* equals *to circumvent.* "The lawsuit was filed *for the purpose of intimidating* the mayor" (*filed to intimidate*). See also *so as to, in order to.*

**for the (simple) reason that.** Excess verbiage for *because.* Beyond this, the use of *simple* insults the reader's intelligence.

**fortuitous, fortunate.** *Fortuitous* means simply *chance* or *accidental,* as in a *fortuitous encounter.* It is incorrectly used in the sense of *fortunate,* as in a *fortuitous* deal.

**fouled up.** This slang expression seems to have come into general use via the Navy during the war. *Fouled,* in a legitimate nautical sense, means *tangled;* it is generally said of anchors whose chains are wound around them, and two crossed, fouled anchors form the insigne of a Navy officer's hat. Let those who may see a touch of poetic justice in this. Nothing seems more natural than the conversion of *fouled* into *fouled up,* meaning *hopelessly confused.* This gave rise in turn to *snafu* (situation normal; all fouled up), now being forgotten. But *fouled up* may be distasteful, not because it is slang, but because of the repulsive suggestion of *fouled* in its most general sense.

**fractions.** Pp. 98-99.

**Frankenstein.** P. 145.

**free pass, free gift.** A pass by definition is free, as is a gift.

**friendlily.** A perfectly good word, but seldom used because of its awkward sound.

**from.** Vs. *of,* p. 47.

**from where, whence.** "This was their last meeting place, *from where* they were sent on individual missions." This construction is sometimes criticized on the ground that *where* is an adverb and cannot be the object of a preposition. *Where,* however, may also be a pronoun. Even so, *from where,* though fairly common, cannot be said to have any real pretensions to good usage. The prejudice against it has some inconsistencies. Invert the word order, and it is acceptable: "*Where* did the cake come *from?*" equals "*From where* did the cake come?" but the latter is clearly less acceptable English. *Here* has established itself in similar constructions (*From Here to Eternity*), and no one objects. So has *there*: "*From there* the trail winds through a meadow." And so, some day, may *where,* but the day is not yet here. *Whence* will grammatically take the place of *from where* (and *from which*), but it has a bookish sound. Nevertheless, *whence* (like *thence, from that place*) might usefully be placed in common service. *From whence* is technically redundant (*the port from whence he will sail*) but some critics regard this as a quibble. In summary, prepositions before *where* (*to where, from where*) are noticeably avoided.

**front runner.** P. 145.

**fulsome.** Means *excessive* or *disgusting,* not *ample* or *abundant.* Fulsome praise is objectionable, not lavish, praise, contrary to what many writers think.

**furlough, leave.** *Furlough* is no longer in use; all branches of the military now say *leave.*

**furnish.**   You say you're not superstitious? All right, put your little hand in mine and we'll walk under a ladder. Superstition holds that *furnish* is not properly used in the sense of *supply;* you can *furnish* a home, the argument runs (i.e., equip it with furniture), but you cannot *furnish* the beer for a picnic (linguistically, that is). If this is one of your pet notions, Webster has a jolt for you. He says the word means "provide . . . equip; fit out or up." A corollary, as a superstition, is that *furniture* is what you put in a house, and *furnishings* what a men's store, for example, sells. *Furnishings* is correct in both senses.

**further.**   See *farther*.

**fused participle.**   This is the name invented by Fowler to designate a subject of a gerund that is in the objective, rather than the possessive, case. "I object to *him* being appointed," then, is an example of the fused participle; "I object to *his* being appointed" is supposedly the correct form. The principle applies to nouns as well as to pronouns: "She resented *John's* ringing the doorbell."

The possessive is far from invariable in this construction, however. Curme, who went into the subject more exhaustively than Fowler, cites numerous examples from good writers to show that the possessive is often impossible or undesirable, and that the tendency is to use the objective ("I object to *him* being appointed") even when the possessive *is* possible. The possessive is most likely to be used when the subject of the gerund is a pronoun. But Curme writes: "We regularly use the accusative [that is, objective] when the subject is emphatic: 'She was proud of *him* doing it.' The emphasis often comes from contrasting the subjects: 'We seem to think nothing of *a boy smoking,* but resent *a girl smoking.*' "

Fowler expressed the pious hope that his discussion would leave readers sick to death of the fused participle, but the sad truth is that most of the examples he cited to bring on this mortal illness do not even make us queasy today.

**future.**   In redundancies, p. 54.

**future plans.**   Redundant, as is *advance plans,* since plans, unless otherwise qualified, are inevitably for the future.

## G

**gag, gagged.**   See *quip, quipped*.

**gauge.**   This word gives so much trouble, often being misspelled *guage,* that it's a wonder the simpler variant *gage* has not displaced it. *Gage* is generally preferred in technical writing, perhaps because of this difficulty.

**gendarme.**  As pointed out in *Watch Your Language*, a gendarme is not the counterpart of an American policeman, but rather of a sheriff's officer or state policeman. French cities have policemen; villages and other small communities have what we would call constables. The use of *gendarme,* then, in indiscriminate reference to any French police officer is inaccurate, and in reference to an American policeman is heavy, worn-out humor.

**general public.**  Says nothing that *public* alone does not, when there is no contrast with some segment of the public.

**geographical descriptives.**  Pp. 103-104.

**gerunds.**  Gerund construction (*the ——ing of*), pp. 65-66; case of subject of gerund, see *fused participle*.

**get.**  See *got; secure, obtain*.

**Ghana, Ghanaian.**  P. 103.

**gibe, jibe.**  *Gibe* means *jeer at*: "The hazing went no farther than *gibing* at the freshmen." *Jibe* means *match* or *correspond with*: "His performance did not *jibe* with his campaign promises." It is true that *gibe* is recognized as a variant of *jibe*, but careful usage preserves the distinction. Confusion is encouraged by the fact that the words are pronounced identically.

**glamour, glamor, glamourous.**  *Glamour* is the preferred American spelling (as well as the British) although generally *o* is preferred in America where the British use *ou*: *labor* (*labour*), *honor* (*honour*). But *glamorous* is the preferred spelling for the adjective (not *glamourous*).

**gobbledygook.**  The use of this term in its present accepted sense (the turgid language characteristic of bureaucracy) was established by Maury Maverick in an article that appeared May 21, 1944, in the *New York Times Magazine*. *Governmentese, federalese, officialese,* and, in England, *pudder,* are sometimes used in this sense, but *gobbledygook* predominates. Curiously, the word is sometimes spelled gobbledegook; this is the way it appears, for instance, in the *American College Dictionary*, but Webster and the OED recognize only *gobbledygook*. The *y*-version is commoner, and, in any event, is the one Maverick used. Such versions as *gobble-de-gook* and *gobbledygock* must be regarded as errors.

Perhaps the best illustration of *gobbledygook,* and its cure, developed in a wartime press conference at which President Franklin D. Roosevelt read an order concerning blackouts that had been prepared by the director of civilian defense:

"Such preparations shall be made as will completely obscure all federal buildings and nonfederal buildings occupied by the federal government during an air raid for any period of time from visibility by reason of internal or external illumination. Such obscuration may be obtained either by blackout construction or by terminating the illumination. This will of course require that in building areas in which production must continue during a blackout, construction must be provided that internal illumination may continue. Other areas, whether or not occupied by personnel, may be obscured by terminating the illumination."

After the reading of this order had been interrupted several times by laughter, Roosevelt directed that it be reworded:

"Tell them that in buildings that will have to keep their work going, put something across the windows. In buildings that can afford it, so that work can be stopped for awhile, turn out the lights."

**got, gotten.**   An uneasy idea persists that *gotten* is improper. This may grow out of the fact that the form has passed out of use in England. Where Americans say *have gotten,* the English say *have got. Have gotten* (meaning *have obtained,* as in "We *have gotten* the provisions") is correct and idiomatic in the United States. "We *have got* the provisions," the English version, sounds affected here, although this might be said as an intensive of *have.* As for *got,* efforts to avoid it by substituting *obtained,* or any other word the writer must strain after, are misspent. When *got* comes naturally, it should be used.

**graduated, was graduated.**   There are those who still insist one cannot say a student *graduated* from college, but must say he *was graduated.* The passive form is not only clumsy, but unsupported by usage. In bygone days, the superstition that only *was graduated* was correct held full sway, but this is now all but forgotten except by pedants.

**'gras (asparagus).**   Newcomers to the great Delta region lying between San Francisco and Stockton, Calif., are temporarily puzzled by newspaper references to *'gras,* especially in headlines. Before long they find out that *'gras* is Westernese for *asparagus,* one of the most valuable crops of that region. Now how in the name of all that's agricultural does *asparagus* become *'gras?* Well, asparagus, both in this country and England, has been known as sparrowgrass, an expression explained as an illiterate corruption. Hence *'gras,* although this abridgment of a corruption is in such common use and apparently has been established so long it is hard to find a user of it who knows its origin.

**gray, grey.**   *Gray* is the preferred spelling in America, *grey* in Britain.

**group words (collectives).**   Pp. 70-71.

**guild.**   See *newspaper terms.*

# H

**had.** It is pedantically and, as usually follows, erroneously argued that such wording as "The man had his driver's license revoked" is objectionable. It suggests, the critics say, that the man deliberately instigated the revocation. This, however, is wrongheaded. Such constructions are correct in every way and their meaning is clear. One of the definitions of *have* in Webster is "to suffer or experience from an external source; as, he had his back broken."

A related idiom is illustrated by "The woman broke her back in a bobsled accident." This is criticized on the same grounds as the foregoing, and with the same lack of basis. Those who say such a sentence will be understood as meaning that the injury was self-inflicted ought to have their heads examined. Anyone who objects to *the woman broke her back* would also have to object to *I broke my leg,* or *He stubbed his toe,* or *She cut her finger.*

**hail, hale.** *Hale,* in the sense that concerns us here, means *haul*; people are *haled* (not *hailed*) into court. *Hail* means *call, shout a greeting,* or *acclaim*: "We *hailed* a taxi"; "The new king was *hailed* by the multitude."

**handle in routine fashion.** Overelaboration of *handle routinely.*

**handsome.** See *attractive.*

**hang.** See *hung.*

**healthful, healthy.** The difference between *healthful* as meaning *conducive to health* ("Eating apples is *healthful*") and *healthy* as meaning *possessing health* ("The children are all *healthy*") is a fading distinction. *Healthy* is pretty well accepted in both senses ("this climate is *healthy*"). *Healthful* may disappear, since it never does duty for *healthy.*

**heart attack.** The idea that *heart attack* conveys an attack upon, or by, the heart, and thus cannot be used to describe a seizure is absurd. The expression is part of the language, and certainly it is preferable to the newly prevalent *coronary* and *cardiac* in reference to heart attacks. Technical language is best left to those equipped to use it exactly. *Coronary* properly is an adjective, but it is metamorphosing into a noun ("He had a *coronary* [i.e., *heart attack*] last November"). See also p. 62.

**height, heighth.** *Heighth* is a common misspelling of *height* that probably grows out of a mispronunciation. But *height* is pronounced *hite* and not *highth.*

**he or she; his or her.** P. 109.

**helicopter.** Mispronunciation as *heeliocopter* may cause a written error, *heliocopter*. *Helio* is the prefix used to indicate some connection with the sun, as in *heliograph,* a device that transmits messages by using the sun's rays, and *heliotrope,* a flower that turns toward the sun. It all goes back to Helios, a Greek name for the sun god. But *helicopter* (correctly pronounced *hell*—you should pardon the expression—*icopter*) comes from *helix,* meaning *spiral,* and *pteron,* meaning *wing.*

**high, highly.** Although *high* may be an adverb ("The plane circled *high* above the city"), the choice between *high* and *highly* appears to be governed by idiom. As an attributive modifier (before what it modifies), *highly* seems preferable; as a predicate modifier (after what it modifies), *high* is required. *Highly paid executive* is preferable to *high-paid executive.* Yet *highly priced* is intolerable for *high-priced.* (*High-price,* as in *high-price advice,* is deplorable for *high-priced.*) *High-strung* and *high-toned* are also established before and after what they modify.

**highlight.** Although some dictionaries make two words of *highlight* as a noun ("The song was the *high light* of the concert"), the fact that there is general agreement on one word as a verb ("The speech will *highlight* education"), and the consensus of usage of both forms, in addition to the way it is spoken, indicate that *highlight* is to be preferred. *High light* may be momentarily taken to mean a light that is high, rather than a prominent feature.

**hike.** Journalese for *raise* or *increase*: "Wages were hiked as a result of the strike."

**historic, -al.** The difference between these words is subtle, but their incorrect use is nonetheless jarring. *Historical* means *pertaining to history*: *A historical account. Historic* means *contributing to,* or *making, history*: *A historic expedition.* A historical novel is one based on, or dealing with, history; a historic novel is a literary landmark, one that makes history. "The *historical* ranch changed hands recently" contains a palpable error; the word should be *historic.*

**hold steady.** This is an idiom, and he who makes it *hold steadily* is painting the lily.

**holdup.** See *burglary.*

**Homeric.** This word, obviously, means *pertaining to Homer*. Homeric laughter is defined as inexpressible or inextinguishable laughter. But there appears to be no occasion to use *Homeric* in the sense of *heroic* or *Herculean,* as in "The managers show no gratitude for the *Homeric* services done them." Such misuses as this may be productive, in scholarly quarters, of Homeric laughter.

**home town, hometown.** See *back yard.*

**honeymoon.** This is another of the words sometimes forbidden by the muttonheads who compile style manuals; in its stead they prescribe *wedding trip.* But *honeymoon* also has a larger meaning, as in figurative application of "The *honeymoon* is over."

**honor.** To honor is to pay tribute to; the word should not be used in the sense of *mark* or *observe,* as in "The community will *honor* Public Schools Week." Only beings or their deeds can be honored.

**honorary degrees.** P. 107.

**hooky.** (*Play hooky from school.*) Often misspelled *hookey.*

**host.** As a verb, *host* is not acceptable ("The East Side Club *hosted* the convention") although society writers love it. *Host* may well be left to them, together with *chair* as a verb, *benedict, justweds,* and *nuptials.*

**hot-water heater.** *Hot* is surely redundant in this expression, but it may be solidly enough established to have passed beyond criticism.

**however, how ever.** *However,* both as an adverb meaning *in whatever manner* and as a connective meaning *nevertheless,* must be distinguished from the adverbial pair *how ever,* an emphatic form of *how*: "It was a mystery, *however* he carried it off" (*in whatever manner*); "We noticed, *however,* that the money was not refunded" (*nevertheless*); "The neighbors wondered *how* they *ever* managed to pay off the mortgage" (*how*). In the last sense, *how* and *ever* properly are separated.

The main question about *however* as a connective is where to put it. The idea that it must not come first in the sentence is a superstition. Its function is to indicate a contrast, and it should not break a sentence except for that purpose. In "We noticed, however," the stress of contrast is laid against *We noticed.* If the arrangement were *We, however,* the stress would be against *we,* contrasted with others. If *however* comes first, the stress is against all that follows. The writer should decide what element of his sentence contains the contrast and place *however* accordingly. *But however,* as Fowler noted, is a redundancy; one or the other should be excised. When *however* is used as a connective, it is preceded by a semicolon: "Several topics of interest will be discussed; however, election of officers will be the main business of the meeting." The semicolon is necessary to relate *however* to the second clause.

**huddle.** Saying that city officials, for example, are going into a huddle is using an overworked figure.

**huge throng.** Redundant. A throng, by definition, is huge.

**huh-uh.** See *ah, aw*.

**human, -s.** *Human* as a noun (*Humans are sentient beings*) is not wrong, but is likely to sound either technical or quaint. The Evanses hold it desirable as a substitute for *men,* which, they say, serves double duty in representing all human beings (that's what they said—*human beings,* not *humans*) and males only. But what about *person* and *people*? These are the natural words to distinguish, for instance, between the human and the nonhuman. "The cast consists of nineteen humans and one goat" would sound better with *nineteen people*.

**humble opinion.** It may be arguable that the truly humble do not have opinions, but humbly adopt the views of their betters.

**hung.** Purists decry the use of this word for execution, holding that only *hanged* is proper in this sense. They say pictures are *hung,* people are *hanged*. Nonetheless, *hung* is prevalent and acceptable in both senses.

**hurl.** Often an overexcited variant of *make* or *throw,* especially in *hurl a charge,* a conspicuous concretion of the news columns. The great advances in rocketry have, among other things, given *hurl* another leg to stand on. Now satellites are invariably *hurled into orbit*. Yet this cliché, though newer than the other, is already just as tiresome.

**hyphens.** In compound modifiers, pp. 75-76; with figures, p. 76; used in dividing words, p. 77; with prefixes and suffixes, pp. 77-78; in phrasal verbs, pp. 76-77; with adverbs ending in *-ly,* p. 76.

**I**

**I.** Vs. editorial *we*, pp. 72-74.

**-ic, -ics.** Pp. 25-26.

**if . . . then.** The use of *then* to begin the conclusion that follows a conditional clause starting with *if* usually contributes an unnecessary emphasis, and may indicate an immature style. "If he can't be a bullfighter right away *then* he'd like to be a steeplejack." "If one Democrat deserts to a united opposition, *then* the vice-president can cast the deciding vote in the Senate." Delete the *thens*.

**if, whether.** The notion that these words are not interchangeable where they make sense is a superstition. "I do not know *whether* he will come" and "I do not know *if* he will come" are equally correct.

**ilk.** In spite of the objections of purists, *of that ilk* is no longer a strictly Scottish expression meaning *of the same* (*name, surname, place*). Its use in the sense *of that kind* ("a development *of that ilk*"; "a swindler *of that ilk*") is established, though facetious.

**ill.** See *sick*.

**illusive.** See *allusive, elusive, illusive*.

**immigrate.** See *emigrate, immigrate*.

**imminently.** See *eminently, imminently*.

**impact.** This word is equally the darling of the newswriter and of the composer of official prose. The newswriter likes it because it is easily invoked to convey the specious sense of drama and excitement he loves so well. *Impact* has a distinct connotation of collision. Even allowing the plea of figurative use, it hardly seems appropriate as a substitute for *effect* or *influence* in "For years scientists have recognized the *impact* of the immense Greenland icecap on the North Atlantic climate"; "The full *impact* of today's mortgage restrictions and tight money won't be felt until next spring or summer"; and "The president's advisers are concerned over the *impact* of high interest rates on school-building." The writer of gobbledygook likes to talk about *federally impacted areas,* meaning those in which the presence of federal activities have had noticeable effects on the local economy. This is true gobbledygook, because it requires translation, except for the initiate.

**impervious.** This means *impenetrable,* not *oblivious* or *indifferent*. The wrong choice was made in "The people of Berlin are not *impervious* to the dangers surrounding them."

**implement.** Unlike *finalize, implement* as a verb is recognized in the sense of *accomplish, fulfill, complete, carry out*: "The farm program will be *implemented* in the fall." But it is so characteristic of gobbledygook that the fastidious shun it, and it is regarded by many as not having legitimate standing.

**imply, infer.** To imply is to hint at, or suggest; to infer is to draw a conclusion. It may help in keeping them straight to remember that only the speaker can imply, but either the speaker or the hearer can infer, though usually it is the hearer. *Infer* is often used where *imply* is called for, and although such a distinguished linguist as Kemp Malone has pointed out that this is long-established usage in English, the fact cannot be blinked that what is written with care maintains the distinction these days. "He *inferred* that we were rascals." The writer meant "He *implied* [*hinted, suggested*] that we were rascals," but the statement as made is open to misconstruction as "He drew the conclusion we were rascals."

**impresario.**    Often misspelled *impressario*. The word has no relation to *impress*. *Impresario* comes from the Italian *impresa,* enterprise; *impress* comes from the Latin word meaning *press upon*.

**in, at.**    P. 47.

**inasmuch as.**    This is the correct form; not *in as much as* or *inasmuchas*. *Inasmuch as* is a clumsy expression whose idea can usually be expressed more neatly by *because, since,* or *for*. "Double sessions were instituted *inasmuch as* [*because*] the school was overcrowded."

**inaugurate.**    Journalese for *open, begin, start*. See also *launch*.

**in back of.**    A gaucherie for *behind*. *In front of,* however, serves a purpose that *before* does not: "The car was parked *in front of* the house." *Before* is possible here but less likely to be used. *Behind* might also be considered before *at the rear of* is set down. See also *upwards of*.

**include.**    Often inexactly used in the senses belonging to *comprise, consist of,* or *be composed of*. That which includes is not all-inclusive, careless usage to the contrary. A writer should not say "The group *includes* . . ." unless he intends to omit some members of the group. In introducing an all-inclusive list it is preferable to say "Members of the group are . . ."

**in connection with.**    Excess verbiage for *in,* as in "Two arrests were made *in connection with* the shooting."

**individual.**    The word is not wrong, of itself, as a noun, as many seem to think, but it is undesirable where *person* will do. It is proper only for emphasis of single identity. Thus "Several *individuals* accompanied the artist into the hall" is questionable, but "*Individuals* and organizations have different rights" is correct. The use of *individual* for *person* is a pretentious illiteracy, as was demonstrated by its highly appropriate use by Adelaide in the musical "Guys and Dolls." Adelaide was a girl of no education who took excessive but misguided pains to create a good impression by her choice of words.

**indorse.** See *endorse*.

**infer.** See *imply*.

**infinitive.** Split, pp. 33-34; of purpose, pp. 34-35; misleading, pp. 35-36.

**inflammable.** See *flammable*.

**informal.** *Informal* and *informally* are words for which misguided fondness is often shown. Subjects of interviews have been known to be described, for example, as "perched informally on top of a desk." The absurdity of qualifiers is sometimes illustrated by substituting their opposites, which, presumably, the writer fears the reader might otherwise assume. We may ask, then, is it possible to perch *formally* on top of a desk? *Informal* and *informally* are all right to set the tone when necessary, but they are not necessary, and in fact are foolishly superfluous, when the tone has already been set by the words they modify. *Chats,* often described as informal, can hardly be anything else. "The president," we are informed, "makes some of his most informal cracks while posing for pictures." What's a *formal* crack—calling a columnist an s. o. b. in a full-dress speech?

**in front of.** P. 55.

**in (his, her) own right.** This expression is ordinarily used of members of a family, and indicates individual ownership of something that might otherwise be held in common. In figurative use, if a man is a poet, it would be correct, in speaking of his wife, to describe her as a poet in her own right. But if a man is a religious leader, it is meaningless to describe his wife as following some other line of endeavor in her own right: "Each morning, the mystic's fourth wife, a poet in her own right, massaged him with oil for two hours in accordance with Hindu practice." Since the mystic was not a poet, his wife should have been designated simply as *a poet*.

**ink a contract.** A hopeless figure. Someday a sportswriter will tell of a player *signing* a contract, and will be acclaimed as a phrase-maker.

**in-migration.** See *emigrate, immigrate*.

**in nothing flat.** The ultimate, perhaps, in clichés as well as in speed.

**inoculate, vaccinate.** These words for the process of immunizing by the injection of vaccine are interchangeable. *Vaccinate,* however, has been firmly established by custom as the word for immunization against smallpox. *Inoculate* is favored for immunization against polio and other diseases, such as diphtheria. *Inoculate* is often misspelled *innoculate*.

**in, on behalf.**   See *behalf.*

**in order.**   This phrase, when followed by an infinitive, as in "He bought the suit *in order* to impress his girl" can usually be omitted without loss. The same is true of *so as.* See also p. 55.

**in regard (s) to.**   See *regard.*

**insigne, insignia.**   The first is the singular, the second the plural.

**install.**   In such constructions as "He was *installed* president," idiom calls for *as* with *install*: "He was *installed as* president."

**insure.**   See *ensure.*

**integration.**   As applied to racial mingling, *assimilation* might have been a better choice than *integration,* which means *combining into a whole,* but *integration* got there first.

**interesting.**   It is simple-minded of a writer to inform the reader that a fact he is relating is interesting. Interest is a subjective consideration, and the reader will make his own judgment about it. By being told he is expected to feel interest in something, he may even be deterred from it.

**interment, internment.**   *Interment,* a favorite in obituaries, is burial: "The good is oft *interr'd* with their bones." *Internment* is a form of imprisonment, and is generally used to describe what happens to aliens living in an enemy nation during wartime.

**intermittent.**   See *continuous.*

**internecine.**   This word has acquired a generally accepted meaning that departs from its strict sense. Basically, *internecine* means simply *destructive.* Fowler explained this, and went on to argue that the idea of mutuality (that is, *destructive of one another*), then becoming widespread in connection with the word, "is what gives the word its only value, since there are plenty of substitutes for it in its true sense—*destructive, slaughterous, murderous, bloody, sanguinary, mortal,* & so forth." The dictionaries now admit the idea of mutuality, but it is observable that good usage has gone one step farther in restricting the meaning. We now understand *internecine* as relating to conflict within a family or nation. World War II was certainly an internecine struggle, in the original sense, between the Allies and the Axis, but the word is not used in that way, and if it were, it would be misunderstood. We now think of internecine war as civil war. ("An *internecine* war over the corpse of Karl Marx has threatened to split the party for decades.") The tendency of popular usage usually is to broaden meanings of words. In this curious instance, the meaning has been narrowed.

**interpretative, interpretive.** Fowler preferred *interpretative* as conforming to the Latin derivation. The word is clumsy, however, compared with *interpretive,* which seems to have gained the majority vote. Preferences based on reasons like Fowler's have been steadily cast on the ash heap, very likely because there is hardly anyone around any more who can be affronted by distortions of Latin. See also *preventative, preventive.*

**in the altogether.** See *altogether.*

**in the event that.** Excess verbiage for *if.*

**into.** A preposition that should be used with care in some constructions, which call for *in to.* "A man wanted as an Army deserter for fifteen years turned himself *into* the sheriff's office last night" suggests an implausible transformation. See also p. 47.

**intrigue.** Still sometimes stigmatized in the sense *arouse interest of*: "The handsome stranger *intrigued* her." Fowler scorned it as an interloper from France, but it has become thoroughly well established.

**invective (s).** *Invective,* coupled with *hurl,* is a stock expression of journalese. This is so much the worse when it becomes *hurl invectives,* for *invective,* like *abuse* and *profanity,* is a general term that has no plural.

**invent.** See *discover, invent.*

**inversion.** In sentences, p. 64.

**in view of the fact that.** Excess verbiage for *since* or *because.*

**invited guest.** Redundant. Being invited is essential to guesthood. Uninvited guests are gate crashers.

**irregardless.** See *regard.*

**-ise.** P. 84.

**Israel, Israeli.** P. 103.

**issue.** See *noncontroversial issue.*

## J

**Jap, Japanese.** *Jap* was freely used during World War II, with malicious satisfaction in the fact that it is derogatory. Since then, *Japanese* is carefully used nearly everywhere, as both noun and adjective: *four Japanese*;

*Japanese* ships. The derogatory implication of *Jap* is so clear it is avoided even in newspaper headlines, despite the pressure of small space. *Nip,* as a clipped form of *Nipponese,* is considered equally reprehensible.

**jeweler, jeweller.**    *Jeweller* is the British preference in spelling.

**Jew, Jewish.**    P. 103.

**jewelry, jewels.**    There is a superstition to the effect that *jewelry* is properly applied to what is in a jeweler's window, and that when worn, the same ornaments must be called *jewels.* By this principle, the crown jewels, if on display, would have to be called the crown jewelry. *Costume jewelry,* it may be observed, is an invariable term, applied regardless of whether the jewelry is being worn or displayed. If there is a distinction, it is that *jewelry* is a collective likely to be applied to a number of items of the jeweler's art considered as a group, and that *jewels* is a plural applied particularly to gems.

**jibe.**    See *gibe, jibe.*

**job, position.**    Usage does not substantiate the idea that *job* necessarily connotes manual labor. It is the homelier word of the two, and certainly *position* would never be applied to ditch-digging. *Job,* sometimes qualified by *big,* is applied casually to employment of all ranks. *Position* is sometimes suspect because it is used to confer a spurious dignity, and those who are sensitive to this avoid it, especially in relation to their own jobs.

**joke, -d.**    See *quip, -ped.*

**journalese, journalism, journalistic.**    Before 1954, when pressure was successfully brought to bear against the G. & C. Merriam Co. by Sigma Delta Chi, the professional journalistic society, the definition of *journalistic* in the Merriam-Webster dictionaries was more or less equated with that of *journalese;* it was as if the words were really *journalese* and *journalese-tic.*

  *Journalese* is what the linguists like to describe as a pejorative; that is to say, a word that depreciates. It applies to all that is bad in journalistic writing. *Journalistic,* on the other hand, properly means *pertaining to journalism,* and ought not to have any derogatory connotation. Nor does it, ordinarily. The old Webster definition of *journalistic* was "Characteristic of journalism or journalists; hence, of style characterized by evidence of haste, superficiality of thought, inaccuracies of detail, colloquialisms, and sensationalism; journalese." In the new definition, the derogatory aspects are replaced by "appropriate to the immediate present and phrased to stimulate and satisfy the interest and curiosity of a wide reading public —often in distinction from *literary*."

The Evanses remark that "As a term for all newspaper writing, *journalese* is a snob term. There is just as good and effective writing in the best newspapers as in the best books, and the faults that are commonly classed as journalese are to be found in all writing." This is a fair judgment, but something more may be said on the subject of snobbery. *Journalese* is seldom applied to all newspaper writing, and when it is, the tone is so bitter that there is little hope of bringing the critic to reason. The truly snob term is *journalism,* applied, as Webster would have it, in distinction to *literature*.

Often, when used in this way, *journalism* is preceded by *mere*: *mere journalism,* says the reviewer, and thus consigns the subject of his comment to perdition. Such judgments are generally stupid, and amount to depreciating folk music by comparing it with classical music. Journalism and literature nurture each other, as do folk and classical music. Much that is unpretentiously journalism is superb, as for example the kind of writing found in *The New Yorker* and the *Reporter*; much that aims at being literary is atrocious.

Faults that are described in this book as journalese are prevalent in news publications, but by no means peculiar to them, because they exert tremendous influence on usage generally. See throughout, and esp. Part III.

**judgment, judgement.**   *Judgement* is the British preference in spelling.

**junket.**   Not a simple synonym for *trip, journey,* or *excursion,* for *junket* has a derogatory connotation, and accordingly should be used with care. A junket is a trip taken by a politician at public expense, ostensibly on public business but really for his own enjoyment. "The word 'junket' will henceforth be taboo in the deliberations of the Foreign Press Association of New York. On motion of Britishers on the executive board it has been decided to substitute the term 'facility trips'."—*Overseas Press Club Bulletin,* April 16, 1960.

**jurist.**   As a variant of *judge, jurist* is inexact, and its use resembles the substitution of *attorney* for *lawyer*. "Winners & Sinners," the *New York Times* critique, commented: "A jurist is merely one who is versed in the law. Therefore, although a judge is, or should be, a jurist, a jurist is not necessarily a judge." Nonetheless, there seem to be few opportunities to use the word in its explicit sense, and newswriters are so afraid of using the same word twice that *jurist* is likely to become established as an exact synonym for *judge*.

# K

**Kan., Kas., Kans.**  Pp. 80-81.

**kerosene, kerosine.**  People who read things not for the usual reasons—pleasure or information—but only to see if they can find any mistakes may think they see one in the occasional spelling *kerosine*. It is not an error, however, but a legitimate variant of *kerosene*. You'll have to go to an unabridged dictionary to find *kerosine,* but Webster says it is preferred by some technical authorities. In some parts of the country, kerosene is called coal oil, an expression all but unknown in other areas.

**kick off.**  Either as a verb (*kick off the campaign*), or as an adjective (*a kick-off dinner*), this frayed figure from the football field has been done to death.

**kick over the traces.**  We are all aware in a general way that this means *to defy* or *escape restraint,* but a generation has grown up that does not know what traces are in this sense. Well, Junior, they are the straps or chains by which horses used to pull wagons.

**kids.**  A generation ago, teachers busily instructed their pupils that kids could only be young goats, but the real goats were the kids who swallowed this pedantry. Some of them grew up to be editors with a prejudice against *kids* for *children.* The word is well established colloquially in this sense, however.

**knots.**  Landlubbers sometimes find themselves at sea when they use nautical terminology; for example, *knots per hour* is a recurrent bit of flotsam. It's redundant, of course, for a knot is a nautical mile per hour; the word is a measure of speed, not distance. A nautical mile is about one and one-seventh land miles.

# L

**labor (a point).**  See *belabor*.

**labor disputes.**  Pp. 153-154.

**lacerations.**  P. 53.

**lady.**  See *woman, lady*.

**(a) large number of.**  Excess verbiage for *many*.

**last, latest, past.**  Some insist that *last* can only mean *final,* and that *past* must be used for *immediately preceding,* as in *during the past week, the* *past year*. This, however, is quibbling. As in *during the last week, the last year, last* is commonly used in the sense of *just past* without ambiguity, since occasions for referring to the end of the world are few. *Latest* is suitable in other references to mean *immediately preceding* where *last* could be misunderstood as *final*: "The *latest* issue is dated Dec. 15; the one to be published in January will be the *last*."

**late.**   Redundant in *widow of the late*.

**latter.**   See *former, latter*.

**launch.**   Journalese for *open, begin, start*. See also *inaugurate*.

**law concern.**   Not idiomatic; a better term is *law firm*. Otherwise, *concern*, like *firm*, is properly used in the sense of a *business establishment*. See also *firm*.

**lawyer.**   See *attorney*.

**lay.**   See *lie, lay*.

**layman.**   The primary meaning of this word is "of or pertaining to the laity, as distinct from the clergy." It is well established, however, to designate one outside some other profession or field of endeavor. Thus *layman* may be used in contradistinction to *doctor, lawyer, engineer, teacher*, etc., as well as *clergyman*.

**lead.**   The past tense of the verb is *led*: "They *led* us to the mouth of the tunnel." Sometimes it is rendered *lead,* perhaps by confusion with the name of the metal, which of course is pronounced *led*. In the cant of printing, however, *lead* is a verb, pronounced *led,* meaning to space out lines of type by inserting strips of metal. In a commendable effort to prevent confusion, the *Linotype News* has invented the spelling *ledd* and *ledding*. Such efforts, no matter how well intentioned, seldom succeed, and it remains to be seen what will come of this one.

**lead pencil.**   See *steam shovel*.

**leapfrog.**   Pp. 110-111.

**leave.**   See *furlough, leave*.

**leave, let.**   Although *leave* [for *let*] *me alone* is widely seen and heard, a useful distinction is lost by neglect of *let*. *Leave* means *go away from,* and *let* means *permit* or *allow*. *Leave me alone* strictly means *leave me by myself; let me alone*, which is usually intended, means *don't bother me*. *Leave* has become popular, with a humorous tinge, in the imperative sense where *let* is called for: *Leave us go*. To corrupt George Washington:

"*Leave* us raise a standard to which the wise and honest can repair." This is in fact a revival of an archaic usage. "About half the American people turned their clocks ahead for daylight-saving time, while the other half *left* their clocks alone." *let*. "This publisher *leaves* his editors alone, while he concentrates on business matters." Ambiguous as it stands; the editors are undisturbed, rather than in solitude. *lets*.

**legitimate.**   The use of this word to designate dramatic performances given on a stage does not imply that those given in movies, on television, or on the radio are illegitimate, however strongly this may be suspected.

**leisurely.**   Although both an adjective and an adverb, *leisurely* is used so seldom as an adverb that it has an uncomfortable sound: "He walked *leisurely* along." It seems almost as if it should be *leisurelyly*.

**lend, loan.**   The idea that *loan* is not good form as a verb is a superstition. There is no basis for the prejudice, and in fact, *loan* seems to be gaining favor. Part of the explanation may be that *lent,* the past tense of *lend,* looks funny, and even wrong, to some people, though of course it's correct.

**lengthy.**   *Long* has apparently been barred from newspaper prose in favor of *lengthy,* which is unobjectionable except that it is longer, or lengthier. What did *long* ever do to journalists that they should boycott it?

**less.**   See *fewer, less*.

**let.**   See *leave, let*.

**letters to the editor.**   Pp. 136-137.

**level.**   *Level a charge* (or *accusation,* or whatever) has no apparent advantage over simply *charge* (or *accuse*).

**liable.**   See *apt, liable, likely*.

**lie, lay, laid.**   The chief difficulty here is remembering that the past tense of *lie* is *lay,* not *laid*—"After dinner, we all *lay* down"; "The book *lay* on the table"—and that the participle is *lain,* not *laid*—"The tools have *lain* in the grass since Sunday." *Laid* is the past tense and participle of *lay* (meaning *place down*): "She *laid* the silver in the closet"; "The table was *laid* for seven." The confusion of the forms of these verbs is so bad, however, and the tendency to use *laid* for *lay* and *lain* so strong, that it may yet be legitimized. This may even extend to the use of *lay* for *lie*: "Let us *lay* [correctly, *lie*] down in the shade."

**lift.**   *Lift* in the sense of *pick up, retain,* or *revoke* is slangy, just as it is in the sense of *steal*. It does not serve any purpose that is not met as well or better by standard expressions. "The new French premier has *lifted* most of his predecessor's program." *retained, adopted, kept.* Here *lift* has the unhappy suggestion of thievery. "The TVA has *lifted* the license of a luncheonette operator who refused to serve Negroes." *revoked.*

**like.** As a conjunction, pp. 41-43.

**likely.** See *apt, liable, likely.*

**literal, -ly.** The trouble here is that these words are unliterally used to mean (a) *figuratively,* (b) *almost* or *virtually,* or (c) nothing much at all. Seldom are they employed in their exact sense, which is *to the letter, precisely as stated.* Some examples: "The actor was *literally* floating on applause." The word wanted is *figuratively,* unless levitation did in fact occur. "George is the proud owner of a bristly, 20-pound porcupine that *literally* dropped out of a tree at his feet." The writer did not mean that was exactly what happened; and so adept have we become at translating such misuses, we are not likely to read it that way. "Flowing through the buttes and deep washes of South Dakota, the Missouri River *literally* cuts the state in half." *Literally* here is excess baggage, for the sentence is more forceful without it. So also in "A marble bust of Tom Paine may soon leave Philadelphia, where it *literally* has been a controversial object for seventy-eight years." The habit of demanding that the reader be thunderstruck by commonplaces, which the meaningless use of *literally* exemplifies, is a tiresome one. After all this, it is fair to ask whether the word has a legitimate use. It does indeed, and here is a sample: "He took literally my suggestion that he jump in the lake."

**little man, people.** In an author's note to *McSorley's Wonderful Saloon,* Joseph Mitchell wrote:

> "The people in a number of these stories are of the kind that many writers have recently got into the habit of referring to as 'the little people.' I regard this phrase as patronizing and repulsive. There are no little people in this book. They are as big as you are, whoever you are."*

*The little man,* a near relative, has incurred the distaste of the Canadian Press, whose stylebook enjoins:

> "Do not use the term *little man* in referring to the population generally or any segment of it. The term has no precise or defensible meaning in that connection and has long since become objectionable."

There is no question that both these expressions are patronizing, and therefore objectionable. Oddly enough, *little woman,* as a fond epithet for

* Copyright 1939, 1940, 1941, 1942, 1943 by Joseph Mitchell. By permission of Duell, Sloan & Pearce, Inc.

*wife,* is something entirely different, and seems unlikely to fall under any ban. Louisa May Alcott, come to think of it, got away with both *Little Men* and *Little Women.*

**lives with his wife.** The wording *He lives with his wife at* has an unhappy ring, because it seems to suggest the alternative of separate maintenance. Something like *He and his wife live at* or *The Tannenbaums make their home at* sounds more agreeable.

**Lloyd's (of London).** *Lloyd's* is the name of the underwriting combine; *Lloyd's of London,* often seen, gained attention from the movie of that name, and the fatal allure of alliteration did the rest.

**loan.** See *lend.*

**loath, loathe, loathsome.** *Loath* is the adjective meaning *reluctant,* as "I am loath to criticize him." *Loathe* is the verb meaning *detest,* as "I loathe spinach." The correct form is *loathsome,* not, as sometimes spelled, *loathesome.*

**locate, situate.** It was once deemed improper to say "The house is *located* [rather than *situated*] on the wrong side of the tracks." *Situated* is as correct as it ever was, but *located* is so usual in such contexts that *situated* may sound a bit precious. *Located* is also both usual and acceptable in the sense of *settled* or *living*: "Where are you located now?" *Locate,* of course, also means *find,* or *fix the position of,* as "You can *locate* the North Star by finding the Big Dipper." In the sense of *situated,* however, *located* is often superfluous: "The house is [*located*] on the wrong side of the tracks."

**lone.** See *poesy.*

**loom.** Journalese in the sense of *threaten, be expected.*

**lulled.** *Lulled into a false sense of security* is what users of this expression must be as to the force of their prose.

**-ly.** P. 76.

# M

**majority.** The word expresses a distinction that seems worth preserving; that is, in its exact sense it means *more than half.* Many say *a majority of* when *most of* would be better. *Most* certainly is the stronger expression for the idea of preponderance. *Majority* might well be saved for elections and the like, where its technical sense applies.

**major portion of.**   Excessive for *most of*.

**mania, phobia.**   A mania is a craze (*a mania for cards*); a phobia is a fear (*a phobia of snakes*). *Mania* takes *for*; *phobia* (like *fear*) takes *of*. Why *phobia* should be confused with *mania* is unexplainable, but it is: "They had a *phobia* for cards." *mania*.

**married, was (were) married.**   There is a delicate and fairly widespread conviction that the man *marries,* but the woman *is married to,* or, rarely, *by*. The idea behind it is that the man is, or is supposed to be, the aggressor in marriage. In these days of equality of the sexes, however, there seems no warrant for preserving this polite fiction, and it appears to be disappearing. It attracts no notice to say a woman *married* a man, instead of *was married to* him. *Was married to* is unavoidable with both sexes to express the idea of duration: "He *was married to* the actress from 1945 to 1950." Sometimes a reverse twist on the basic prejudice appears: "He was then *married* and divorced by two heiresses." As to divorce, of course, the identity of the aggressor is a matter of legal record. Sometimes there is regrettable clumsiness: "After World War II, Markevitch *married* a second time, to Donna Topazia Caetani." *Married to* is hardly defensible; even the supposedly feminine version, *was married to,* would be preferable.

The phrases *married his wife, married her husband* contain an absurd redundancy. It can be avoided by saying simply "He *married* [or *was married*] in 1933" (instead of "He *married* his wife in 1933."). "He and his wife were *married* in 1933" may be technically open to the same objection but sounds less objectionable. "The actor wants a divorce *from his current wife* on the grounds of adultery" illustrates the love of superfluity. The italicized words should be cut out.

**masterful, masterly.**   Although some dictionaries show these words as synonyms, careful usage preserves the distinction that *masterful* means *domineering* and *masterly* means *skillful*. "This book contains a collection of *masterful* photographs." *masterly*.

**masthead.**   See *newspaper terms*.

**materialize.**   The word means to take material, or physical, form. As a pretentious displacement of *develop, arrive,* or *appear,* it is journalese: "The clear skies expected for the weekend failed to *materialize*." The *Dictionary of Contemporary American Usage* cites a Lucely written example from *Time*: "No new angles *materialized*" (in a murder trial).

**may.**   See *can*.

**may or may not.** This expression rather stupidly stresses the idea of uncertainty: "The matter *may or may not* be presented to the City Council tonight." *May* alone fully poses the alternatives.

**M. C.** (for *member of Congress*). See *M. P.*

**media, medium.** *Media* is in increasing use to refer to the means by which advertising, particularly, is disseminated ("The *media* used were newspapers, magazines, and television"). It is not always recognized, however, that *media* is the plural of *medium,* and thus *medias* is impossible. Nor should *media* be used as a singular: "In the debate over toll TV the mathematics peculiar to a mass *media* [properly, *medium*] have tended to run away with common sense."

**mediocre.** Whether we like it or not, this once-weak word has grown strong. Its strict sense, which is the only one yet recognized in dictionaries, is *average* or *commonplace.* But we may as well face the fact that *mediocre* in effect means *lousy*—not *infested with lice,* but *pretty bad.* A musician described as having given a mediocre performance would be mortally affronted, and with good reason. If the critic means the performance was of average quality, he had better say so, and not allow himself to be betrayed by *mediocre.*

"In this wonderful printing and electronic age, we are surfeited with *mediocracy*—mediocre music, mediocre writing, mediocre speech." Yeah, but the word is *mediocrity*—unless one was being coined for the occasion, of which there was no indication. Anyway, *mediocracy,* if there were such a word, would mean *an ordinary government,* or maybe a lousy one. Perhaps we should add spelling to that surfeit of mediocracies, or mediocrities.

**meet.** There is an unreasoning prejudice among the compilers of style manuals against the use of *meet* as a noun. Yet it is unqualifiedly recognized by dictionaries in this sense. Usually the ban is imposed on the use of the word in headlines, where it fits when *meeting* would not. In text, the use of *meet* is a matter of idiom, and rarely raises any valid question. In *track meet,* particularly, it is established and invariable.

**meet, pass.** Although these words are carelessly interchanged with respect, for example, to trains on parallel tracks or to automobiles on the same highway, a distinction is worth encouraging, especially to make accounts of accidents clearer. *Pass,* in these connections, at least, might be reserved to mean *overtake,* or better, be abandoned in favor of *overtake.* The suggestion sometimes advanced that *meet* indicates a collision is nonsense; it indicates, as *pass* does not, that the vehicles are traveling in opposite directions.

**meeting notices.** Pp. 152-153.

**mental telepathy.** It may be too late to attack this redundancy, but telepathy is thought transference, and hence inescapably mental.

**Middle East, Mideast.** Mideast appears to be a coinage that grew out of the attention concentrated in recent years on what was formerly known as the Middle East. Its usefulness, especially to headline writers confronted with *Middle East* as an alternative, is hardly to be gainsaid. At a congressional hearing in 1957, Representative Walter H. Judd of Minnesota explained that *Middle East* originated in British military and colonial policy. In terms of distance from England, Asia Minor (mainly Turkey) was the Near East, beyond the Suez Canal through the Persian Gulf to India was the Middle East, and from there on was the Far East.

**Midlands.** The application of this term, which is best known as applying to the interior of England, to the American Midwest is an affected importation.

**military.** In spite of suspicions to the contrary, *military* properly applies to all branches of the armed forces, including the Navy. Such descriptives as *military and naval forces,* then, are redundant. It is true, however, that the word comes from one meaning *soldier,* and thus its application to sailors and airmen is an extension.

**military publicity.** Pp. 150-151.

**militate, mitigate.** To mitigate is to soften ("His apology *mitigated* the accusation"); to militate (with *against*) is to have an effect on ("The rumor *militated* against her success").

**minimize.** "Its influence on modern American architecture cannot be *minimized*." What this says is that the influence is so small nothing could diminish it; what the writer meant is that the influence cannot be overstated or overestimated. For a similar error, see *underestimate.*

**misquotation.** Pp. 144-147.

**Miss.** P. 103.

**misrelated appositive.** Pp. 24-25.

**mitigate.** See *militate, mitigate.*

**modern, modernistic.**   As applied to design, these words have different meanings. What is modern is contemporary, more or less, by whatever standards apply to the art or field in question. *Modernistic* applies to a jagged, angular school of design that lived and died in the '20s and '30s, and the word now generally is derogatory.

**modifiers.**   Adjectives, pp. 21-22; articles, p. 27; redundancy in, pp. 55-56; piled up, pp. 21-22; limiting, p. 22; nouns as, p. 27; ending in *ic, ics,* pp. 25-26; prepositional, misplaced, p. 65; participles, pp. 22-24.

**Mohammed.**   John Gunther, in *Inside Africa,* noted:

"There are at least a dozen ways to spell *Mohammed.* Most correct is *Muhammad,* and do not forget the dot under the *h.* I am conforming to simplified American usage in saying *Mohammed.*"*

Among the variants, *Mahomet* is fairly frequent, but for the sake of consistency it would be well to settle on *Mohammed,* since it is by far the most prevalent version.

**Mohammedan, Moslem, Mussulman, Muslim.**   Moslems are said to object to the term *Mohammedan* as wrongly implying that Mohammed is the object of worship, that is to say, a deity, but the term is so firmly established without any derogatory intention that this specialized quibble is not likely to make any headway. *Moslem,* which Moslems prefer, means "those who submit to the will of God." *Muslim* is the version favored in Britain. *Mussulman* is a variant of *Moslem.*

**moot.**   This word is almost invariably used as an adjective in the sense of *debatable,* and usually modifies *point* or *question*: "Whether the city had a case was a *moot* point." A *moot court,* however, is a mock court set up for law students to practice in.

**Moslem.**   See *Mohammedan,* etc.

**most times.**   A gaucherie for *usually, generally,* etc.: "Sterility is *most times* due to physical causes."

**motor.**   See *engine, motor.*

**M. P.**   *M. P.,* for *member of Parliament,* has been solidly established for a long time, and its solidity is probably assisted by the fact that the letters are the usual form of reference. But the attempt to establish *M. C.* for *member of Congress* does not seem to have caught on, although some congressmen use it in signing letters. *M. C.,* unhappily for its sponsors, just does not happen to be used by itself the way *M. P.* is.

---

* Gunther, John. *Inside Africa,* New York: Harper & Brothers, 1955.

**Mr.**  Pp. 101-102.

**Mrs.**  P. 102.

**Muslim.**  See *Mohammedan,* etc.

# N

**nameplate.**  See *newspaper terms.*

**names.**  Handling in publication, p. 104; quotation marks with nicknames, p. 143; nicknames in obituaries, p. 150; possessive forms, pp. 67-68.

**narcotic, -s.**  P. 26.

**national.**  A national is a person belonging to a country or nation, and the word should no more be capitalized than *citizen* or *countryman. National* has come into great currency in the phrase *Mexican national,* as applied to crop workers brought into the United States.

**native.**  A native of a place is a person who was born there, a fact that ought to be clear by analogy with *nativity,* although it appears that many do not know that *the Nativity* means *the birth* (of Christ). A mutton-headed naval officer was once the subject of a biographical sketch that appeared in the newspaper published for the station he commanded. The editor had based the sketch on an official Navy biography that said the officer was born in Albany and grew up in Buffalo. So he wrote that the officer was a native of Albany. On reading this, the officer grew purple with rage, and, as was his custom, summoned the editor to his office for a dressing down. The editor falteringly tried to explain that the source of his information was official, but to no avail. "I was born in Albany," the officer bellowed, "but I'm a *native* of *Buffalo!*"

There is, however, a specialized use of *native,* in distinguishing inhabitants from visitors, that does not necessarily imply birth in a place. It is commonest in New England, and may be what led the officer astray.

**negative.**  See *affirmative, negative.*

**Negro.**  A certain amount of tightrope-walking is practiced in the use of racial terms. The most conspicuous development in this field in recent years has been the spread of rules against regularly identifying Negroes as such in the press. Editors have increasingly concluded that in general there is no more reason to characterize a person as a Negro than as a Jew, a Swede, or a Chinese.

There are instances, of course, when identification by race is essential, and sometimes it is hard to decide where to draw the line. Such an instance, involving adultery and miscegenation on the part of a fairly prominent couple, was a top news story for several days. One editor could not find it in his heart to use the wire services' identification of the man in the case as a Negro. This was in accordance with his paper's general policy, strictly construed, of not using racial identifications unless essential. On the other hand, it was the racial element in this story that gave it point. Furthermore, only the dullest reader could have failed to know, from accounts in other newspapers, news magazines, and newscasts, what the situation was. Relief finally came to this editor's tortured soul when, after a couple of days, photos of the couple came through clearly showing that the man was a Negro.

Some publications proscribe *colored* in the sense of *Negro*. *Colored* is not explicit, although in the United States there is little likelihood of its being misunderstood. But the reason sometimes given for banning it is that Negroes consider the word offensive. There seems no way to square this explanation with the use of it in the name *National Association for the Advancement of Colored People*. In South Africa, *Colored* is applied to a special type of mulatto. Elsewhere, it may be applied to non-Caucasians other than Negroes, but this is not done in the United States.

The *American College Dictionary's* definition of *negrophile* is "one regarded as *too* [my italics] friendly to Negroes," but its definition of Anglophile is merely "one who is friendly to or admires England . . ." To Webster, however, a *Negrophile* (with a capital *N*) is, disinterestedly, "One friendly to the Negro." What dictionary d'ya read?

Sometimes the word *Negro* is not capitalized, and some use this form to refer to people of mixed ancestry. This distinction has no recognized standing, however, and failure to capitalize the word may be interpreted as an intention to demean.

A newspaper that took great pains to avoid offense in racial matters found itself in a quandary over what to call a neighboring community regrettably named Nigger Hill. The problem was solved by rechristening the place Negro Hill as far as references to it in the paper were concerned —regardless of maps, general usage, and the befuddlement of its own residents.

**new construction.**  P. 55.

**new innovation.**  Carelessly redundant. An innovation is by definition new. For *new* in other redundancies, see p. 55.

**news.**  P. 70.

**newspaperman.**  The old goat who says he used to be a newspaperman himself often turns out to be a former circulation man, or an alumnus of some other than the news department of a paper. The consensus seems to be that a newspaperman is a member of the editorial department; that is, one whose duties are writing or editing. This is no aspersion on the other kinds of specialists whose services are necessary to the production of a newspaper, but there is a continuous, though ineffectual, attempt to arrogate *newspaperman* (or, on a tonier level, *journalist,* to which the same reasoning applies) by those who have no title to it. No newspaperman, however, has ever been known to pass himself off as a member of some other than the editorial department.

**newspaper terms.** Certain such terms have mildly surprising histories. Who would have thought, for example, that a deadline was originally the line drawn around a military prison, beyond which a prisoner might be shot?

*Tabloid* had its genesis in a trademark registered in 1884 by Burroughs, Wellcome & Co. of London, who used it for a pill, and attached to the term the idea of concentration. The expression passed into general use, and in 1902 was first applied to a newspaper format. Although a tabloid is no longer necessarily a pill, some tabloids have been described as hard to take.

The union of white-collar newspaper employees is the American Newspaper Guild. *Guild* had its first use in trade in the Middle Ages. At that time, guilds were associations of masters; that is, employers or owners, and not employees. Guild members of those days had objectives opposite those of modern union members.

Now consider *masthead,* likely to be misapplied by newsmen. The masthead, contrary to general assumption, is not the name of the paper as displayed at the top of the front page. That's the *nameplate,* sometimes referred to as the *flag.* The masthead is what used to be commonly found at the top of the editorial column. It usually contains a reduced version of the nameplate, the terms of subscription, etc. There is a tendency now to drop it in at random on an inside page. Time was when the information in the masthead usually included the names of the chief editorial executives, but that was before editors were put in their place by publishers and business managers.

**nice.** He who hews undeviatingly to the line that *nice* means *exacting* and must not be used in the sense of *pleasant* or *agreeable* is not so much a purist as a bigot. It means both, equally acceptably, and the context always shows which. The meanings attached to this word at various times have a long and tortuous history, which will not be gone into here. Suffice it to say that the word or its forebears have meant everything from *foolish* to *delicately balanced.*

**nicety.** This word, which preserves a specialized sense of *nice,* does not mean something pleasant or agreeable, any more than *unpleasantry* (which see) means something unpleasant. In general, a nicety is a detail or a minute distinction, as "The *niceties* of formal etiquette are seldom observed today."

**nicknames.** See *names.*

**Nip.** See *Jap, Japanese.*

**noisome, noisy.** That which is noisome stinks, and so does the use of this word to mean *noisy.*

**non-.** Pp. 78-79.

**noncontroversial issue.** A pertinent observation for this age of controversy was made by Robert M. Hutchins, the educator, in *Look*: "An issue is a point on which the parties take different positions. A noncontroversial issue, therefore, is as impossible as a round square. All issues are controversial; if they were not, they would not be issues." By the same token, the often-seen *controversial issue* is redundant.

**none.** P. 69.

**noon luncheon.** Redundant. By definition, a luncheon is at noon.

**normalcy.** Whatever his other sins, President Warren G. Harding has been unjustly held accountable for *normalcy* as an illegitimate coinage. *The Dictionary of Contemporary American Usage* points out that Harding was employing a perfectly good, though at that time little-used, word. Either the attention attracted to it by Harding and his critics, or the inscrutable currents of language, have given it far greater currency today, so that now it is not boggled at. *Back to normalcy,* however, is less likely to be rendered *back to normality* (the word Harding's critics thought he should have used) than *back to normal.*

**not, not all.** The problem of the placement of *not* is similar to that of the placement of *only* (see *only, not only*). Fowler, who usually insists on exactitude and no nonsense, takes a liberal view in both instances, which may only illustrate that even oracles have their foibles. Perhaps this was his way of paying off some early teacher for what he considered pedantry in this connection. Those who wince at the misplacement of *not* wince oftenest, probably, at "All is *not* gold that glitters" (correctly, it's *glisters,* as Fowler quoted it, but no one says that anymore). We all know, of course, what is meant; not, as might be perversely construed, that everything which glitters is not gold, but "*Not* all that glitters is gold."

A more modern example, outside the sacred precincts of Shakespeare: "Every story with an unusual feature does *not* call for a humorous headline." We all know here, too, what is meant: "*Not* every story with an unusual feature . . ." Fowler held it not worthwhile to make any great point of this misplacement. He predicted, however, that *all . . . not* for *not . . . all* would pass away in time. But the time is not yet.

**not only.**   See *only, not only.*

**not so (as) . . . as.**   P. 44.

**not too.**   *Not too,* as the successor of *not very,* is a prevalent peculiarity that bears watching. To begin with, the legitimate meaning of *too* in this phrase, and the one likely to be assumed, is *more than enough. Not too* is clearly objectionable as it is often used. *Not very,* although it also may be open to objection, at least has established itself as an idiom, and conveys a clear meaning (*not very satisfactory; not very honest*). A case against *not too* may be constructed on the grounds that it is often illogical, sometimes misleading, and not found in careful writing. It appears to be a sample of the timid understatement favored by mealymouthed writers who hesitate to commit themselves even to "It's a nice day out," no matter how fine the weather, without toning things down or qualifying them in some way.

Let us look at some examples:

"She testified that her husband was very restless and did *not* like to stay put *too* long."

"The fact that the device will not accurately fix the position of an enemy plane is *not* considered *too* important."

"The gross national product next year may *not* be *too* far below the peak."

"Elsewhere, apparently, there was *not too* much resistance against the price-support program."

"Since the primaries set a pattern, the new system should *not* mean *too* much change at election time."

These sentences will strike the critical reader as open to a charge of absurdity. *Not very,* substituted for *not too* in each instance, sounds more acceptable, somehow. But neither *very* nor *too* is necessary. As an experiment, strike the *too* out of the quoted examples: "She testified that her husband . . . did not like to stay put [too] long." Nothing meaningful is lost by the omission of *too,* and a certain directness is added.

There are sentences in which the lurking illogicality looms over everything:

"Mrs. Eisenhower's health is *not* always *too* good, either." Is it possible for anyone's health to be too good? Even one's enemies may stop short of conceding this. *Not always good* seems preferable.

"The candidate is *not too* prosperous." Much the same criticism applies here. If *not prosperous* is too blunt, how about *none too prosperous, prosperous but not rich,* or *only moderately well off?*

"The expert said farmers do *not* need *too* much rain, but some moisture would be beneficial." Too much rain would be a flood, or at any rate more than enough, and it takes no expert to say the farmers do not need it.

There are occasions when *not too* could be useful in a literal sense. But if someone says "It's *not too* hot out today," we may understand him as meaning either "It's not unendurably hot" or merely "It's not at all hot." We have reached the scene too late, for the spurious *not toos* have already made sentences like this hopelessly ambiguous.

**nouns as adjectives.**   P. 27.

**now.**   See *presently.*

**nth.**   Fowler was in a testy mood the day he leveled his lance at the popular usage of *to the nth. N,* in the language of mathematics, he explained,

> "does not mean an infinite number, nor the greatest possible number, nor necessarily even a large number, but simply the particular number that we may find ourselves concerned with when we come to details; it is short for 'one or two or three or whatever the number may be . . .' "

Unless we are going to shut our eyes, however, we must concede that *to the nth degree* is now permanently established in the sense of *to the utmost* or *infinitely.* Webster gives us "indefinitely large or little," but this is primarily the mathematical, not the popular, meaning. Let us steel ourselves while Fowler lays on the lash: "Those who talk in mathematical language without knowing mathematics go out of their way to exhibit ignorance."

Aw, come on, H. W., technical terms are constantly being taken up by the populace, and out of either ignorance or blithe disregard of the proprieties, are used to mean something different. We mathematical ignoramuses are likely to stretch the meaning of $x$, the symbol for an unknown quantity, to cover the technical sense of $n$ as an indefinite number.

**number.**   Of collectives, pp. 70-71; of *none,* p. 69; of *pair, couple,* p. 71; of *number,* p. 71; plurals, pp. 71-72.

**numbers.**   General, p. 95; vs. words in text, pp. 96-98; in compound modifiers, pp. 71, 76.

# O

**obituaries.** General, pp. 149-150; use of *of* in listing survivors, pp. 87-88; use of *Mr.* in, p. 102.

**obtain.** See *secure, obtain.*

**occupational titles.** Pp. 100-101.

**occur, take place.** The consensus of usage is that what occurs is accidental and unforeseen ("The explosion *occurred* while shifts were changing"), whereas what takes place is planned or arranged ("The coronation will *take place* May 12").

**-odd.** With numbers, p. 99.

**of.** Vs. *from,* p. 47; vs. *to,* p. 47; *of* phrases (identifying), pp. 87-88.

**offence, offense.** *Offence* is the British preference in spelling.

**officer.** The idea that, with reference to policemen, *officer* should be applied only to those holding a rank, such as sergeant, lieutenant, or captain, may have merit, but the weight of usage does not support it. Police themselves, no doubt, would be delighted to see *cop* (which see) supplanted by *police officer,* a term of much more dignity.

**official, -ly.** Overused in contexts where there is no occasion to think the action described could be unofficial, as for example the conduct of business by public bodies. *Official,* as might be expected, runs rife in officialese. Bureaucrats take deep satisfaction in speaking of their duties as *official business.*

**off of.** P. 47.

**O. K., okeh.** Now and again some wounded scholar raises a plaintive cry in favor of *okeh,* accompanied by a denunciation of *O. K.* as impure. I have read moving accounts of how *okeh* is the way Hiawatha, or some other literary Indian, spelled it. Woodrow Wilson, too, is said to have given his benison to *okeh,* possibly as a diverting interlude in the drafting of the Fourteen Points. *Okeh,* at least, has lasted longer than the League of Nations, that other monument to his fame. It is still with us, though failing fast.

The outraged proponents of *okeh,* who want it imposed on everyone by fiat, overlook an all-important point: people generally do not favor *okeh,* no matter how pure it is. What probably denied *okeh* a fair start in life is that it does not look as if it sounds like what everyone says.

The legalists in the audience may be interested to hear that the matter apparently was settled, as far as derivation is concerned, by Allen Walker Read in an article, "The Evidence on O. K.," in the July 19, 1941 issue of what was then known as the *Saturday Review of Literature*. Read traced *O. K.* back to the O. K. Club, a Democratic organization formed in New York in 1840 to promote the re-election of President Van Buren. The initials were those of Van Buren's birthplace, Old Kinderhook, N. Y. In 1936, five years before Read's research was published, H. L. Mcncken listed ten versions of the origin of *O. K.* in *The American Language,* and showed remarkable perspicuity by leaning toward a hint of the explanation Read was to develop.

The latest Merriam-Webster dictionaries list *okeh* only as a variant, and cite Read's article. *Webster's Unabridged* places *okeh* in the small type at the bottom of the page, which looks like the kiss of death, even if the editors do insist that words down there are just as good currency as those above. If Read's explanation is all right with Webster, it ought to be O. K. with the rest of us, especially since *O. K.* has general acceptance in its favor. And so farewell, *okeh!*

**old adage.**   Redundant. Oldness is inherent in *adage*.

**old fashion, old fashioned.**   The correct form of the modifier is *old fashioned*: *an old-fashioned girl*; not, as is sometimes seen, *old fashion*.

**Old Guard.**   (*The*) *Old Guard* is a collective that cannot properly be pluralized into *Old Guards* in reference to individuals. Make it "Members of the Old Guard."

**omission (ellipsis).**   Ellipsis, pp. 56-57; of needed verb forms, p. 57; of pronoun plus *to be,* p. 57; to avoid repetition, p. 58; of *that* and necessary prepositions, pp. 44-45; indication of, p. 58.

**on.**   Pp. 48-49.

**on account of.**   P. 55.

**on behalf.**   See *behalf*.

**one of those who (is, are).**   Such sentences as "I am *one of those who* hope(s) for a peaceful settlement" agitate writers who cannot decide whether the verb should be *hope,* to agree with *those,* or *hopes,* to agree with *I* and *one*. Strictly, the correct form is *hope,* since its subject is *who,* which refers to *those*. Nevertheless, a singular verb (*I am one of those who hopes*) is often found in constructions of this kind, and is regarded as acceptable.

**onetime, one-time.** It is desirable to differentiate *onetime* (*former*) from *one-time* (*single-occasion*). "He is a *onetime* prospector" (at one time, he was a prospector). "It was a *one-time* attempt" (the attempt was made only once).

**only.** Displaced by *lone,* see *poesy.*

**only, not only (not only, but also).** Fowler made a scathing and surprising denunciation of those who would criticize "He *only* died a week ago" as a mistake for "He died *only* a week ago." Not that he would permit *only* to be dropped in just anywhere; he saved his scorn for those who would change its position when there is no chance of misunderstanding.

The placement of *only* is something that warrants close attention, however. This is illustrated by an example in *Word Study* attributed to Professor Ernest Brennecke of Columbia University: Seven meanings result from placing *only* in all possible positions in "I hit him in the eye yesterday." Let us spin this exercise out: "*Only* I hit him in the eye yesterday" (I alone); "I *only* hit him in the eye yesterday" (I did no more than hit him); "I hit *only* him in the eye yesterday" (him, no other); "I hit him *only* in the eye yesterday" (just in the eye); "I hit him in the *only* eye yesterday" (he had just one eye); "I hit him in the eye *only* yesterday" (as recently as yesterday); "I hit him in the eye yesterday *only*" (yesterday, no other day).

Yet authorities agree that too much fuss has been made over the placement of *only*. Its strictly logical position is before the element it modifies, and surely no one will be criticized for meticulously placing it there. Perhaps the thing to do, if you are bound to be meticulous, is to keep your preference to yourself. The problem of the placement of *only* is similar to that of the placement of *not*. See *not, not all.*

Meticulousness is advised, if only because it's a good habit in writing. Laxity with *only* will likely lead to trouble with *not only . . . but also,* and here carelessness is more damaging. "The strike has created problems for the company in maintaining *not only* the goodwill of its customers *but also* of the general public." *Customers* should be balanced off against *general public,* and the only way to do it is: "*not only* of its customers *but also* of the general public."

George Orwell, a highly self-critical writer, permitted himself to say:

"Mr. Auden's brand of moralism is only possible if you are the kind of person who is always somewhere else when the trigger is pulled." Nigglers would insist on *possible only*.

**optimistic.** Optimism is a cheerful or hopeful frame of mind, and thus *optimistic* can be properly said only of a person. It is miscast for *favorable* or *encouraging* in "He cited several *optimistic* factors."

**or.** At beginning of sentence, see p. 94.

**oral.** See *verbal, oral*.

**oscillate, osculate.** An absurd though not uncommon confusion exists here. *Oscillate* means *flutter* or *move to and fro*; a pendulum oscillates. *Osculate* means *kiss,* and the word now is heavy humor. Readers are occasionally amused by references to *osculating fans*.

**other.** "He has more readers than *any* financial writer on a New York newspaper"; "I am more interested in the capture of my wife's murderer than *any* person on earth." In both instances, logic requires *any other*. As pointed out in Perrin's *Writer's Guide,* the rule is that *other* is required in the comparison of things in the same class. *Other* is often used superfluously when there is no need to differentiate: "Three small children and a young woman were killed, and three *other* children were almost asphyxiated"; "The pilot made the mission in a huge Sikorsky helicopter. Three *other* persons accompanied him."

**out-migration.** See *emigrate, immigrate*.

**over.** Among the sturdiest of superstitions is that there's something wrong with *over* in the sense of *more than*. Both accepted usage and Webster show this to be indeed a superstition. Webster gives one meaning of *over* as "more than; as, it cost *over* five dollars." *Over* is also defined as "beyond or above, or in excess of a certain quantity or limit; as, boys of twelve years and *over*." The *Oxford English Dictionary* specifies this sense too. Nevertheless, *over* for *more than* is noticeably avoided in careful writing. For *over* vs. *from*, see p. 48.

**overwriting.** Pp. 120-122.

**owing to.** See *due to*.

**P**

**pachyderm.** Want to pick up some easy money? Make a few bets that a horse is a pachyderm. Refer your takers to Webster, and then collect. The unwritten law against using a word twice, no matter what absurd efforts are necessary to avoid it, has so firmly ensconced *pachyderm* as the synonym for *elephant* that many writers consider it the basic term and use *elephant* as *its* synonym. The fact is that *pachyderm* (*thick-skinned*) is equally applicable to the rhinoceros, the hippopotamus, the tapir, the pig, and perhaps even the politician.

**painful.** As descriptive of a beating or injuries, *painful* is sometimes criticized as superfluous on the ground that there is no such thing as a painless beating or injury. This objection seems captious, since *painful injury* conveys a graphic meaning.

**pair.** P. 71.

**pajamas, pyjamas.** *Pyjamas* is the British preference in spelling.

**pander, -er.** Although *panderer* is favored by the press, headline writers, who are always up against it for space, will be glad to hear that *pander* is equally correct as the noun, and in fact is the basic version of the word.

**parallelism.** Pp. 60-61.

**parentheses.** The problem here is the relative position of the period and the closing parenthesis. If an entire sentence is enclosed, the period comes first. If the enclosed matter is the last part of the sentence, the parenthesis comes first. (This and the following sentence will illustrate.) Such problems, however, are usually left to the printer or proofreader (sometimes inadvisedly).

**parochial titles.** P. 106.

**partially, partly.** That these words should be synonyms in one sense, that of *in part,* is unfortunate, because *partially* has another and widely divergent sense that can cause ambiguity if care is not used, namely, *showing favoritism.* "The testimony was *partially* recorded" may be read as meaning either that it was recorded in part, or that it was recorded in a biased way. The writer who wants to stay out of trouble with these words will use *partly,* not *partially,* to mean *in part.* It is preferable also because it is the simpler word.

**participles.** Dangling, pp. 22-23; and time sequence, p. 24.

**party.** *Party* for *person* is legalese and telephone cant (*the party of the first part; your party does not answer*). Otherwise, the word is out of place, although it is sometimes used humorously. But "Firemen helped police remove the injured *parties* from the car" is objectionable. Some fancy the word as giving a distinguished tone to their utterances, but it is only pompous.

**pass.** See *meet, pass.*

**passion flower, fruit.** It may show something of the preoccupations of our age that, by common consent, these are assumed to be aphrodisiacs in one way or another. But *passion* here is used in reference to the passion of Christ. The name was given because portions of the flower resemble the cross.

**passive.** Used objectionably, p. 39.

**past.** Redundant with *history, experience,* and *records.* See also *last, past.*

**patio.** Purists have inveighed, with the usual results (none), against the American use of *patio.* Properly, a patio is an enclosed court open to the sky. But the patio that is almost standard equipment with modern houses is seldom enclosed in the sense of being a courtyard, and usually is covered.

**penny.** It is an illustration of how far the compilers of style manuals can carry absurdities that some of them forbid *penny* for *cent.* In reference to the coin as such, *penny* is so thoroughly established in America that even a stylebook compiler would be startled to hear his child ask for a cent.

**people, persons.** Pp. 68–69.

**(a) period of.** Usually unnecessary verbiage before a specified interval, as in *a period of five years.*

**permit of.** *Permit of,* as in *statements that permit of no denial,* is accepted usage, but it has a fusty sound, and may even be taken for an affectation, since the meaning is not touched by omitting *of.* "I felt my job was too demanding to permit [*of*] other involvements."

**perpetrate, perpetuate.** Many readers must have done a double-take when they saw the quoted citation that accompanied the award of an honorary degree to an eminent journalist. It praised the recipient as "a worthy perpetrator of an illustrious journalistic tradition." *Perpetrate* means *commit something evil.* And then there's *perpetuate,* which means *give enduring character to.* These words may have something in common, however, in that both a perpetrator and a perpetuator may be thought of as carrying on.

**personal.** The word is often obtrusively used to qualify things that can be nothing but personal: *friend, charm, opinion* are the leading examples.

*Great personal charm* has become a tiresome set phrase. An employer was described as *personally popular with his workers*. There is something distasteful about the idea these examples suggest, that friendship, charm, and popularity have been so devalued as qualities inseparably associated with the person that the words must be reinforced somehow. Potentates and presidents seem to require *personal* physicians; the impersonal ones who treat us ordinary folk apparently will not do. But here the meaning is really that the physician has only one patient.

**persons, people.**   Pp. 68-69.

**persuade, convince.**   The displacement of *persuade* by *convince* flouts idiom. One is convinced *of* a fact, or *that* it is so. This is the customary form of use, and the meaning of *convince* is *to create belief in. Persuade,* on the other hand, means *talk into* or *induce.* One may be persuaded *of* a fact, or *that* it is so, and in these constructions the sense shades into that of *convince.* It is in the strict sense of *talk into,* when *persuade* is followed by an infinitive, that the confusion arises.

Note these examples of incorrect usage: "The director of the museum had *convinced* Brancusi *to part* with the sculptures for awhile"; "The decree of nationalization has all but *convinced* Western capitalists *to zip* shut their billfolds"; "We can only hope Congress can be *convinced to finance* the dam and the canal at the same time"; "He hopes he has *convinced* the prime minister *to await* developments."

In each instance, the word should be *persuade,* or else the infinitive object must be recast to read (*convinced*) *that he should part with, that they should zip shut, that it should finance,* and *that he should await.* Since the revisions are clumsy, it may be assumed that the word the writer wanted in each instance was *persuade.*

**petite.**   Too much of a favorite, perhaps, in connection with brunettes. Why can't blondes be petite?

**phase.**   See *faze, phase.*

**Ph.D.**   Pp. 106-107.

**phobia.**   See *mania, phobia.*

**phony, phoney.**   The correct spelling of the slang expression meaning *not genuine* is *phony.* The error *phoney* may come from some imagined connection with *phone.*

**phrasal verbs.**   Wrongly hyphenated, pp. 76-77.

**pick, choice.**   *Pick* is loosely interchangeable with *choice* or *selection*, but its use in this sense is avoided in careful writing, except in such set phrases as *take your pick, the pick of the crop*. "We are studying American authors, and you are my *pick*" is a disagreeable construction. Sportswriters, when they gaze into their crystal balls, like to speak of their *picks* as the victors in forthcoming contests, but the word sounds no better here either.

**pictures.**   In newspapers, pp. 151-152.

**pier.**   See *dock*.

**pinch hitter.**   P. 145.

**planned withdrawal.**   P. 62.

**plead innocent.**   People who have been charged with crimes are often described as pleading innocent, but technically there is no such plea. What they plead is *not guilty*. A lawyer correspondent of "Winners & Sinners," the *New York Times* critique, wrote, "If a man were let aver that he is innocent, he might be required to prove it, and it is fundamental that no man is required to prove his innocence."

**plough, plow.**   Plough is the British preference in spelling.

**plurals.**   In compound modifiers containing numbers, pp. 71-72; of compound nouns, p. 72; of proper names ending in *s*, p. 72; of letters, figures, and signs, p. 72; inflation by means of, p. 72.

**poesy.**   The gentlemen of the press are sometimes eager to prove that the often humdrum task of reporting the news has not entirely numbed them to the finer things in life. They do this with random poetical touches, like *'twas, 'tis, 'twere,* and *'twill.* Such ornaments may be calculated to make the throat of the reader tighten, but if this happens, it is most likely because he is retching. *Lone* is a more prevalent example of poesy; it has all but supplanted the homely *only* or *sole*: "He cast the *lone* dissenting vote." That must have been the vote against lyricism in inappropriate contexts. Fowler, under the heading "Vulgarization," cited *save* (in the sense of *except*) and *ere* as examples of words abandoned to the journalists, who, he said, had not yet ceased to find them beautiful. Nor have they yet, especially third-rate sportswriters. But perhaps *'twas, lone, ere,* and the like are the only poetry that enters their lives, and to forbid them such expressions might be cruel.

**poetess.**   See *feminine forms*.

**political pot.** To speak of the political pot as boiling, bubbling, simmering, or whatnot is to use one of the creakier clichés of journalese.

**pomposity.** Pp. 116-117.

**pore, pour.** *Pore* (usually with *over*) means *read studiously*; *pour* means *tip out of a container*. One *pores* over a book, but *pours* water. The usual error is something like *pour over a book,* which raises the question what could have been poured over it, and why.

**position.** See *job, position.*

**possessives.** False, pp. 26-27; rules for forming, p. 67; with subject of gerund, see *fused participle*; of inanimate things, p. 68.

**possible, possibly.** *Possible* is impossible in such phrases as *a possible fractured jaw, a possible serious fire, a possible serious accident. Possibly,* or recasting, is called for.

**possibly may.** Redundant. *May* alone conveys the idea of possibility.

**powerful.** As descriptive of the House Ways and Means Committee and like legislative groups, all that remains is for *powerful* to be incorporated into their official titles.

**practicable, practical.** What is practicable is capable of being accomplished, as "Scientists now consider a rocket shot to Mars *practicable*"; what is practical is useful or adapted to use: "*Practical* solutions are better than theoretical ones."

**practically.** Not used by careful writers in the sense of *almost*: "The oranges are *practically* gone." It is used by so many others in that sense, however, that its strict meaning, *in practice* or *in effect,* has been all but eroded away.

**practice, practise.** *Practise* is the British preference for spelling the verb ("The girl was *practising* on the piano"), but *practice* is the preference in both Britain and America for the noun ("This doctor has a large *practice*").

**pre-.** *Pre-* has become the darling of the ad-writers' frantic prose (*precooked, preheated*) and true to the frantic tradition it becomes attached to words where it is redundant: "The secretary of state denied that the president had made a foreign ministers' meeting a *pre*-condition to a treaty"; "*Pre*-registration for the course is scheduled for Tuesday."

**prefixes.** Hyphens with, pp. 77-78.

**preparatory to.** Means *in preparation for*; in the sense of simply *before* it is both wrong and pretentious.

**prepositional phrases.** Misplaced, p. 65.

**prepositions.** At end of sentence, pp. 45-46; *between, among,* p. 46; *in, at, on,* pp. 47-48; *of, from,* p. 47; *off, of,* p. 47; *confess to,* p. 47; *admit to,* p. 47; *dismiss against,* p. 47; *compare to, with,* p. 47; *over,* p. 48; *with,* pp. 49-50; piled up, p. 50; *omitted,* pp. 60-61.

**present incumbent.** *Present* is redundant.

**presently.** *Presently,* in the sense of *now* or *at present,* seems to be exercising an increasing fascination. To those who remember it from fairy tales, it may come as a surprise that it can properly mean anything but *by and by* or *before long.* As Webster is our judge, however, this is one of those unhappy instances in which the same word has contradictory senses. But *presently* in the sense of *by and by* always occurs with a future verb: "The roll will be called *presently*"; in the sense of *now,* it always occurs with a present verb. Although the dual meaning thus does not cause confusion, the current fondness for *presently* often results in needless obtrusion of a time element. For example, "He is presently superintendent of parks" says nothing that "He is superintendent of parks" does not. Likewise, the time elements in "He is *now* living in Brooklyn" and "The children are being cared for *at present* by neighbors" are superfluous, unless there is some reason to contrast the present condition and some other. *Currently* is often used in the same way.

The overuse of *existing* is closely related to these redundancies. We read of "The provisions of *existing* law" instead of "The provisions of the law." Incidentally, there comes to mind the old superstition that nothing can exist which is not alive, but Webster will have no part of this.

**present (-ed) with.** *Present with* is frowned on in some style manuals as excessive in the sense of *give,* and *present* by itself is recommended instead: "He was *presented* a token of esteem." This is faulty advice, however. *Presented with* is good idiom; *present* alone grates on the ear. The real case against *present with* is that it is slightly pretentious. Those who are prejudiced against it would do well to use *give* instead. This, of course, will lead to *was given,* which is afflicted with a prejudice of its own. See pp. 39-40.

**present writer.** P. 73.

**pressure.** *Pressure* as a compression of *put pressure on,* in the sense of *exert influence,* is not yet in the dictionaries, but the day cannot be far off: "The mayor was *pressured* to fire the chief of police." Even so, the use of *pressure* as a verb in the literal, physical sense is questionable: "A muffled concussion *pressured* the eardrums."

**pretence, pretense.** *Pretence* is the British preference in spelling.

**prevent.** See *avoid.*

**preventative, preventive.** *Preventative* is sometimes said to be the noun, and *preventive* the adjective. But *preventive* is preferable as both. Examples: "He took *preventive* measures"; "This medicine is a *preventive.*" *Preventative,* said to be an incorrect formation, gets thumbs down from both Fowler and Webster.

**prexy.** College slang for *president;* it is out of its element when applied to other than college presidents.

**principal, principle.** Often confused. *Principal* is an adjective meaning *chief* or *leading,* as *the principal reason*; it is also a noun meaning *chief,* as *the principal of the school. Principle* is a noun only, meaning *a rule,* as in *a principle of conduct.*

**prior to.** Stuffy for *before.* More at home in a legal document than in everyday speech or writing. The same is true of *prior* as an adjective in the sense of *previous* or *earlier: a prior conviction for drunken driving.*

**private industry.** People who leave government jobs are often described as going into *private industry* or *business.* Since *industry* or *business* alone have no connotation of government ownership, however, they should suffice by themselves.

**probe.** *Probe* may be unavoidable in headlines, but it is not the best English in text in the sense of *inquiry* or *investigation*; or, as a verb, for *inquire into* or *investigate.*

**proceed to.** *Proceeded to open the meeting* is an overblown way of saying *opened the meeting.* The principle holds in the combination of *proceed to* with other verbs. The phrase should be used only to mean *take steps toward,* when some preparatory action is indicated.

**professor.** This title is properly reserved for one who holds the rank; it is not to be indiscriminately applied to college teachers. Some colleges do not have professorships. For much the same reasons that apply in the use of the title *Dr.* (which see) in the academic world, professors often prefer to be called *Mr.* Application of the title *professor* at random to teachers of music is an old-fashioned, small-town quirk that has all but disappeared. It is not done now except humorously.

**promptly.** In many contexts, this word is driving *at once, immediately,* and *right away* to the wall, and not entirely justifiably. Promptness implies action that meets a demand or limitation of some kind: "We pay our bills *promptly*"; "Meet me at the theater *promptly* at eight." *Promptly* seems inexactly used of an act that merely follows upon something: "When he won the lawsuit, he *promptly* tore up the contract." Is *promptly* worth preserving in the sense of meeting an obligation or requirement? Choosy writers, to judge from the way they use the word, seem to think so.

**pronouns.** Avoidance of, pp. 108-109; masculine gender in reference to both sexes, p. 109; omission of relative pronoun, pp. 44-45.

**proof.** As applied to alcoholic content, this is a baffler that everyone pretends to understand until asked to explain it. It is the percentage of alcohol multiplied by two. Thus *200 proof* would be pure alcohol, *180 proof* 90 per cent alcohol, and so forth.

**prophecy, prophesy.** Often confused. *Prophecy* is the noun ("He uttered a *prophecy*"), and *prophesy* is the verb that describes what the prophet does: "He *prophesied* rain." Confused only in writing, for *prophesy* ends with "sigh" and *prophecy* with "see."

**proportions.** Correct in the sense of dimensions: "It was a storm of cloudburst *proportions*." But it is often criticized as wrong in this sense, perhaps because in the singular it denotes merely a relationship, having nothing to do with size. Newswriters are unduly fond of it, however, as a substitute for *size, dimensions, extent, magnitude,* and the like. The example cited will be recognized as journalese.

**proposition.** As a verb ("The woman said she had been *propositioned* in the bar"), *proposition* is slang for *make an indecent proposal to,* and had best not be used in the decent sense of *make a proposal to.*

**prostate, prostrate.** Prostate, the name of a male sexual gland that often gives trouble in later years, is sometimes ignorantly rendered *prostrate,* which means prone.

**prostitution.** "She told the grand jury that the trade of prostitution was used to gather scandal for the magazine." The revelation offered here is less shocking than the reference to prostitution as a trade, when we all know it is not only a profession, but by common consent the oldest profession in the world.

**protagonist.** There seems to have been a revival lately of the old fuss over the use of this word. The natural assumption is that *protagonist* is the opposite of *antagonist,* and that since *antagonist* means fighter against, *protagonist* means *fighter for.* But such an assumption is enough to make purists, especially those who know Greek, writhe. It happens, I am informed by a reliable Greek, that *agonistes,* the root of both words, has two meanings. One is *fighter* and the other is *actor. Antagonist (fighter against)* developed from the first sense, plus *anti,* and *protagonist (leading actor)* from the other sense. The *pro* here does not mean *favoring,* but rather is *prot* from *protos,* meaning *first.*

Chances are, however, that even when *protagonist* is used in its correct sense of *leading actor,* it will be understood in the sense of *fighter for,* so prevalent has the misuse become. Lost and losing causes are the sad lot of the purist. The lostest causes of all may be those based on the knowledge of a language that has become the property of a handful of pale classicists, and has long since ceased to be the distinguishing mark of an educated man.

**prototype.** The word means the original or model after which something is copied; an experimental model of an airplane may be the *prototype* of the production model. It does not mean merely a predecessor, instance, sample, or example. "Miss Smith, who is in charge of a program marking National Secretaries Week, is a *prototype* of the businesswoman being honored." The writer of this strained for a word he did not understand; he might better have said that Miss Smith *exemplified* the businesswoman.

**proved, proven.** A notion has been set afoot and fostered, largely in style manuals, that *proven* is incorrect. Both forms are acceptable, however, and *proven* is the more often used. The *Dictionary of Contemporary American Usage,* which is very canny about national distinctions, reports that *proved* is preferred in Great Britain. The *Oxford English Dictionary* recognizes *proven,* although Fowler aspersed it as not the regular past participle.

**provided, providing.** *Provided* is often considered preferable to *providing* in the sense of *if,* but there is no valid basis for such a preference. The writer who is tempted to write either *provided* or *providing* in this sense, however, should try *if,* and if it fits, use it.

**pupil, student.** It is sometimes represented that *pupil* may be applied only to one attending an elementary school, but neither usage nor definition supports this. The best that can be said is that ordinarily those attending elementary schools are called *pupils* and those attending high schools are called *students,* but *high-school pupils* is often heard and hardly objectionable.

**purist.** A purist is anyone whose ideas of grammar and usage stand to the right of those held by the user of the word. It is, of course, a deprecatory epithet, much like *Puritan* on the lips of a libertine. In this book, *purist* and *purism* are used for the most part concerning rules and distinctions that have no standing in usage and no effect on meaning.

**purple passage.** Purple passages are characterized by ornate, highly rhetorical writing; *purple* does not mean risqué, as in: "The novel had difficulty finding a publisher because of some *purple* passages." This was a case of confused colors, for *blue* has the meaning, in a literary sense, that the writer intended.

**purpose.** *"With* [or *for*] the *purpose* of advancing," or whatever, is redundant for "to advance"; unintentional expression of purpose by misuse of infinitive, pp. 35-36.

## Q

**qualified expert.** Redundant. An unqualified expert is no expert.

**quandary, quandaries.** Often misspelled *quandry, quandries.*

**quartet.** P. 96.

**questions.** The restatement of a question indirectly does not make the restatement itself a question: "He asked the director of the museum whether the paintings on display were originals?" The question mark is wrong. This error appears also with speculative statements, as "I wonder whether my application has been considered?" The statement is declarative, not interrogative, although it describes a state of indecision. Another example: "What he would like to know is how the police found out about this?"

**quiet, unassuming.** These descriptives are so often linked as to be truly a cliché.

**quip, quipped.** "Martha Raye gave her age as thirty-seven, but later quipped to newsmen, 'Confidentially, I'm fifty-seven.' " This use of *quipped* amounts to digging the reader in the ribs with a big fat thumb and saying, "It's a joke, kid—get it?" The use of *quipped* with any direct quotation is a fit candidate for outlawry. Perhaps there is a place for it in those rare instances when the reader has no way of knowing the speaker is joking. Even then, it seems, some more explicit indication of levity is called for. Otherwise, if a quip is too weak to stand on its own legs, why bother to quote it?

*Cracked,* as a truncated form of *wisecracked,* is in the same league with *quipped,* like *wisecracked* itself, *joked, jested,* and *gagged.* "Questioned whether Italy's long siestas have anything to do with its overpopulation and housing problem, Scelba cracked, 'In Italy, a siesta is a time for rest, not work.' " Look, Ma—Scelba made a funny! Instead of beating the defenseless reader over the head with them, let us take the standing advice of the *Chicago Tribune's* "Line o'Type" column: "Hew to the line, and let the quips fall where they may."

**quite.**    The lexicographers say that, formally, *quite* means *entirely, wholly,* or *altogether*; colloquially, it means *fairly, somewhat, moderately.* We may as well concede that the colloquial sense has all but driven the other out. "I was *quite* happy with the editorial," said a legislator who had received an accolade. Although the purist might accuse him of ambiguity, everyone else will understand immediately that the legislator was pleased though not carried away. Thus also in "The franc is *quite* stable"; "These big ships are still *quite* vulnerable"; "Christian Dior has done something to the female bosom that might prove *quite* startling." Yet careful writers tend not to use *quite* in any sense but *entirely.*

**quotation marks.**    Pp. 142-143.

**quotations.**    Misquoted, pp. 144-147; wrong person in, pp. 143-144.

## R

**raise, rear.**    It is grammatical folklore that children are reared, animals are raised. *Reared,* however, has a flossy sound. Speaking of children as *raised* is earthy American idiom and beyond cavil.

**raise, rise.**    These words are sometimes confused in connection with increases in pay. The established form is *a raise*; *a rise* can be defended, but is little used in America. In Britain, *rise* is preferred.

**rarefy.**    Often misspelled *rarify.*

**ravage, ravish.**   To ravage is to damage or destroy; to ravish is to rape, abduct, or enchant. A building may be ravaged by fire; a woman may be ravished, ravishing, or both.

**readjust, -ment.**   See *adjust, readjust.*

**realistic.**   P. 62.

**reason is because.**   *The reason is that* is better usage than *the reason is because.*

**receipt, recipe.**   Usage has differentiated these words to the extent that it now attracts slightly surprised attention to use *receipt* to mean a formula for cooking, although this sense is technically correct. The word for the formula is now almost invariably *recipe; receipt* is all but exclusively used to mean a written acknowledgment, as *a receipt for a payment.*

**receive.**   See *suffer, sustain, receive.*

**receptive.**   See *acceptable.*

**recipe.**   See *receipt, recipe.*

**reconvert.**   This word threatens, as a redundancy, to drive out *convert,* especially in connection with the adaptation of buildings to new uses. Homes, for example, are erroneously spoken of as being *reconverted* to apartments. What is *re*converted must already have been converted. *Re-convert* gained currency after the war, when industrial plants that had been converted to war production were reconverted to their original uses.

**recur, recurrence.**   See *reoccur, reoccurrence.*

**red-faced.**   This expression may have some virtue as the invariable sub-stitute it has become for *embarrassed,* but if so, the virtue is not apparent. Account might be taken of the fact that most people are embarrassed without blushing.

**redundancy.**   General, pp. 54-55; in defining modifiers, pp. 55-56; in meet-ing notices, pp. 152-153.

**redwood.**   Now and then Californians are startled to hear it said that *Sequoia gigantea,* the big tree of the Sierra, is not a redwood. There are two species of sequoia in California: *S. sempervirens,* otherwise known as the coast redwood, and *S. gigantea.* Precisians who hold that the term *redwood* applies only to the coastal variety will find some comfort in Webster. But this is a bookish distinction supported by neither general nor expert usage, and Webster may as well come down out of that tree.

**re-enforce, reinforce.** These words are synonyms, but the second form is predominant, as in *troop reinforcements, reinforced concrete.*

**refer.** See *allude, refer.*

**reference, problems of.** Pronouns, pp. 108-109; reference to both sexes, p. 109; leapfrog (gap in identification), pp. 110-111.

**refute.** To refute an argument is to demolish it, not merely to contradict or rebut it.

**regard.** *Regard* leads us to two barbarisms: *irregardless* and *in regards to. Irregardless* is beyond the pale, and no more need be said, except perhaps that it comes from heedless analogy with *irrespective. In regards to* is an illiterate variant of *in regard to. In regard to, with regard to,* and *as regards* are not actually crimes, but the writer who is neat will eschew all three for *regarding, concerning,* or *about.*

"National politics are different *in some regards* from state politics" will offend the discriminating, who would prefer *respects.*

*Regard,* in the general sense of *consider,* takes *as.* Fowler expressed concern over the omission of *as* ("He was *regarded* a bum"), but this fault appears to be rare, having been succeeded by the unwanted pairing of *as* with *consider* (which see).

**relation, relative.** As the word for *kinsman, relative* is preferable because it is favored by current usage. *Relation* is acquiring a tinge of quaintness, though it remains established in set phrases like *poor relations* and *friends and relations.*

**relative clauses.** Restrictive, nonrestrictive, pp. 90-92; cancel pronoun plus *to be,* p. 57.

**relative pronouns.** Omission of, pp. 44-45.

**relieve.** *Relieve* in the sense of *deprive of* or *take away from* is facetious, and the writer who is using it in that sense should be aware of this. "The city initiated action to *relieve* the bus line of its franchise" and "The pickpocket *relieved* several tourists of their wallets" are examples of such use. *Relieve* in the first example is so inappropriate it must have been used unwittingly.

**religious.** As a noun ("Two *religious* were kneeling in prayer" and "The pilgrimage was made by a party of *religious* and laymen"), the word is churchly cant, so seldom seen in ordinary prose as to cause a moment of puzzlement.

**remind.** Although Webster designates *remind* as both transitive and intransitive, that is, either taking or not requiring an object, the transitive use is so predominant the other sounds strange: "Taxes will be due April 1, the collector *reminds*." This may leave the reader up in the air, so to speak, groping vainly for the missing object. The more usual and satisfying use is along these lines: "Taxes will be due April 1, the collector *reminds* property-owners." Interestingly, the *Oxford English Dictionary* designates *remind* only as transitive, and so does the *American College Dictionary*.

**render.** It is not true, as style-manual superstition would have it, that only lard is rendered. The word is correct in the sense of *sing* or *play,* but it is now both pretentious and quaint.

**rendezvous.** This word has been aspersed as a verb ("The searchers *rendezvoused* at Horner's Corner"), but its use in this way is reputable, even though an English ending has been grafted onto a French word. It probably gained popularity from frequent use in naval operations during World War II.

**reoccur, reoccurrence.** Needless variants of *recur, recurrence.*

**repast.** See *banquet.*

**repetition.** Of defining modifiers, pp. 55-56; of facts in news stories, pp. 123-124.

**replica.** The commonest misuse of this word is in the sense of *model* or *miniature*; it should be kept in mind that a *replica* is a copy in the same size. The word has a specialized application in the fine arts, meaning a copy by the person who made the original.

**reportedly.** *Reportedly,* my spies inform me, has been sneered at and even proscribed on the ground it is not to be found in dictionaries. Now, the fact that a word is not in the dictionary is no reason it should not be used. If everyone took this attitude there would be (a) no words, and (b) no dictionaries, for, of course, words come first and dictionaries later. *Reportedly* has a vigorous present and a bright future. Some newspaper editors asperse it on the ground that only verifiable fact should be reported, arguing that this leaves no place for *reportedly*. Such views are matters of policy and have nothing to do with the virtue of the word. They would also rule out *allegedly, supposedly, reputedly,* and other speculative expressions. Publications that print only verifiable fact, incidentally, must be pretty bleak propositions. I had a little trouble finding *reportedly* myself, but it does appear in the small type at the bottom of page 2113 of *Webster's New International.*

**restrictive, nonrestrictive clauses.** Pp. 90-92.

**Rev. (reverend).** P. 105.

**review, revue.** Confusion of a sort appears in applying *review* to a stage show. Though it is technically justifiable, usage has fastened *revue* on such performances.

**revise, revision.** *Revise* is often loosely and improperly used for *rearrange*, *reorganize*. Revise has to do with changing or amending something that is written; printers' proofs and laws may be revised. "The lower courts were *revised* in California in 1953" should be *reorganized*. For *upward revision*, *downward revision* as euphemisms, see pp. 61-62.

**right-to-work laws.** It is generally realized that this is a political euphemism, concocted to make a kind of law that labor considers repugnant palatable to the voter. As a result, most publications now designate such legislation as *so-called right-to-work laws*. The purpose of such laws is not to preserve any right to work, but to outlaw the union shop. See also *fair-trade laws*.

**rime, rhyme.** *Rhyme* is the established preference, and *rime* in this sense, though technically correct, is an affectation. Thus it was in Fowler's day, and it is all the truer now. *Rime* is best reserved to mean hoarfrost or frozen mist.

**Rio Grande River.** See *Sahara*.

**robbery.** See *burglary*.

**rock, stone.** Some editors specify that *stone* must be used concerning what is of small size, for example what can be thrown, and *rock* concerning only a large mass, for example a boulder or mountain. Literary usage, especially in England, pretty well follows this idea of applying *rock* only to what is large, such as *Rock of Ages*. But in this country *rock* is indiscriminately applied to all sizes. He who insists otherwise may be regarded as having stones in his head. *Stone*, on the other hand, has also been reputably used for objects of considerable size, as for example in reference to the stones that were rolled away from the sepulcher of Jesus.

**romance.** Those who would criticize the use of *romance* as a verb must differentiate its senses. With the meaning of *exaggerate, invent*, it is a reputable word whose use goes back to 1671. "The clergyman's wife had nearly been *romanced* out of a $203,000 inheritance," although aspersed, was certainly both clear and acceptable in its use of *romance*. It may be that *romance* here was interpreted by the critic in the sense *make love*, but obviously the meaning intended was that the money was nearly lost to a

storyteller. *Romance* for *make love*, as "There is much *romancing* in the
moonlight," may be described as Hollywoodese and slangy, though this
sense may easily gain in reputability.

**round.**   See *around, round.*

**rout, route.**   *Rout* means *drive out*: "The troops prepared to *rout* the in-
vaders"; *route* means *select,* or *send along, a path*: "Hannibal planned to
*route* his army through the Alps." The past tense (*routed*) is the same for
both words.

**routine training mission, flight, exercise.**   Usually redundant. Drop *routine*.

**rule of ten.**   In handling numbers, p. 97.

**rustic.**   *Rustic* has acquired a specialized sense in the lingo of Western real-
estate dealers and, perforce, their customers. To them, a rustic house is
not one charmingly countrified, but one having wooden outer facing, as
distinguished from stucco or brick. This usage is spreading to the East.

# S

**Sabbath.**   The Sabbath is not necessarily Sunday; to Jews and Seventh-Day
Adventists, the Sabbath is Saturday, and to Mohammedans it is Friday.

**Sahara.**   Those versed in Arabic, and some others, are aware that *Sahara
Desert* is redundant, for *Sahara* means *desert*. Similarly, to those in the
know, *Sierra Nevada,* the name of the great rocky spine of California,
means *snowy mountains*, and *Rio Grande* means *big river*. Some are dis-
tressed by the illegitimate but common plural *the Sierras*, rather than *the
Sierra*. But those who would trim down *Sierra Nevada Mountains, Rio
Grande River*, and *Sahara Desert* might as well give up. It is pedantic to
insist on distinctions based on knowledge of the languages from which
these terms have emerged into currency in English. Those who do so
should consistently object to *City of Minneapolis* and *City of Indianapolis*
as redundant, too, since the suffix *-polis* means *city*.

**said.**   *Said* as an adjective in the sense of *aforementioned* (*the said editor,
said contractor*) is legalese, and distasteful in other than legal contexts,
but *aforementioned* is hardly to be recommended, either. Almost always,
the definite article (*the*) suffices in reference to what has already been
specified. "The editor of the local newspaper, together with members of
the clergy, refused to take a position in the controversy. *The editor* [not
*said editor*] would not give his reasons, however." For the use of *said* in
attribution, see pp. 140-141.

**salary, wage.** It is sometimes said that a job pays a wage and a position pays a salary. The distinction between *job* and *position* (see *job, position*) is not, however, what it is often thought to be. In general, *wage* is applied to the compensation for work at the lower end of the scale in prestige. A teacher often gets less than a truck driver, but the teacher's pay is not likely to be referred to as a wage, though that of both may be referred to as a salary.

**saloon.** See *bar, saloon.*

**same.** *Same* as a pronoun without *the* ("He collected the money and deposited *same*") is not literate English; it bears an unwholesome odor from the world of commerce. The usage achieved a species of immortality, and perhaps even an appearance of sanction, from "Sighted sub, sank same." Kipling, too, had Tommy Atkins say, "We 'ave bought 'er the same with the sword and the flame." But the military are noticeably fond of adopting commercialese. In good usage, *the same* becomes *it.*

**sanatorium, sanitarium.** He who still seriously argues for a difference between *sanatorium* and *sanitarium* can only be set down as a Latinized fanatic. By derivation, the first is a place to restore health and the second a place to preserve it. Not only are these words easily confused, but the distinction seems of little use. So little has it been used, in fact, that Webster cites *sanatorium* and *sanitarium* as synonyms, although generally a preference is shown for *sanatorium* in names of institutions for the treatment of tuberculosis. *Sanitorium* is simply an error.

**savant.** As a random variant for *professor, scholar,* or *scientist, savant* is journalese.

**save.** See *poesy.*

**saving, savings.** As modifiers, these words have distinctive uses in two common connections. It's *savings bank* (a bank where savings are kept); but *daylight-saving time* (time that saves daylight). Thus *saving bank* and *daylight-savings time* are both wrong.

**saw, see.** Scholars will have to tell us whether the uses of *saw* (and less often, *see*) noted here are indeed dialectal, as they seem to be. At any rate, they sound questionable.

"Winds up to 20 miles per hour are expected to *see* a recurrence of the dust storms today." *bring* or *cause.*

"He disbanded his chorus after nine seasons that *saw* more than 1,500 concerts around the world." *included.*

"Subsequent proceedings *saw* the closing of the place and the sale of its equipment." *resulted in.*

"The fiscal year *saw* a total of 300 million dollars appropriated for highways" is sanctioned, however, by one dictionary meaning of *see* (witness as present or contemporary), which apparently has been stretched to cover the other examples cited here.

**scattered.** *In all directions* is redundant with this word.

**scent, sense.** According to the style sheet of the *Ottawa Journal*, a man does not *sense* trouble, he *scents* it. Yeah, but what about the kind of trouble that doesn't smell?

**scientist.** See *engineer, scientist.*

**Scot, Scotchman, Scotsman.** Much as the inhabitants of San Francisco object to having their city called *Frisco*, inhabitants of Scotland object to being called *Scotchmen. Scotchmen*, however, is a reputable term, and the only reason for avoiding it is to keep from giving umbrage to Scotsmen (the term they prefer). *Scot* is the original name for inhabitants of Scotland. For practical purposes, *Scot, Scotchman*, and *Scotsman* are synonyms.

**seasonable, seasonal.** What is seasonable comes at the right time; what is seasonal is connected with a season. Snow in winter is *seasonable*; some jobs are *seasonal.*

**secure, obtain.** The use of *secure* in the sense of *obtain* is old and reputable, though often denounced. But, as the Evanses comment, *get* is often preferable to *secure, obtain*, or *procure*. "The reporters *secured* complete details from the police." Pretentious for *got.*

**see.** See *saw, see.*

**senior citizen.** A distasteful, but perhaps irresistible, euphemism for *the aged, the old*, or *oldsters*, beloved of *Time. Senior citizens* has been pickled in the names of organizations and buildings.

**sententious, sentient.** Although *sententious* has the sense of "terse and energetic in expression; pithy," it is used almost entirely in the derogatory sense of "marked by pompous formality." It may be said that only this latter meaning survives; we can hardly expect a word to bear two nearly opposite senses. *Sententious* is sometimes unhappily confused with *sentient* (*capable of sensation*). Neither word means *wise,* as is sometimes assumed.

**sequence of tenses.**   Pp. 31-33.

**sequoia.**   See *redwood*.

**series.**   Commas with, pp. 92-93; colon with, p. 94.

**service.**   As a verb meaning *provide service to*, this expression is well established and in some connections has no convenient synonym, as when we speak of servicing an automobile. Its use is questionable, however, where *serve* will serve, as in "The bus line *services* [better, *serves*] the northern suburbs." *Service* also has an agricultural meaning (as a synonym for *breed*), a fact the city-bred are not always aware of, and one that should discourage its indiscriminate use. Readers of John Steinbeck's *The Grapes of Wrath* are not likely to forget this:

> "See that sign 'longside the road there? Service Club. Luncheon Tuesday, Colmado Hotel? Welcome, brother. That's a Service Club. Fella had a story. Went to one of them meetings and told the story to all them businessmen. Says, when I was a kid my ol' man gave me a haltered heifer and says take her down an' git her serviced. An' the fella says, I done it, an' ever' time since then when I hear a business man talkin' about service, I wonder who's gettin' screwed."*

**sewage, sewerage.**   Much is made by the finicky of the distinction that *sewage* is what is carried off, and *sewerage* the system that carries it off, the act of carrying it, or the descriptive applying to either. As a practical matter, however, *sewage* is predominant as both noun and adjective ("The *sewage* is treated in four plants"; "A *sewage* system has been installed"). *Sewerage* is rarely seen as a noun ("The *sewerage* was faultily designed"); the choice in this sense generally is *sewage system*. *Sewerage* is falling into disuse, but no irreparable harm is being done, for the distinction between it and *sewage* serves no useful purpose, and, what is more to the point, is little observed.

**shall, will.**   Pp. 37-39; vs. *am to, is to,* p. 36.

**shambles.**   It is sometimes said that this word may be correctly used only of a slaughterhouse, or, by extension, a scene of carnage. Dictionaries, however, now recognize it also in the sense of *a scene of destruction or wreckage*. The really valid criticism of the word is that newspaper writers and many others like it too well.

**shatter.**   Journalese at its most histrionic as used in *shatter a production record, shatter a precedent*.

* John Steinbeck, *The Grapes of Wrath*. New York: The Viking Press, Inc., 1939. Used by permission.

**shear, sheer.** *Shear* means cut off: "The runaway car *sheared* [not *sheered*] a power pole." *Sheer*, as a verb, is most commonly used in the sense *veer away*: "The wheels hit a rock, and the car *sheered* away from the cliff."

**shepherd.** Don't ask why, but in the sheep-raising areas of the West the man who tends the flocks is not a *shepherd*, but the comparatively clumsy variant, *sheepherder*. *Shepherd*, for some mysterious reason, seems on the way to becoming literary.

**shipshape.** The sentence "Cities like Chicago and Milwaukee plan to spend millions to get their docks in *shipshape*" may give an old salt a touch of seasickness, for *shipshape* is an adjective, not a noun. *Make their docks shipshape* would be better. Any analogy with *in shape* is false.

**should, would.** Pp. 37-39.

**shutter.** "The historic old theater shuttered its doors this week." This use of *shutter* is a curiosity. Windows can be *shuttered* (i. e., covered by shutters), but doors, it would seem, can merely be shut. If the doors of the theater were boarded up, it would have been well to say so, for a boarded door is not shuttered; a shutter, even if mounted on a door, would be a movable closure.

**sick, ill.** The idea that *sick* means only *nauseated*, or *sick at the stomach*, reflects British usage, not the realities of American speech. In this country, *sick* and *ill* mean the same thing. *Ill*, however, has a stilted sound, and in an everyday context may seem affected.

**Sierra Nevada.** See *Sahara*.

**similar.** *Similar* means *resembling*, and should not be used in place of *same* or *identical*: "Rice exports through the first seven months of this year were 20 million pounds greater than during a *similar* [actually, *the same*] period last year." The writer did not mean any seven months last year, but the same seven. If two men were accused of skulduggery, and one of them were exonerated, it would be inexact to speak of the dismissal of a *similar* charge against the other. It would be an *identical* charge.

**since.** It is a delusion that *since* may be used only as an adverb in a temporal sense ("We have been here since ten o'clock"). It is also a conjunction meaning *for* or *because*: "*Since* it is raining, we had better take an umbrella." For *since* vs. *as*, see p. 43.

**sir.** See *dame*.

**situate.** See *locate, situate*.

**skid road, row.**   Which is it, *skid row* or *skid road*? This question will have little interest in New York, where it's the *Bowery*. Elsewhere, in a nation increasingly socially conscious, more and more references are being made to the quarter of town where bums, winos, and migrant crop workers foregather, and there is disagreement over what to call it. *Bowery* has spread beyond New York, for that matter. If memory serves, this term is applied in Duluth to the district that is the hangout of waterfront toughs. *Bowery*, incidentally, comes from the name of a street, which in turn comes from *bouwerij*, a Knickerbocker word for *farm*.

*Skid road* comes from lumbering operations in the Northwest, where logs are slid down a kind of channel made of other logs that have been peeled and sunk in the ground. The connection between such a slide and a resort for derelicts is none too clear. It seems, rather, that the resort should be *skid row* instead of *road*, the *skid* derived from *on the skids* and the *row* from the sense of a street and its buildings, as in *Rotten Row*. Regardless, *skid row* is more prevalent than *skid road*, which is what counts. Dictionaries of slang tend to favor *skid row*, when they do not give both versions. True, *Webster's New International* does not recognize *skid row*, listing only *skid road*, but this is not the only instance in which Webster is out of step with usage. Webster defines *skid road* as a Westernism meaning "the part of a town frequented by loggers." That ain't the skid row we know, from which any loggers have long since taken to the woods.

Herb Caen, when he was writing for the *San Francisco Examiner*, coined the picturesque expression *Skid Rowgue*, which seemed to be a vote for *skid row*. But otherwise he referred to *skid road*, perhaps in deference to the *Examiner's* style. If this is the explanation, it is plain that wit is not always in style.

For meekly venturing the opinion that *skid row* seems to be more prevalent than *skid road*, I once brought on my head an impeachment in the editorial columns of the *Portland Oregonian*, which took me to task for cavalierly giving *Webster's New International* the back of my hand. Curiosity then prompted me to ask the Webster people what their files show on this expression, and they replied that *skid row* had snuck into the addenda section, apparently while I wasn't looking. And so I am constrained to turn the front of my hand to Webster, the while glancing sidewise in the direction of the *Oregonian*.

The Webster files showed *skid row* to be commoner in the East, and *skid road* in the West, especially in Los Angeles and Seattle. I question instancing Los Angeles, after seeing that an official city commission there on slum clearance or something even incorporated *skid row* in its name.

But I will not cavil at their citing Seattle, or for that matter the whole states of Washington and Oregon, where the use of *skid road* seems to be practically a religion—a fact of which I was dimly aware from the outset. As a religion, its high priest is the author, Stewart Holbrook, who if he had not gained fame otherwise, might have won it by his incessant and impassioned public endorsements of *skid road*.

**slate.** Perhaps undeservedly frowned on in the sense of *schedule*. The verb *slate*, in any event, has a legitimate sense of *register on a slate*, and does not mean solely *censure* or *reprimand*, as the folklore of style manuals would have it.

**slow, slowly.** *Slow* is equally an adverb and an adjective, so that *go slow* is just as correct as *go slowly*. An Englishman was outraged by a road sign that read DRIVE SLOW. Reacting violently and misguidedly, as people often do when their linguistic prejudices are crossed, he knocked it over. When he was haled before a magistrate for damaging public property, he pleaded that the sign was ungrammatical—it should have read DRIVE SLOWLY. As it happened, however, the magistrate was enough of a scholar to be able to show him he was all wrong, and had the additional pleasure of fining him.

**small in size.** Redundant; omit *in size*. Similar to *large* (or *small*, or *many*, or *few*) *in number*; *rectangular* (etc.,) *in shape*; and the like.

**smog.** In its pristine sense, smog was a mixture of smoke and fog. The term originated in the East. What has plagued Los Angeles and other parts of California is not smog in this sense, but a substance generated by the action of sunlight on pollutants in the atmosphere. St. Louis and Pittsburgh had smog, in the true sense. This is offered only as curious linguistic lore, for everyone knows only too well what smog is, and if Los Angeles did not have the original title to the word, it has certainly earned one.

**so.** At beginning of sentence, p. 94; with *not,* p. 44.

**so as to.** *So as* is excessive verbiage with an infinitive construction; *so as to overcome* equals *to overcome*. See also *in order to, for the purpose of*.

**so-called.** P. 143.

**social disease.** P. 61.

**solon.** This word, which comes from the name of the Athenian lawgiver, is journalese in the sense of *legislator*. It may be inescapable, and thus grudgingly admissible, in headlines, where *legislator, senator,* or *representative* cannot be made to fit, but in text it is to be avoided.

**some, -odd.**   P. 99.

**some, some of us.**   *Some* for *somewhat* is dialectal and not good English: "The weather warmed up *some*"; "The wounded Nicaraguan leader was reported to be *some* better." The possessive pronoun that follows *some of us* depends on whether the speaker regards himself as part of the group designated: "Some of us lost *our* heads" is correct if the speaker lost his head and is willing to admit it, but if not, he would properly say "Some of us lost *their* heads."

**something, somewhat (of a).**   Although *something* and *somewhat* are sometimes sanctioned as interchangeable in such expressions as *somewhat of a coward*, it is noticeable that *something* is preferred in careful writing. The reason may be that *somewhat* as a noun is obsolete and rarely seen, and sounds out of place in that role.

**some time, sometime, sometimes.**   *Some time* is an adverbial phrase denoting an interval or period: "He stayed *some time* [not *sometime*]." *Sometime* is an adverb indicating an indefinite occasion: "He will come *sometime*, I am sure." *Sometimes* means *occasionally* or *at one time or another*: "*Sometimes* it rains in the summer in the desert, but very seldom."

**son of a gun.**   A harmless and once-popular expression that has fallen overboard, perhaps since Harry Truman put the presidential seal on another breed of son. It is said that in the days when ladies of easy virtue were brought aboard warships for the diversion of the crews, they were always entertained on the gun deck, and consequent offspring, officially fatherless, came to be referred to as sons of guns. In those days, *son of a gun* were fighting words.

**sonic wall.**   The Style Guide of the Aerojet-General Corporation says:

> "An example of a misused word that contributed to confusion among both technical men and laymen in recent years was 'the sonic *wall*.' When pilots first approached the speed of sound, they found that aircraft control was difficult and uncertain. The difficulties were first referred to as 'obstacles' to supersonic flight, then as a 'barrier,' and finally as a 'wall.' This last term became so popular with journalists that, after the speed of sound had been exceeded repeatedly, they felt called upon to announce the 'discovery' that there was no 'sonic wall.' "

**so . . . that.**   In the pair *so . . . that*, no comma should be used before *that*: "The car was so badly damaged [,] that it had to be towed away."

**Southland.**   California news editors must be disconcerted by those national weather summaries that refer to the South as *the Southland. Southland,*

in California, means *Southern California*, which is practically a separate
state, if not an empire. Used in California as a synonym for *the South*
(the Ole South, that is), *Southland* will cause either confusion or indignation. If those wire-service weathermen cannot be content with *the South*,
maybe they could make it *Ole Southland* for California consumption.

**spearhead.**    Journalese for *lead, head, direct*: "A banker will *spearhead* the
Community Chest campaign." Excessive use has blunted its point.

**specie, species.**    *Specie* is coin: "The payment was made with a combination of *specie* and paper money"; *species* is a distinct scientific category of
animal or plant: "Monkeys of this *species* are found only near the
equator."

**spelling.**    General, pp. 82-84; British preferences, p. 84; as humor, pp.
84-85.

**split infinitives.**    Pp. 33-34.

**split-verb constructions.**    Pp. 36-37.

**spokesman.**    A spokesman is one who speaks on behalf of others. The writer
who told of "a fluent *spokesman* of idiomatic English" meant "a fluent
*speaker*."

**sport.**    As a verb, *sport* is appropriate only of something that would be displayed or flaunted; a man might *sport* a moustache, or a red necktie, but
hardly thick-lensed glasses, as a news magazine reported. *Sport* as a verb,
in any event, is overused in newswriting.

**sporting.**    As an adjective in the sense of *pertaining to sports, sporting* is
now old hat. *Sporting editor* is redolent of a generation that is all gone; the
sporting editor's successor is the sports editor. *Sporting* in the sense of
*sports* may prompt a snicker because it suggests the sense of *sporting
house*. The latter, however, is also an anachronism. Yet all this does not
impugn such expressions as *a sporting proposition*. And *sporting goods*
survives without a shadow.

**sportswriting.**    Is there anything to the assumptions that sportswriting is
more creative than other kinds of newswriting and that the sports page
has been the launching pad for numerous literary rockets? One cynic said
nothing more is needed to demolish this idea than to lay a number of
sports stories beside other kinds of news stories, all selected at random,
and compare them for evidences of creativity. It is true that sportswriters
generally enjoy more latitude in choice of language, and in exhibiting indi-

viduality, if any, in their work. What use do they make of this latitude? We have two opinions, separated by more than thirty years. One of them was expressed by H. W. Fowler in *Modern English Usage* in 1926, incidental to his discussion under the heading *sobriquets*:

> . . . games and contests are exciting to take part in, interesting or even exciting also to watch, but essentially (i. e. as bare facts) dull to read about, insomuch that most intelligent people abandon such reading; the reporter, conscious that his matter & his audience are both dull enough to require enlivening, thinks that the needful fillip may be given if he calls fishing the gentle craft, a ball the pill or the leather, a captain the skipper, or a saddle the pigskin, & so makes his description a series of momentary puzzles that shall pleasantly titillate inactive minds.

The following comments were made by Bergen and Cornelia Evans in *Dictionary of Contemporary American Usage*, under the heading "sports English":

> Because it deals with struggle, sports writing is required to be vigorous, and because it scorns formality it must be slangy and colloquial. But slang is particularly unfitted for frequent repetition and sports writing is, above any other type of contemporary writing, repetitious, laden with clichés. The wretched sports writer, with slight material and often (one suspects) even slighter interest, is compelled to assume concern he does not feel and to conceal his yawns under forced shouts of excitement . . . No one, apparently, using only the normal resources of the richest language known, can make sports interesting . . .
>
> A legend has grown up that the sports pages have produced an immense number of writers who have gone on to literary triumphs. But as Nunnally Johnson asked, after Lardner, Broun, Kieran, Pegler, Gallico, Reynolds, and Considine, who is there? Johnson's characterization of sports writing is not flattering. "Bad writing, grammar-school humor, foolish styles, threadbare phrases, spurious enthusiasm and heavy-footed comedy . . . nauseating sentimentality and agonized slang . . . [and] above all, breeziness, breeziness, breeziness!"

An able newspaperman who started his career as a sportswriter asked, after two or three years, for another assignment, even though it would mean loss of income. When asked his reason, he said he could no longer endure to deal with and write in awestruck tones about sports figures, whom he characterized as phonies, cases of arrested development, or both at once.

**sprawling.** The greatest love affair of all time is not that between Romeo and Juliet, nor that between Abélard and Héloïse, but between many writers and this word, as used to describe an extensive building.

**stage.** Journalese for *present, exhibit, offer, put on, perform.* There is a tendency to discourage its use except in reference to performances that are given on a stage, and this appears to be the most acceptable sense. *Stage a comeback,* which Webster cites as an example of colloquial use, is a cliché. *Stage* as a verb in the senses under discussion here is so worn that it might as well be avoided.

**stalk.** Outworn in connection with death personified, as "Death stalked the highways," which is warmed over and served up after every holiday.

**stalling for time.** Redundant. *Stalling* is inevitably for time.

**state-name descriptives.** P. 104.

**statuesque.** Excessively used to describe beauties of larger-than-average size.

**statutory charge, offense.** These are euphemisms, now less used than at one time, for charges or offenses relating to sex, such as rape, sodomy, and incest. The expressions are carefully nondistinctive in themselves, for all crimes are defined in statutes of one kind or another. The result of using *statutory offense* only in connection with sex crimes is that the expression is taken as applicable only to such crimes.

**steam shovel.** A number of style manuals clear their throats and self-importantly intone something like this: "Don't write *steam shovel.* The steam shovel is obsolete. Make it *power shovel.*" Then they solemnly proceed to more important, or often even more trivial, matters. Why this particular expression should have been seized on to flaunt editors' grasp of modern technology (even if it does hark back thirty years) is hard to explain. Moreover, the ban on it seems like nonsense, because *steam shovel* has gone into the language, and thus serves a purpose even if most mechanical shovels are no longer run by steam. Steam is out of style for steam rollers too, and next we can expect some editor to insist that legislation which fits the description is power-rollered, rather than steam-rollered, through.

Lead pencil is even more of an anachronism than *steam shovel,* because probably no one now alive can remember when lead really was used in pencils, rather than graphite. What about *cables* and *cabling?* No effort is made to distinguish between messages actually sent by cable and those sent by radio. Any such effort would, of course, be ridiculous. Since *steam roller, lead pencil,* and *cable* have escaped the wrath of style dictators, it seems only fair that *steam shovel* should be excused, too. Shame on you, dictators! Let's go after bigger game.

**stercoraceous.** Editorial writers who feel they cannot accurately appraise certain politicians or political proposals without using words that are out of place in a family medium may be overlooking *stercoraceous*.

**sterling.** As applied to silver, *sterling* is sometimes regarded as meaning the same thing as *pure*, but this is not quite right. It means 92.5 per cent pure, or a little less so than Ivory soap.

**still and all.** See *well and good*.

**still remains, continues.** Redundant for *remains, continues*.

**stone.** See *rock, stone*.

**stormy petrel.** The stormy petrel, once a numerous species, appears to be extinct as a metaphor. Too bad. I used to imagine them angrily dipping and screaming in the troughs of the waves that bring the tempest. Is it possible that Billy Mitchell was the last of the stormy petrels? Come to think of it, latter-day petrels seem less stormy than petulant.

**streamline, -d.** Interchangeable as adjectives: *a streamline (streamlined) train. Streamlined*, however, seems predominant.

**stricture.** In the physical sense, a stricture is a contraction or narrowing, as in a tube; in the nonmaterial sense, it is censure or adverse criticism.

**student.** See *pupil*.

**stuffy writing.** P. 51.

**style.** Capitalization, pp. 107-108; stylebooks, pp. 133-134.

**subliminal.** This word, used to describe advertising flashed on a screen so quickly the watchers don't consciously perceive it, often is printed *sublimal*. This is going from the subliminal to the pediculous, as far as spelling is concerned.

**suddenly collapsed.** Redundant. Suddenness is the essence of collapse, unless the word is otherwise qualified.

**suffer, sustain, receive.** Properly speaking, people suffer *injuries*, and such wording as "The driver *suffered* a broken leg" is frowned on by some critics because they think it means, in effect, that the driver suffered a leg. Such criticism has dubious foundation, for the writer said *broken leg*, i.e., *the breaking of a leg*, and that is how all but the captious will read it. "The driver *received* a broken leg" offers no refuge from these critics, who have been known to respond to such intelligence with "How? By parcel post?"

In any event, such sentences seem open to improvement: "The driver's leg *was broken*." There is no good reason why one should not write "The driver *suffered* [or *received*] a fracture of the leg," however. See also *break, broke,* and *have, had.*

It is sometimes held by those who have never looked up the word that *sustain* means only *hold up.* It is a proper synonym for *suffer* or *undergo.*

**suffixes.**   Hyphens with, p. 77; see also *-wise.*

**suffocate.**   By itself, this word cannot be relied on to indicate fatality. *Suffocated to death* may sound like a redundancy, and indeed it is, in view of one meaning of *suffocate.* But another meaning is merely *to stifle* or *choke. Suffocate* in its fatal sense, then, should be used only in contexts that indicate a fatal result.

**supply.**   See *furnish.*

**survive.**   Pp. 149-150.

**survivors.**   Listed in obituaries, pp. 87-88.

**suspected.**   Injustice is done by referring to a person accused of being a spy, for example, as a *suspected* (or *accused,* or *alleged*) *spy,* Theodore M. Bernstein points out in *Watch Your Language.* The implication is that the person *is* a spy, and not simply accused of being one.

**sustain.**   See *suffer, sustain, receive.*

**swing into high gear.**   As a figure of speech, this expression unmistakably shows its age.

**T**

**tabloid.**   See *newspaper terms.*

**take.**   See *bring, take.*

**take place.**   See *occur.*

**tar.**   Some sailors on liberty once got into trouble with the police, and the headline on the resulting story referred to them as *tars.* Now, as it happened, these fellows were Negroes, and a delegation from the local Negro community shortly appeared in the editor's office, demanding an apology for what they considered an unnecessary racial slur. They got it, too. But although *tar* and *tarbrush* sometimes have a racial connotation, it does not exist in the use of *tar* for *sailor.* The expression is variously described as a shortened form of *tarpaulin* and as a reference to the tar sailors once smeared on their pigtails. See also *Negro.*

**taunt, taut.** *Taunt* means *jeer at* or *tease*: "The losing team was *taunted* by the students." *Taut* means *stretched tight*: "The clothesline was not *taut* enough." *Taunt* is often misused for *taut*.

**technic, technique.** Though these forms are interchangeable, *technique* has a long running start. In any event, the word is always pronounced tek*neek*. *Technic* may as well be abandoned.

**technical terms.** Pp. 53-54.

**telecast, televise.** The technical distinction that *telecast* means to broadcast by television, and *televise* to record by television apparatus and then to broadcast, may be useful to those in the field, but they are the only ones aware of it.

**tenses.** Sequence of, pp. 31-33; in time elements, pp. 125-127; in cutlines, p. 152; in participles, p. 24.

**tenterhooks.** These are hooks on which curtains are stretched, and the term was once applied to hooks from which poultry was hung in a shop. The word is now usually used figuratively in the phrase *on tenterhooks*, meaning *in suspense*, and sometimes misrendered *on tender hooks*.

**term as.** See *consider*.

**that.** Omitted as conjunction, p. 44; before a direct quotation, p. 45; vs. *which*, p. 92; omitted in relative clauses, pp. 44-45; *that of, in* wrongly omitted (false comparison), p. 60.

**the.** Omitted, p. 28; used carelessly, p. 30; with *Congress*, p. 28.

**theater, theatre.** *Theatre* is the British preference in spelling.

**thee, thou.** See *-eth*.

**theft.** See *burglary*.

**there.** Max J. Herzberg, as the editor of *Word Study,* found that three subjects got his readers' dander up higher than anything else: the split infinitive, proposals to dispense with the apostrophe, and the use of *there is* or *there are* to begin a sentence. This latter construction is often criticized as objectionably indefinite and a product of lazy thinking. Nonetheless, it is frequent in good literature, particularly the Bible: "*There were* giants in the earth in those days"; "Now *there arose* up a new king"; "The fool hath said in his heart, '*There is* no God' ", and "*There were* in the same country shepherds . . ." Other examples have been cited: "*There is* a pleasure in the pathless woods" (Byron); "*There is* the smack of ambrosia about it" (Lowell).

It seems apparent that the *there* construction is used advisedly, rather than lazily, in these examples, to avoid the undesirable emphasis on the true subject that would come of placing it first. "*Giants* were in the earth in those days" would lay an undesired stress on *giants*. In any event, the rearrangement kills the rhythm and force of the line. If "Now *there* arose up a new king" became "Now a new king arose up" *a new king* would take emphasis from *arose up*. Considerations of rhythm also enter here.

The *there* construction may be clumsy and objectionably indirect after a passive auxiliary: "As in the previous ruling, *there was* no jail sentence imposed." Surely "no jail sentence was imposed" would be better. "Yesterday *there were* four more cases of polio reported." Better: "Yesterday four more cases of polio were reported." The clumsiness is aggravated when *has* or *have*, as auxiliaries in passive constructions, follow *there*: "*There have been* thousands of people killed"; "*There have been* two surveys taken."

It is not considered good practice to begin a sentence with a figure, and there is reason to believe that the rule against it causes some writers to shy away even from starting a sentence with a number that has been spelled out. They resort to the *there* construction: "*There are* eleven organizations representing health, welfare, and youth groups in the county"; "*There were* nineteen military experiments connected with the explosion."

This timidity in the presence of numbers unnecessarily carries over to those beginning clauses, rather than sentences: "At present, it is said, *there are* 102 of the county's 167 dairies shipping milk into the area." *There are* only defeats the prominence that *102* deserves, and gives the sentence a woolly sound. Besides, the verb *are shipping* is unidiomatically divided by a prepositional modifier. Unidiomatic division of verb forms also figures in the unhappy sound of the passive constructions cited earlier.

Whether any ground has been gained in this little review of the problem the reader must decide for himself. These points may be made, at any rate: The *there* construction is not to be condemned out of hand; it is both idiomatic and common in the best literature; it is clumsy and to be avoided with a passive verb; and in view of the prejudice against it, the writer who uses it should take heart and be prepared to defend himself, for defense is indeed possible.

**therefor, therefore.** *Therefor* is usually found in legal or other fusty contexts, and it means *for that* or *for it*: "He explained the cause of action and the basis *therefor*" (that is, *the basis for it*). *Therefore*, a familiar friend sometimes displaced by *therefor*, means *consequently, as a result*: "The conclusion, *therefore*, is that we have no case."

**think.** See *feel*.

**this, these.** There are two misuses of *this* as a pronoun. One consists in using it at the beginning of a sentence or clause in reference to something specific of what has gone before, rather than to the general idea preceding. "The Senussis established what has been called a theocratic empire, spilling over political frontiers. *This* [better *It,* or *The empire*] was then broken up." An example of correct use: "Because of inherited venereal disease, their population remains static. *This* worries the elders of the tribe."

Otherwise, the demonstrative *this* should not be used when personal pronouns will do. "We were much impressed by the chief. *This* [better *He,* or *This man*] is an able and progressive citizen." "Since 1927 he has lived in his studio, and it has long been his wish that *this* [better, *it*] be kept as a museum after his death."

*These* as a demonstrative pronoun tends, like *this,* to be misused in the place of personal pronouns. "Her heartbeat tripled and her rate of breathing was three or four times normal, but as the rocket reached its orbit, *these* [better, *they*] tended to return to normal." "She digs up whole pages of evidence and serves *these* [*them*] hot." "I get all the oysters I want at home, but *these* taste like brass doorknobs." The demonstrative *these* is proper here, the context showed, because the writer was contrasting the oysters at home with others.

**this writer.** P. 73.

**thrifty.** In careful writing, this word is all but invariably applied to people: *a thrifty housewife.* Ad-ese, however, loosely and liberally applies it to products: *a thrifty shortening, a thrifty toothpaste,* a usage that is distasteful to the discriminating, who would use *economical* in such contexts. Whether this distinction will be done in by the brevity and breeziness of *thrifty* vs. *economical* remains to be seen.

**time elements.** Tenses misused in, pp. 125-127; *today,* pp. 129-130; day of the week, pp. 130-131; misplaced, pp. 127-129; in cutlines, p. 152.

**'tis.** See *poesy.*

**titles.** Capitalization, pp. 107-108; clerical designations, pp. 105-106; see *Dame;* doubled, p. 101; *Dr.,* pp. 107-108; false, p. 100; see *feminine forms; Miss,* p. 103; *Mr.,* pp. 101-102; *Mrs.,* p. 102; occupational, pp. 100-101; *Rev.,* p. 105.

**to.** vs. *of,* p. 47.

**today.** *To-day,* p. 80; as a time element in news stories, pp. 129-130.

**tortuous, torturous.** *Tortuous* means *twisting* or *winding,* as a *tortuous mountain road; torturous* means *giving torture,* as *a torturous stiff collar.*

**toss.** There is no good reason why *toss* should be putting *throw* and similar expressions out of business, but it is.

**tot, tote.** Often confused in their past tenses, *toted* and *totted*. *Tote* is a dialectal expression meaning *carry*: "We *toted* our own wood for the fire." *Tot* means add up: "The accountant *totted* up the column of figures."

**totally (or completely) destroyed (or demolished).** Redundant for *destroyed* or *demolished*. It is true, of course, that something may be *partly destroyed*, but without a qualifier the sense of the words is absolute.

**tour of duty.** Military lingo that may best be left to military connections. A writer infatuated with inappropriate cant, however, may speak of a policeman going off duty as "ending his tour of duty." Properly, a tour of duty is an assignment to a locality or post for a considerable period, and is not applied even by the military to a watch or shift.

**transpire.** The use of *transpire* for *occur* or *happen*, Webster says, is "disapproved by most authorities but found in the writings of authors of good standing." When any authority as conservative as Webster concedes this much, however, the battle against any disputed expression may be considered over. One more thing, however, remains to be considered: that *transpire* is likely to be regarded as a somewhat hifalutin substitute for *happen or occur*.

**tread, trod.** The use of *trod* (its past tense) for *tread*, and of *trodding* (no such word) for *treading*, is a ludicrous gaffe: "He's *trodding* softly, meanwhile, on that borrowed oriental rug"; "She will *trod* the boards tomorrow." Next thing we know they'll be giving us:

> " 'Will you walk a little faster?' said a whiting to a snail
> 'There's a porpoise just behind us, and he's *trodding* on my tail.' "

No doubt, too, they will rush in where angels fear to trod.

**trigger.** In an age of armament races, wars, and rumors of wars, the popularity of *trigger* as a verb meaning *cause, begin, set off*, and the like is probably inevitable. Like many other words fancied as contributing drama, however specious, this one is mournfully overworked.

**trio.** P. 96.

**trod.** See *tread, trod*.

**trooper, trouper.** A trooper is a soldier; a trouper is an actor, or member of a troupe.

**true facts.** Redundant. What are not facts are not true. See *fact*.

**trustee, trusty.** Both are people in whom trust has been reposed, and the confusion arises generally in the plural forms: *trustees, trusties.* A trustee is a member of a controlling board, as of a college or foundation. A trusty is an inmate of a prison who enjoys special privileges because of his trustworthiness. Regrettably, it is not unknown for irresponsible trustees to end their careers as trusties.

**tsk, tsk.** An ad published nationally by a radio station carried an incidental reminder: "Have you registered to vote? Tch, tch—better do it now." Deviations like this must be nipped in the bud, for a tsk is a tsk is a tsk—and not a tch.

**turn in, into.** P. 47.

**tuxedo.** There is a sneaking idea that *tuxedo* is an expression inferior, somehow, to *dinner coat* or *dinner jacket.* This is not so, and further, the prevalence of *tuxedo*, and especially *tux*, is now such that people know them who do not know that *dinner coat* and *dinner jacket* are the same thing. *Tuxedo*, incidentally, comes from the name of a club at Tuxedo Park, N. Y. The term as applied to clothing dates from 1899.

**'twas, 'twere, 'twill.** See *poesy.*

**twelve noon, midnight.** Redundant. Noon and midnight are both twelve.

**twit.** A transitive verb; twitting is done by one to another, and is not reciprocal. "When he courted Jane Hadley, Kentucky *twitted* with him; when he finally won and married her, Kentucky rejoiced with him, too." *Twitted with* is unidiomatic; *twitted him.*

**type.** There are several things to be said about the misuse of this noun as an adjective (*the intellectual type employee, athletic type persons, a nonparalytic type polio, a new type antenna, a different type Communist dictator, an adventure type show*). The first is that no one with any sensitivity to the nuances of expression uses the word in the way illustrated by the examples, in either speech or writing. Such locutions are characteristic of the untutored speech of New York's lower East Side or the Bronx, as reproduced so amusingly in the fiction of Arthur Kober. A hyphen between *type* and the modifier preceding it at least brings this construction within the pale: *the intellectual-type employee, a nonparalytic-type polio.* The trouble with this way out is that those who fancy *type* as an adjective are the type who cannot be depended on to have any appreciation of the role of hyphens, either. As noted in *Watch Your Language, type* with a hyphen is most acceptable in technical connections, as in *V-type engine,*

*O-type blood, cantilever-type bridge.* Let's face it: It is necessary to say *type of* (*the intellectual type of employee, a new type of antenna*) or be set down as an ungrammatical type.

**typewriter tricks.**    I would be ashamed to offer these open secrets if I did not know that there are writers who have functioned for decades and never learned about them. First, the number *1* is formed on the typewriter by striking the lower-case *l* (ell, that is), not the *I*.

The dash is formed by striking the hyphen twice, and it is standard practice to leave no space between the strokes or at either side of the dash. A hyphen with a space at either side is not a proper dash.

The exclamation point is formed by striking the apostrophe and the period one at a time while holding the space bar down.

Reasonably satisfactory brackets ([ ], used to enclose interpolated matter) can be made, if absolutely necessary and worth the trouble, by use of the underline (_) and the virgule, or slant(/). To form the upper horizontal lines, the underline must be struck on the line above that on which the bracket is being formed. A box may be made by joining a pair of such brackets.

Reasonable facsimiles of diacritical marks are also possible with the typewriter, if you are not unreasonably critical. The double quotation mark over a letter will serve as an acceptable umlaut, and the single quote will serve at least as a gesture toward the grave or acute accent, although of course it will not be possible to tell one from the other. Perhaps this mark is better made by hand with a pen. A cedilla may be made by striking the comma under a *c*.

# U

**uh-huh, unh-unh, etc.**    See *ah, aw*.

**umlauts.**    See *diacritical marks*; *typewriter tricks*.

**underestimate.**    "It would be a mistake to *underestimate* the Russian leadership," pontificated a news magazine. Well, yes; a mistake is indeed a mistake. Similarly, "The role that his wife played in this new and immense shot in the arm for the importance of his office cannot be *underestimated*" should read *overestimated*. See also *minimize*.

**under way, weigh; aweigh.**    *Under way,* which was born on the foam but has become firmly settled ashore, and the title of that fine old chantey, "Anchors Aweigh," are likely to get tangled, like neglected lines. *Way,* to a sailor, generally means *power,* so that a ship under way is one under power, or not moored or anchored. *Under way,* of course, has come into general use in the sense of *getting started* or *in motion,* and there is a noticeable tendency, resisted by purists, to make it one word.

*Under weigh* is neither fish, flesh, nor good red herring. *Under weigh* is the spawn of confusion with *anchor's aweigh,* a shipboard report better known as the name of the Navy song. An anchor is aweigh when, in effect, it is being weighed by the ship—that is, free of the bottom and hanging by the chain. "Anchor's aweigh, sir," is what the boatswain reports to the officer of the deck. Thus *anchor's away,* a version sometimes seen, is meaningless.

**unhealthful, unhealthy.** See *healthful, healthy.*

**uninterest.** See *disinterest, uninterest.*

**unique.** The doctrine that *unique* is an absolute modifier that cannot be qualified may be a noble one, but it has no connection with the facts of usage. When used without a qualifier, as in "His outlook on the world was *unique,*" it means *without a like or equal.* There are so few unique things under the sun that generally the word is used with a qualifier. This simply extends its meaning without diminishing its force as an absolute when used alone. "So *unique* then was a ship carrying only tourists that port officials greeted them with alarm" and "The college shares with other private schools several points of *uniqueness*" are not open to criticism. *More unique, most unique, quite unique,* and the like are equally acceptable.

**unpleasantry.** "There have been no acts of disorder, no disturbance, and no unpleasantries at our schools." Thus was a governor quoted in a news magazine. Fowler might have placed *unpleasantry,* if it had appeared in his time, in his category "Facetious formations." Dictionaries do not recognize *unpleasantry,* which, sad to say, appears to be an illiterate back-formation from *pleasantry. Pleasantry* is a good word, but it means *a jest,* not *pleasantness.* In spite of this, *unpleasantry,* which turns up every now and then, may become one of Fowler's sturdy indefensibles that outlive their critics. *Unpleasantnesses,* the obvious alternative, is certainly clumsy. Since there is no such thing as the opposite of a joke, *unpleasantries* can hardly be misunderstood.

**unveil.** Journalese for *announce, display, reveal, exhibit.*

**up.** As a verb (*prices have been upped*), journalese.

**upcoming.** Journalese for *coming*: "Plans have been made for the up-coming festival." This word has no standing, nor is there any occasion for it. It is part of the cant of news-gathering, but it should not find its way into print.

**Up Style.** P. 108.

**upwards of.** Clumsy for *more than*. It is in the same league with *in back of* for *behind* and *close to* for *nearly*.

**usage, use.** *Usage* relates to a customary practice, *use* to the act of employing something. Often *usage* has a technical sense; when it applies to language, as it often does in this book, it means a standard of use. It may also apply to customs, traditions, rituals, and the like: *the usages of the church*. In "the unprecedented *usage* of power," the writer would have been better advised to use *use*.

**utterance by proxy.** Pp. 141-142.

## V

**vaccinate.** See *inoculate, vaccinate*.

**variation.** To avoid unnecessary repetition, pp. 58-59; the geographical fetish, p. 59.

**various.** See *different, various*.

**veep.** Now and then *veep* is applied to any and all vice-presidents, including those of colleges, clubs, and corporations. Yet the consensus seems to be that there was really only one veep, namely, the late Alben B. Barkley, and that applying this expression, which was peculiarly his, to any other vice-president is a species of misappropriation. If this be sentiment, make what you will of it.

**verbal, -ly.** *Verbal* means *in words,* either spoken or written. If the intention is convey the idea of spoken, rather than written, words, the expression wanted is *oral,* whose opposite is *written.* "He *verbally* assaulted the committee" illustrates a correct, if not altogether explicit, use. We know that the assault was in words, rather than physical, but we cannot be sure whether the words were written or spoken. Probably the words were spoken, for *verbal* is often loosely misused in this way, as in *a verbal contract.* If exactness is of any consequence, the writer should choose between *oral* and *written,* and not take a chance with *verbal.*

**verbs.** Compound, divided, p. 36; omission of needed forms, pp. 56-57; wrongly hyphenated phrasal verbs, p. 76; in time elements, pp. 125-127. See also *tenses*.

**verse.** Is chintziness on the rise? It seems so, when verse is reprinted like this: Twinkle, twinkle, little star/How I wonder what you are/ Up above the world so high/Like a diamond in the sky. Quoted poetry once was set up line by line, as it ought to be. This takes a little more space than running the lines together. But running the lines in tends to kill the effect of verse as such.

**very.** It is true that *very* is a four-letter word, but this hardly justifies the opprobrium that has been heaped on it in style guides and otherwise. Some newspapers, for example, interdict its use entirely in the news columns, a ban they attempt to justify on the ground that *very* implies a judgment by the writer. One deep thinker in the newspaper profession adjured his reporters, when tempted to use *very,* to set down *damn* instead. This may be clever, but it is not damn (or *very,* if you prefer, as I do) smart. An outright prohibition on the use of any word that is not indecent only reflects on the judgment of the prohibitor.

What is so bad about *very*? Overuse, say its critics. It appears, however, that the prejudice has outlived the vice that produced it, for no objectionable number of *verys* is evident these days. This is not to say the word is never misused. But the most conspicuous misuse is seen in misguided attempts to strengthen words that are already strong. The result of fastening *very* to them is that they are weakened, not strengthened. *Wonderful* is a frequent victim. *Wonderful* is wonderful, but *very wonderful* is less so. The reader is left with the impression that the writer doth protest too much. Likewise *lovely* (*a very lovely singing star*), *splendid* (*a very splendid performance*), and *excellent* (*a very excellent dinner*). The writer who wants to damn can do it not only with damns, like the captious editor we have referred to, but by tacking *very* onto what would otherwise be veritable praise. We may say that *very* is often invoked when the writer is straining for an effect he does not quite believe in, and its use generally shows this.

Fowler cited instances in which *very* could not be correctly used with a passive participle. *A very worried official,* he said, is right, but *The Government, very worried, withdrew the motion* is wrong. It seems hardly worthwhile to go into the ins and outs of this, because it is now a dead issue. A writer's ear will tell him whether he is using *very* idiomatically. The substitution of *much* for a *very* that sounds questionable (*I was much inconvenienced*), as recommended by Fowler, jars on the American ear.

But *very much* (*I was very much inconvenienced*) will solve the problem, if problem this be.

**via.**   *Via* means *by way of*. It is a great favorite with the journalese artist, who uses it to inflate *by* and in other distasteful ways. The proper use of *via* is only in the sense of *by way of*: "We traveled to San Francisco from Chicago *via* New Orleans." *Via train* would be better *by train*. Basketball writers like to tell of scores being made "*via* the free-throw route" when they mean "*by* free throws." Mayhem is often reported as being committed "*via* the knife route," instead of "*with* a knife."
"An electronic device fits around the dog *via* a harness." *by means of*.
"They talk *via* ham radio to their relatives and friends." *by* or *over*.
"The museum will open its new gallery *via* an exhibit of fifty paintings." *with*.
"Dr. Young's pigs were born *via* Caesarean section." *by*.

**visionary.**   The word means existing in imagination only, hence chimerical or impractical. It usually has a derogatory connotation, and cannot be used in the sense of *farsighted, prophetic,* or *imaginative*. "The speaker closed with an appeal to city officials in the audience to do some *visionary* planning." *farsighted, imaginative*.

**voice.**   In *voiced objections, voiced praise,* and the like, unnecessarily roundabout for *objected, praised*.

**vow.**   As a verb, *vow* means to take an oath. It is all but extinct in common parlance, except that in journalese it is a favored variant of *say* or *promise*. "We'll win the next one, the coach *vowed*," not making a bloody sacrifice on an altar but merely being wistful. The use of *vow* where *promise* will do implies an inappropriate solemnity. The fondness for *vow* has something in common with a preference for *lone* over *sole* or *only*.

# W

**wacky.**   The slang term for *mentally unbalanced* or *eccentric* is thus spelled, not *whacky*.

**wage.**   See *salary*.

**was a former.**   Pp. 126-127.

**was given.**   Pp. 39-40.

**we (editorial).**   Pp. 72-74.

**weather stories.**   Pp. 148-149.

**well and good.** The two most inane expressions of recent years are *well and good* and *still and all*. *Well and good* apparently reflects the influence of radio announcers, who seem unwilling to trust any word to convey an idea by itself, especially when they are ad-libbing, but must bolster it with a synonym. *Still and all* (sometimes rendered *still in all,* which surely means no less) has even found its way into the ordinarily well-culled pages of the *New Yorker*. May the shade of Harold Ross be placated.

**well known.** *Well known* has been placed under interdiction in some quarters on the fussy assumption it is an error for *widely known*. There is nothing to this. *Widely known* is perfectly all right, of course. So is *well known*. It is solidly enough established to be in the dictionary, and the expressions are synonymous.

Now and then we encounter *well breeding,* apparently the misshapen descendant of *well bred,* as in "The apology showed well breeding." *Well* cannot be used as an adjective in the sense of *good,* and what is meant is "The apology showed *good breeding*." *Well breeding* will have to be reserved for the breeders of wells, presumably well-drillers.

Naval officers use the peculiar expression, "That's well," to express approval, usually to subordinates. They don't always mean simply "That's good" by it, but sometimes "That's enough."

Expressions like *well known* are hyphenated when attributive (that is, when they come before what they modify, as *the well-known human race*), and unhyphenated when predicative (when they come later, as in *his fondness for liquor was well known*).

**welsh, welch.** *Welsh* enjoys marked preference over *welch* as the form for the word meaning to swindle someone in a bet, or to go back on a commitment. Welshmen have been known to object to the use of this term as unjustly aspersing them. It is unlikely that anyone has Welshmen in mind when using it, however, and the *Oxford English Dictionary* diplomatically describes its origin as obscure. In any event, *welsh* in this sense is never capitalized.

**wha.** A kittenish reviewer, after giving a generally rough time to the movie version of *Brigadoon,* asked, "Scots, wha' this?" Sometimes it doesn't pay to get cute. *Wha* in Scots dialect means *who,* not *what* or *what's*. Robert Burns wrote:

> Wha will be a traitor knave?
> Wha can fill a coward's grave?
> Wha sae base as be a slave?

Wha, indeed?

**wharf.** See *dock*.

**whence, from whence.**   See *from where*.

**where.**   See *from where;* also (restrictive, nonrestrictive clauses), pp. 90-92.

**whether.**   See *if, whether*.

**whether or not.**   Although some insist *or not* is redundant here, the form is so well established they may as well turn their attention to weightier matters. *As to* preceding *whether* ("The question *as to whether* he had dinner") is useless.

**which.**   Vs. *that,* p. 92; may be omitted with forms of *to be,* p. 57; see also *and which*.

**while.**   As a conjunction (for *and, but, although*), p. 43.

**whodunit.**   Since this word is solidly established in the dictionaries as the designation for a murder mystery story, the frequent renderings *who dun it, whodunnit,* etc., seem hardly excusable.

**who, whom.**

"If a boy ignores his arithmetic teacher and states that 8 times 7 are 63, he will be laughed at by his friends; but if he *obeys* his English teacher and says, '*With whom* are you going to the party?' instead of '*Who* are you going to the party *with?*' *he will also be laughed at.* Grammar, at least as taught by many old-fashioned teachers, is almost purely directive and bears little relation to the way English is actually spoken and written."—*Language in Thought and Action,* S. I. Hayakawa.

In a survey by Norman Lewis, "How Correct Must Correct English Be?" in *Harper's,* March, 1949, "Who did you meet?" was given 43 per cent acceptance in an opinion poll of 468 high-school and college teachers of English, authors, editors, journalists, radio commentators, lexicographers, and a random sampling of subscribers to *Harper's.* Kyle Crichton, associate editor of *Collier's,* commented:

"The most loathsome word (to me at least) in the English language is *whom.* You can always tell a half-educated buffoon by the care he takes in working the word in. When he starts it I know I am faced with a pompous illiterate who is not going to have me long as company."

The *Oxford English Dictionary* calls *whom* "no longer current in unstudied colloquial speech." *Whom* is regularly nominated for oblivion. Yet there remain a good many people to whom its strictly correct use, whatever that may be, is the touchstone of education. The chief among these, possibly, are the editors of the *New Yorker,* who steadily note misuses under the snide caption, "The Omnipotent Whom."

It appears that critics of the supposed misuse of *who* or *whom* are on shaky ground. *Whom,* of course, is the objective (or accusative) form, and seems to be required as the object of a verb or of a preposition: "You chose *whom*?" "This is the man to *whom* I spoke." But "You chose *who*?" is acceptable, at least in speech. *To who* is unlikely, however.

Most of the trouble with *whom* comes in relatively complex constructions that must be taken apart to determine what is subject and what is object. Most of us, especially in view of the ambiguous standing of *whom,* pay no attention to which form is used. There are those, however, to whom the appearance of either *who* or *whom* is as a red flag waved before a bull, and they cannot wait to parse the sentence, in hope of finding an error.

"He summoned the officer, *whom* he said had just been commissioned." *Whom* is not the object of *summoned,* as may appear, but rather the subject of *had been commissioned,* and should be *who.*

"She explained her presence to the Hungarian hussar, *whom* she hoped would fall in love with her." *Whom* is not the object of *hoped,* but the subject of *would fall,* and should be *who.*

These sentences illustrate the commonest "misuse" of *whom.* Yet when the critics of such errors must indict the translators of the Bible, together with Keats and Shakespeare, as having known no better, their preachments take on a hollow ring:

"Young Ferdinand *whom* they suppose is drown'd"; "Arthur, *whom* they say is killed tonight." Shakespeare.

"*Whom* say ye that I am?" Matthew 14:15.

"I have met with women *whom* I really think would like to be married to a poem." Keats.

The consensus is that either *whom* or *who* is correct in these constructions.

There is general agreement among grammarians that a preposition or verb following *who* does not make it *whom* even if *who* is the object. Thus "*Who* are you going with?" and "*Who* did you invite?" are not only correct, but preferable to *whom. Than whom* is an idiom: "An architect *than whom* there was none more clever."

In Boston, according to Ernest Weekley, the owls say "To-whit, to-*whom.*"

See also *and which, and who*; and for omission of *who* plus forms of the verb *to be,* see p. 57.

**whopping.** *Whopping* long ago had all the whop whopped out of it. *Whacking* and *thumping,* as modifiers, are coming to the same end.

**whose.** Correctly applicable to things as well as to people: "The tree *whose* leaves were falling." *Of which* is correct, but unnecessary and usually clumsy.

**widow, wife.** Pp. 149-150.

**will.** Vs. *shall,* pp. 37-39.

**-wise.** *Wise* words like *dollarwise, saleswise, productionwise* have been widely jeered as samples of the Madison Avenue mind at its worst. It was only to be expected, then, that a man who wrote "*Budget-wise* housewives are looking for economical buys," should be taken to task, as indeed he was. But the critic was barking up the wrong avenue that time. If the victim had written, "*Budgetwise,* housewives are confused," he would have been guilty as charged, for there, indeed, is one of the excoriated species.

It appears that the *wise* in a true *wise* word is a suffix meaning *in terms of* or *with respect to. Wise* words often are used as adverbs, taking the place of prepositional phrases modifying the whole sentence: "Sales are up, *dollarwise*" (in terms of dollars). But the *wise* in *budget-wise* housewives is the adjective that means *possessing wisdom.* What the writer had in mind were housewives who are wise in the ways of budgets. *Budget-wise* in this instance is not to be blamed on Madison Avenue. The use of *wise* in this way (as a word in its own right, serving as part of a compound adjective, rather than as a mere suffix) is long established and highly respectable. The saying "Penny-wise, pound-foolish," for example, is surely old enough to be virtuous. Why should *budget-wise* be any more objectionable than any other compound modifier: *large-scale* (map), *next-door* (neighbor), *money-back* (guarantee)?

True *wise* words, on the other hand, seem to have developed on the model of certain reputable expressions in which *wise* is a suffix having a slightly different sense, namely, *in the way,* or *manner, of.* Some of those words are *lengthwise, clockwise, likewise, otherwise.* Since we have seen a false accusation against the compound adjective *budget-wise*, it may be well to administer loyalty oaths to *lengthwise, clockwise, likewise,* and *otherwise,* before they are hauled up for guilt by association.

When that rock was first turned over, exposing *wise* words to public scorn, I didn't like them any better than anybody else. It now looks, however, as if some of them have a future, at least in conversation. They shorten expression in a way that is undeniably handy, however loathsome it may seem while it is still relatively new. Certainly it is easier to say "This scheme is clumsy productionwise" than "This scheme is clumsy with respect to production" (or "when it comes to production"). Snobbery and imitation play large roles in the rejection or acceptance of such devices. Some people are delighted by the economy of *wise* words, and after becoming aware of their possibilities, go at once and do likewise at every opportunity. There is a tendency to jump overboard: "Solano is the largest county populationwise and assessed valuationwise." *Wise?* Unwise. Others are jarred by the compression and bluntness of *wise* words, and even more important, are overimpressed by having read they are disdained in some quarters.

Some Madison Avenooers have denied inventing, using, or even hearing used among their associates the expressions blamed on their kind. Observation shows that *wise* words, at least, were being manufactured long before Madison Avenue existed as a mythical institution, or as a fount of supposedly defiled language.

**wisecrack.**  See *quip, quipped*.

**with.**  Vs. *of,* p. 47; *with* phrases, p. 49.

**with regard to.**  See *regard*.

**with the exception of.**  Redundant for *except* or *except for*.

**with (for) the purpose of.**  See *for the purpose of*.

**witness.**  Often a pretentious substitute for the simpler and more direct *see, watch, observe. Witness* has a legal or official connotation that is out of place in its usual contexts: *witness a ball game, witness a school play.* Used in this way, the word is journalese.

**woman, lady.**  Rudyard Kipling's cavalier verdict was that "A woman is only a woman, but a good cigar is a smoke." Many of that sex are likely to go up in smoke themselves at hearing the term *woman,* rather than *lady,* applied to them, and in their indignation might not even notice any unfavorable comparison with a cigar. The conflict between *woman* and *lady* in American usage is a curious thing to behold. In one widely accepted view, *woman* suggests commonness, if not vulgarity, while *lady* suggests breeding and refinement. It is this idea, no doubt, that has led to the rejection of *women's* in such names of organizations as *Ladies' Aid* and *Ladies' Auxiliary*.

Go up a few notches in the social scale, however, at least as far as pretensions are concerned, and you will find organizations with names like *Woman's Club* and *Women's Alliance.* This choice is common among the country-club, study-group, and college-alumnae sets. Why should these women, who surely have an equal claim to refinement and breeding, have forfeited the chance to call themselves ladies? Can it be that they would rather have any such tribute conferred upon them than arrogate it to themselves?

Newspapers commonly forbid the use of the word *lady* in their columns as a synonym for *woman,* holding that *lady* belongs only in titles (Lady Astor) and in references to their holders. This seems to be an unduly restrictive attitude. Anyhow, no newspaper has been known to insist that ladies' aids are women's aids. At the same time, *neighbor woman, widow woman,* and *the Smith woman* are discouraged as poor usage (see *Miss*).

*Lady* is in general use as a courtesy, as in the salutation *ladies and gentlemen.* Few of us, in directing a remark at a group, would say *you women* rather than *you ladies.* The upshot seems to be that *lady* remains useful when a touch of courtliness is desired, but like all tributes sounds more graceful when it is not self-applied. *Woman* is the workaday word for the female of the species, and the idea that it carries a hint of disparagement is a delusion.

**word as a word.**   Set off, p. 89.

**word division.**   P. 77.

**word order.**   Inversion, p. 64; placement of prepositional phrases, p. 65; placement of time elements, pp. 127-129.

**worsen.**   A suspicion is abroad that *worsen* is not all it should be, even in the sense *get worse,* to say nothing of *make worse.* But the OED describes it as having been reintroduced to literature about 1800 to 1830 by writers like Southey and DeQuincey, and Fowler also endorses it.

**would.**   Past tense of *will,* pp. 32-33; and *should,* p. 38.

**would have.**   Often used, quasi-literately, in conditional sentences where *had* belongs: "If a doctor *would have* been on the premises, a death certificate *would have* been signed." The first *would have* should be *had*; the second is, of course, correct.

**wraps.**   In reply to a reader who wrote in asking about the sentence, "Will they really put the wraps on the senator?" *Newsweek* explained: "*Wraps* is a sports term meaning: 'A turn of the reins around the jockey's hands to restrain a horse, hence, restraint.' " All very interesting, but the expression is constantly used and interpreted in a less esoteric fashion, to wit, in the sense of *wrappings.* Most readers probably visualized the senator as muffled or gagged, rather than drawn up short. *Newsweek* itself uses *wraps* in this way: "The army demonstrated its latest antitank weapon and removed some of the secrecy wraps that have surrounded the project for several years."

**wreathed in smiles.** It may be that this expression is itself ready to be wreathed—and interred.

# X

**Xavier, etc.** Many are unaware that the initial *x* is pronounced with the sound of *z*. Thus they say *ex-avier* rather than *zavier*, *ex-ylophone* rather than *zylophone*.

**Xmas.** *Xmas*, popular assumption to the contrary, is not an irreverent, commercialized form, nor a space-saving form invented by headline writers, but rather a reverent form that originated in the early Greek church. *X*, the first letter of Christ's name in Greek, has often been used as a holy symbol. No etymology will remove the taint of derogation that many people see in *Xmas*, however.

# Y

**you-all.**
"All the South, however, has one word in common and that is the *you-all* (*y'all* or *yawl*) that Yankees usually mess up. It is used only in a collective sense and takes a plural verb." *James Street's South*.

**yous, youse.** *Yous*, as an attempt to make a distinct plural form of *you*, and otherwise, is depreciated as "not standard" in the *Dictionary of Contemporary American Usage*. It is depressing to see such inattentiveness exhibited by such learned commentators. Granting its questionable status, the word is *youse*, not *yous*. This was incontrovertibly established by the judgment, "Fagin, youse is a viper," which was a stock feature of Billy de Beck's "Parlor, Bedroom, and Sink," a sideshow to his comic strip, "Barney Google," some years ago.

**youth.** Attempts have been made to set an age limit for this term, as a discouragement against applying it to those who are no longer young. Such limits are difficult to enforce, however, since it is evident that youth, like beauty, is in the eye of the beholder, and perhaps even more so in the mind of the possessor. We all know circles of elderly men and women who refer to each other as *boys* and *girls*. *Youth* as applied to individuals means only males (*four youths were sauntering down the walk*); as a general term (*the youth of the nation*) it includes both sexes. See also *elderly*.

# Z

**zoom.**    Technically, this word means to make an aircraft climb briefly at an angle sharper than it would be capable of in sustained flight. In this sense it apparently dates from Army pilot training in World War I. There are those who still insist that *zoom* cannot apply except in an upward direction. That is a distinction all the dictionaries still recognize. But its use in the sense of a burst of speed in any direction, and even sustained, as "The car *zoomed* down the incline" and "The jet *zoomed* across the Atlantic" is now so prevalent that dissent seems like quibbling.

# Bibliography

*American College Dictionary*, New York: Random House, 1957.

Bernstein, Theodore M., *Watch Your Language*. Great Neck, N. Y.: Channel Press, 1958.

Colby, Frank O., *Practical Handbook of Better English*. New York: Grosset & Dunlap, Revised Edition, 1947.

Curme, George O., *Syntax*. New York: D. C. Heath and Company, 1931.

Davies, Hugh Sykes, *Grammar Without Tears*. New York: John Day Company, 1953.

Evans, Bergen, and Evans, Cornelia, *A Dictionary of Contemporary American Usage*. New York: Random House, 1957.

Flesch, Rudolf, *Art of Plain Talk*. New York: Harper & Brothers, 1946; and *Art of Readable Writing*. New York: Harper & Brothers, 1949.

Fowler, H. W., *A Dictionary of Modern English Usage*. London: Oxford University Press, 1926.

Fowler, H. W. and F. G., *The King's English*. London: Oxford University Press, 1906.

Gowers, Sir Ernest, *Plain Words, Their ABC*. New York: Alfred A. Knopf, 1954.

Hayakawa, S. I., *Language in Thought and Action*. New York: Harcourt, Brace and Company, 1949.

Jones, Easley S., *Practical English Composition. New York*: Appleton-Century-Crofts, Inc., Third Edition, 1956.

Montague, C. E., *A Writer's Notes on His Trade*. London: Pelican Books, 1952.

*Oxford English Dictionary*. London: Oxford University Press, 1888 et seq.

*Oxford Universal Dictionary*. London: Oxford University Press, Third Edition, 1955.

Partridge, Eric, *Usage and Abusage*. New York: Harper & Brothers, Second Edition, 1942.

Perrin, Porter G., *Writer's Guide and Index to English*. New York: Scott, Foresman, Third Edition, 1959.

Potter, Simeon, *Our Language*. London: Penguin Books, 1950.

Strunk, William Jr., and White, E. B., *Elements of Style*. New York: The Macmillan Co., 1959.

Vallins, G. H., *Pattern of English*. London: Penguin Books, 1957.

*Webster's New International Dictionary*. Springfield, Mass.: G. & C. Merriam Company, Second Edition, 1958.

*Webster's New Collegiate Dictionary*. Springfield, Mass.: G. & C. Merriam Company, 1956.

*Word Study*, a periodical published by G. & C. Merriam Company, Springfield, Mass.

## THE AUTHOR AND HIS BOOK

*Roy H. Copperud has had a varied career, predominantly as a newspaperman, but embracing also work in the publications end of public relations and as a technical editor. Born in 1915 in Michigan, he grew up and began as a newspaper reporter in the iron-mining region of northern Minnesota. He graduated from the University of Minnesota as a member of Phi Beta Kappa, and has been a member of the editorial staffs of the* Baltimore Evening Sun *and the* Milwaukee Journal. *During World War II he served with the Navy in the Pacific, ending as executive officer of a destroyer-transport. At present he is chief editorial writer and music critic for the* Pasadena Independent *and* Star-News. *Since 1954 he has written a column, "Editorial Workshop," dealing with the use of language, for* Editor & Publisher, *the leading journal of the newspaper field. He, his wife, and their three children make their home in Altadena, California.*

*WORDS ON PAPER (Hawthorn, 1960) was designed by Ernst Reichl, and completely manufactured by George McKibbin and Son, Brooklyn, N. Y. The body type was set in Times Roman, originally designed for use by* The Times *of London.*

## A HAWTHORN BOOK